SHOWTIME'S
ACT ONE FESTIVAL
of One-Act Plays
1994

To John & Janey -

Your love AND support
are like gRavity in
A chaotic world.

with all my love -

1/29/95

Smith and Kraus *Books For Actors*

THE MONOLOGUE SERIES

The Best Men's / Women's Stage Monologues of 1994
The Best Men's / Women's Stage Monologues of 1993
The Best Men's / Women's Stage Monologues of 1992
The Best Men's / Women's Stage Monologues of 1991
The Best Men's / Women's Stage Monologues of 1990
One Hundred Men's / Women's Stage Monologues from the 1980's
2 Minutes and Under: Original Character Monologues for Actors
Street Talk: Original Character Monologues for Actors
Uptown: Original Character Monologues for Actors
Ice Babies in Oz: Original Character Monologues for Actors
Monologues from Contemporary Literature: Volume I
Monologues from Classic Plays
100 Great Monologues from the Renaissance Theatre
100 Great Monologues from the Neo-Classical Theatre
100 Great Monologues from the 19th C. Romantic and Realistic Theatres

YOUNG ACTORS SERIES

Great Scenes and Monologues for Children
New Plays from A.C.T.'s Young Conservatory
Great Scenes for Young Actors from the Stage
Great Monologues for Young Actors
Multicultural Monologues for Young Actors
Multicultural Scenes for Young Actors

CONTEMPORARY PLAYWRIGHTS SERIES

Romulus Linney: 17 Short Plays
Eric Overmyer: Collected Plays
Lanford Wilson: 21 Short Plays
William Mastrosimone: Collected Plays
Horton Foote: 4 New Plays
Israel Horovitz: 16 Short Plays
Israel Horovitz Vol. II: New England Blue
Terrence McNally: 15 Short Plays
Humana Festival '93: The Complete Plays
Humana Festival '94: The Complete Plays
Humana Festival '95: The Complete Plays
Women Playwrights: The Best Plays of 1992
Women Playwrights: The Best Plays of 1993
Women Playwrights: The Best Plays of 1994
EST Marathon '94: One-Act Plays
EST Marathon '95: One-Act Plays
Showtime's Act One Festival '95: One-Act Plays

GREAT TRANSLATION FOR ACTORS SERIES

The Wood Demon by Anton Chekhov, tr. by N. Saunders & F. Dwyer
The Sea Gull by Anton Chekhov, tr. by N. Saunders & F. Dwyer
Three Sisters by Anton Chekhov, tr. by Lanford Wilson
Mercadet by Honoré de Balzac, tr. by Robert Cornthwaite
Villeggiatura: The Trilogy by Carlo Goldoni, tr. by Robert Cornthwaite
Cyrano de Bergerac by Edmond Rostand, tr. by Charles Marowitz

CAREER DEVELOPMENT SERIES

The Job Book: 100 Acting Jobs for Actors
The Smith and Kraus Monologue Index
What to Give Your Agent for Christmas and 100 Other Tips for the Working Actor
The Camera Smart Actor
The Sanford Meisner Approach
Anne Bogart: Viewpoints
The Actor's Chekhov
Kiss and Tell: Restoration Scenes, Monologues, & History
Cold Readings: Some Do's and Don'ts for Actors at Auditions

If you require pre-publication information about upcoming Smith and Kraus books, you may receive our semi-annual catalogue, free of charge, by sending your name and address to *Smith and Kraus Catalogue, P.O. Box 127, One Main Street, Lyme, NH 03768. Or call us at (800) 895-4331, fax (603) 795-4427.*

SHOWTIME'S
ACT ONE FESTIVAL
of One-Act Plays
1994

Edited by Marisa Smith

Contemporary Playwrights Series

SK
A Smith and Kraus Book

A Smith and Kraus Book
Published by Smith and Kraus, Inc.
One Main Street, PO Box 127, Lyme, NH 03768

Copyright © 1995 by Smith and Kraus
All rights reserved

Manufactured in the United States of America

Cover and Text Design by Julia Hill

First Edition: August 1995
10 9 8 7 6 5 4 3 2 1

Library of Congress Cataloguing-in-Publication Data

Showtime's Act One Festival of one-act plays, 1994 / edited by Marisa Smith. -- 1st ed.
    p. cm. -- (Contemporary playwrights series)
    ISBN 1-880399-96-2 (alk. paper)

    1. One-act plays, American. 2. American drama--20th century. I. Smith, Marisa. II. Series.

PS627.053S56   1995   95-22540
812'.04108054--dc20   CIP

Contents

INTRODUCTION by *Risa Bramon Garcia and Jerry Levine* vii

LYNETTE AT 3 AM by Jane Anderson......................... 1

CALL IT CLOVER by Wil Calhoun.......................... 11

TOM AND JERRY by Rick Cleveland 37

TINKLE TIME by Dana Coen 79

THE OTHER FIVE PERCENT by Bryan Goluboff 97

DICE AND CARDS by Sam Henry Kass 119

THE DYING GAUL by Craig Lucas 135

WALTZING DENIRO by Lynn Martin 149

STICKS AND STONES by Drew McWeeny and Scott Swan.......... 173

JACKIE by David Rasche................................... 195

IRON TOMMY by James Ryan 209

WISH FULFILLMENT by David Simpatico 227

A DEATH IN BETHANY by Garry Williams 245

Introduction

The one-act is one of the most unique, challenging, and ultimately compelling of all dramatic forms. It is the kind of theatre that has been quietly seducing and nurturing writers, directors, actors, and designers for years, pushing the limits of their talents and skills to provide an immediate, intensive and complete experience. The one-act is hard and fast, exploring the most heightened moment in a character's life, an instant in time is captured, relished and untied.

We are thrilled to have the plays from our first one-act Festival, Act One '94 published, to be able to share them with artists across the country. As artists ourselves, the one-act has given us enormous satisfaction and has allowed us to take great risks in our creative growth. For Risa, it was producing and directing years of one-acts at The Ensemble Studio Theatre in New York. For Jerry, it was the experience of mounting the Los Angeles production of the one-act play and subsequent short film and Ace Award winner *Big Al*, written by Bryan Goluboff. Our logical next step was to come together to create Act One, dedicated to the one-act form and ultimately to the marriage of stage and film.

By doing the best theatre we can imagine with a keen eye toward the development of the one-act into other forms, we've witnessed the natural evolution of the one-act from the stage to the screen, where an idea, a circumstance, a character, a moment in time will inspire a short film, a series, even a feature film. The work we do in theatre is as instantaneous and tenuous as it is meant to be while we strive to find a way to translate its power and capture its brilliance for the screen.

Act One '94 was sponsored by Showtime Networks, Inc. and The MET Theatre. Bringing the film and television industry toward a direct sponsorship and a wholehearted endorsement of the work on stage and its future possibilities, Showtime Networks Inc. had the foresight to champion this one-act festival, the first of its kind.

In our search for extraordinary one-act plays, we embarked on a six-month adventure along with our Artistic Committee of 40 dedicated theatre professionals, reading close to 2,000 pieces, selecting and reading approximately 70 one-acts and workshopping the most provocative plays. The best of these plays were presented in Act One Festival of One-Act Plays 1994.

We thank all of the directors, actors, designers, and especially the writers for their talent, incredible energies, and commitment. We extend special thanks to the MET Theatre and their Board of Directors, Casting Director Mary Verniett, Associate Producers Kate Baggott and Michael Koopman, and our Executive Producer Judy Pastore of Showtime Networks, Inc. for making the Act One '94 festival possible.

Risa Bramon Garcia　　　　　*Jerry Levine*
Producer　　　　　　　　　　*Producer*

SHOWTIME'S
ACT ONE FESTIVAL
of One-Act Plays
1994

Lynette At 3 AM
by Jane Anderson

BIOGRAPHY

MS. ANDERSON grew up in northern California and after two years in college, dropped out to move to New York City to train as an actress. In 1975 she appeared in the New York premiere of David Mamet's *Sexual Perversity in Chicago*. She began writing in 1979 when she founded the *New York Writers Bloc* with playwrights Donald Margulies and Jeffery Sweet. She developed a series of characters and performed as a comedienne in New York clubs and cabarets. In 1982, her act was discovered by Billy Crystal and she was brought to Los Angeles to be a regular on *The Billy Crystal Comedy Hour* which was taken off the air after three weeks. Ms. Anderson continued to perform in Los Angeles, receiving critical acclaim for her one-woman show, *How to Raise a Gifted Child.*

For several years she worked as a television writer, working on staff for several series, including *Wonder Years* and creating a short-lived show for Grant Tinker called *Raising Miranda.*

Her playwriting career began in 1986 with *Defying Gravity,* which premiered in L.A. and later received a W. Alton Jones Grant for a production at the Williamstown Theatre Festival. Her plays to follow were *Food & Shelter, The Baby Dance, The Pink Studio, Hotel Oubliette* (recipient of the Susan Smith Blackburn Prize) and several short plays, including *Lynette at 3 AM* and *The Last Time We Say Her,* both winners of the Heideman Award. Her works are published and have been widely produced off-Broadway and in theatres around the country, including Long Wharf, The McCarter, Williamstown Theatre Festival, The Pasadena Playhouse, ACT, and Actors Theatre of Louisville.

In 1993, Ms. Anderson received an Emmy Award and Writer's Guild Award for her H.B.O. movie, *The Positively True Adventures of the Alleged Texas Cheerleader-Murdering Mom,* directed by Michael Ritchie and starring Holly Hunter and Beau Bridges who also received Emmys for their performances.

Her film work includes: *Cop Gives Waitress $2 Million Tip,* renamed for release to *It Could Happen to You* (Tristar). Currently in production is her film adaptation of *How To Make An American Quilt* from the novel by Whitney Otto. It will be released in Fall of 1995 by Amblin/Universal.

Ms. Anderson is a member of the Dramatists Guild.

AUTHOR'S NOTE

I wrote this play because of my bladder. It wakes me up in the middle of the night and I have to crawl out of bed and make my way to the dark bathroom. That's when a soul is most vulnerable, I think, in those moonlit AM hours when the soup in your head is all stirred up from heavy dreaming. It was during one of those endless nocturnal pees when, like Lynette, I touched my bony knees and thought to myself, "My God, someday I'm going to die." Then I crawled back in my bed and burrowed between my slumbering lover and the cats. And before I could torture myself with thoughts of their eventual demise, I grabbed the tail end of a recent dream and willed myself to sleep.

ORIGINAL PRODUCTION

Lynette at 3 AM was first produced at the Showtime's Act One 1994 Festival. It was directed by Jane Anderson with Anne O'Sullivan as Lynette, pat Skipper as Bobby and Yul Vazquez as Esteban.

TIME

Present

PLACE

An apartment in Brooklyn

CHARACTERS

Lynette, who's had trouble sleeping lately.
Bobby, her boyfriend. A man who works too hard.
Estaban, from the apartment below.

Lynette At 3 am

Three A.M. Lynette's apartment in Brooklyn. Lynette is lying awake on the bed with Bobby, who's fast asleep. We hear the toilet running. We hear traffic. We hear a car alarm. It stops. Very faintly, we hear something that sounds like a gun shot. Lynette sits up and listens.

LYNETTE: Bobby. Bobby, wake up.

BOBBY: Uh.

LYNETTE: I heard a gun go off.

BOBBY: (*Still asleep.*) Where?

LYNETTE: I think in the building somewhere.

BOBBY: Where in the building?

LYNETTE: I think maybe in the apartment below.

BOBBY: So what do you want me to do about it?

LYNETTE: You want to call the police?

BOBBY: You call. You're the one who heard it.

LYNETTE: You wanna maybe check in the hall, see if there's anything out there?

BOBBY: What's gonna be in the hall?

LYNETTE: I just thought maybe you should check.

BOBBY: There's nothing to check in the hall. Anything to see would be behind a door. There's no point to the hall. The hall has nothing.

LYNETTE: OK.

BOBBY: If you think you heard an actual gun, if you are certain you heard it, then make the commitment and call the police. But don't say you're not sure and make me get up and go to the hall. That's not what I'm here for. I'm not interested in that.

LYNETTE: OK. (*A beat.*) I just have this funny feeling.

BOBBY: You always get paranoid in the middle of the night.

LYNETTE: If it were a gun then there'd be people yelling. There'd be a commotion, right? (*A beat.*) Maybe it was just a car making a backfire on the street. Or maybe a cat knocked a book offa someone's shelf. You think that's it?

BOBBY: Mmm.

LYNETTE: That's probably it.

(*A beat.*)

Bobby?

BOBBY: Wha.

LYNETTE: Hold me?

(*Bobby rolls over on his back so Lynette can cuddle with him. He flops his arm over her and falls back to sleep. Snores. Lynette jiggles him.*)

BOBBY: Sorry.

(*Bobby goes back to sleep. Lynette has her head on his chest. We hear Bobby's heartbeat. He snores slightly. Lynette jiggles him to stop. She listens to his heartbeat. It beats, stops for a moment then starts up again. Lynette sits up, panicked.*)

LYNETTE: Bobby, Bobby.

BOBBY: Uh!

LYNETTE: Bobby, wake up.

BOBBY: Wha.

LYNETTE: Your heart stopped. I heard it.

BOBBY: No it didn't.

LYNETTE: Bobby, it did.

BOBBY: We don't have heart in my family. We have cancer, we don't have heart.

LYNETTE: I swear to God. I was listening very specifically. I was counting the beats.

BOBBY: What were you counting the beats for?

LYNETTE: Because I love you.

BOBBY: Jesus.

LYNETTE: I love that even though you're sleeping, this little part of you is still awake, working to keep you alive. I think that's a miracle, don't you?

BOBBY: C'mon, Lynette, I gotta get up early. (*Bobby turns over.*)

LYNETTE: Bobby, when you get up to pee in the middle of the night do you ever think about your own death?

BOBBY: No.

LYNETTE: While I was sitting on the toilet I touched the top of my knees and I thought about how someday everything will be rotted away and there will only be bones there. And there will be no point to shaving my legs anymore because there will be no skin on which to support the hair. And it occurred to me that even the act of urination is not a forever kind of thing and it's something I should treasure because someday my bladder will turn to dust.

(*Bobby lets out an impatient breath.*)

Breathing. This is also a special thing. Lungs are not forever. Someday they'll be two dried sponges.

BOBBY: Shit, Lynette, shit.

LYNETTE: I'm sorry.

BOBBY: I'll be fucked if I don't get my sleep. C'mon.

LYNETTE: I know. I'm sorry.

BOBBY: (*Overlap.*) Three hours, I gotta get up...

LYNETTE: (*Overlap.*) I know. Go to sleep. I want you to sleep. Good night.

(*Lynette lays down. She changes position. She changes position again. A beat, she starts scratching herself.*)

BOBBY: Stop it.

LYNETTE: Could we spoon?

BOBBY: Jesus.

LYNETTE: Never mind.

BOBBY: All right.

(*They readjust positions. Bobby wraps himself around Lynette. A beat.*)

LYNETTE: Are you still in love with me?

BOBBY: Why are you asking me this?

LYNETTE: Because usually when we spoon you get a hard-on.

BOBBY: Jesus, Lynette...

LYNETTE: Sorry. (*A beat.*) But you still love me?

(*No response. Lynette settles down. A beat. Bobby snores very faintly. A car with a scraping muffler passes by, Salsa music playing on the radio. Silence. The pipes in the building thud a few times. Silence. Lynette sits up. She takes the remote from the bedside table and turns on the TV. She mutes the sound and just stares at the picture. A beat.*)

Estaban, a young Latino man appears. He's barefoot and dressed in a white T-shirt and white pants. Lynette stares at him.)

ESTABAN: Hello. My name is Estaban. I'm from the apartment below. I just died.

LYNETTE: Oh my God.

ESTABAN: I am sorry to disturb you. I have to pass through so I can go ...(*Points up.*) ...to above.

LYNETTE: Was this like a few minutes ago this happened?

ESTABAN: Yes.

LYNETTE: I thought I heard a gun. Was that you?

ESTABAN: Yes.

LYNETTE: You know, I knew there was something. I told Bobby, I said to him there was definitely a shot. So that was you?

ESTABAN: That was me.

LYNETTE: I was gonna call the police. Should I call the police?

ESTABAN: It doesn't matter anymore.

LYNETTE: Who shot you?

ESTABAN: My brother Jorge.

LYNETTE: Oh my God, your brother?

ESTABAN: I was making love to his wife.

LYNETTE: Oh. Well. That wasn't a smart thing to be doing.

ESTABAN: It couldn't be helped. Lola and me, we fell in love when we were fifteen.

LYNETTE: Really? So this has been going on a long time then.

ESTABAN: Yes. Me and Lola, we grew up in the same village in Puerto Rico.

LYNETTE: I hear Puerto Rico is a very nice place to vacation. Is it nice there?

ESTABAN: Like a paradise.

LYNETTE: I've always wanted to see the islands. But Bobby, he's not a traveler.

ESTABAN: No?

LYNETTE: But you and Lola, I want to hear about. So you met on the island, you were soul mates, go on.

ESTABAN: The first time we made love, it was siesta time. We walked down the street, everyone was asleep. Everything was quiet except for the waves flipping over very soft. It was hot, just a little bit windy from the ocean. Very sexy. I took her to the shade of a vanilla bean tree. We lay down on a blanket. She opened her blouse for me and her skin, it smelled sweet just like the tree. After we made love, I cried.

LYNETTE: I do that. I cry after Bobby and me make love. So you cry too?

ESTABAN: Oh yes. It is because when I make love, my heart leaves my body for heaven. And when it is over and my heart has to come back, it is very sad.

LYNETTE: See, my crying thing is a little different. When I make love and my heart leaves my body I'm always expecting to meet Bobby's heart outside his body. But Bobby's heart – well Bobby has a hard time opening up, if you met his family you'd understand. His heart doesn't really leave his body so my heart is out there all alone waiting while Bobby finishes up. Below. And then he falls asleep and I'm still out there, floating and feeling very lonely. And then I cry and wake Bobby up and he gets annoyed. (*A beat.*) Which is not to say that I don't get a lot of other things from him.

ESTABAN: Yes?

LYNETTE: So how come Lola didn't marry you?

ESTABAN: Her parents said, "Lola, marry Jorge, he make better money than Estaban."

LYNETTE: Aw, that's not fair.

ESTABAN: That is life. Jorge, he runs a car service to the airport. I been working for him. Olmos Limos.

LYNETTE: I hate to fly. I see my own death when I fly.

ESTABAN: See, when I drive someone to the airport I always say before they get out, "Have a safe trip, God bless." Not one of my passengers ever died in a plane crash. It's part of the service.

LYNETTE: That's nice. (*A beat.*) So do you know where you're going? Is anyone gonna be meeting you, like do you have grandparents or anyone who're gonna take you over to the other side?

ESTABAN: No, my family, they're all still alive.

LYNETTE: Are you Catholic?

ESTABAN: Yeh, I grew up with that.

LYNETTE: Do you think the Virgin Mary will be there?

ESTABAN: I don't know.

LYNETTE: Did you go through a tunnel and see a white light?

ESTABAN: No, I haven't even left the building yet.

LYNETTE: Are you scared?

ESTABAN: Why should I be scared? It's nature. Everything dies.

Chickens and dogs and pussy cats and movie stars and cockroaches and grandmommies and guys like me who drive people to the airport. We all gotta do it. So how can something that everybody has to do be so bad?

LYNETTE: But you think there's something to go to? You think there's something else?

ESTABAN: Sure, why not?

LYNETTE: Bobby says all that stuff is bullshit, that when you die you die.

ESTABAN: Oh man, don't listen to him. How can a guy who can't make good love know anything about the afterlife? Geez, no wonder you're such a scared lady.

LYNETTE: I didn't paint a fair picture. He's a very good person.

ESTABAN: What's your name?

LYNETTE: Lynette.

ESTABAN: Ay, Lynetta, Lynetta. Tu eres muy amable y muy hermosa. Deseo que pudiera besarte y tener tus cenos en mis manos como si fueran frutas perfectas, desmasiados bellas para comer.

LYNETTE: What did you just say?

BOBBY: (*Translating in his sleep.*) "You are very kind and very beautiful. I wish that I could kiss you and hold your breasts in my hands as if they were perfect fruits, too beautiful to eat."

LYNETTE: Bobby?

ESTABAN: Pon tu mano en mi pecho.

(*Lynette looks at Estaban.*)

BOBBY: (*Still asleep.*) He says to put your hand on his chest. That's as far as you go, Lynette.

LYNETTE: I didn't do anything, Bobby.

ESTABAN: Eschucha a la musica.

(*Music – very soft mixed in with ocean.*)

Esto es lo que esta entre los pulsares del corazon despues que todo se va.

(*Lynette looks to Bobby. Estaban touches her chin.*)

This is what you hear between heartbeats after everything else is gone.

(*Estaban kisses Lynette. He caresses her face and lays her down on the bed and continues to caress her. Over this, the alarm goes off. Lights come up to indicate morning. Bobby wakes up, punches the alarm, swears to himself. Lynette starts to sit up as if dragging herself up from*

her sleep. Estaban gently pushes her back down. Bobby sits on the edge of the bed, rubbing his face. He gets up, shuffles to the bathroom. We hear a garbage truck. Estaban starts to leave. Lynette pulls him back. They continue their embrace over Estaban's music. We hear the toilet flush, the music fades. Estaban starts to get up. Lynette tries to pull him back but he slips through her hands and disappears as Lynette wakes up.)
(Fade out.)

END OF PLAY

Call It Clover
by Wil Calhoun

BIOGRAPHY

WIL CALHOUN was raised in Baton Rouge, Louisiana, and is a graduate of the Louisiana State University Theatre Program. His work has been produced Off-Broadway at New York's Circle Repertory Company, the Circle Rep Lab, The Empty Space Theatre in Seattle, The Company of Angels Theatre and The Met Theatre in Los Angeles, The Buffalo Theatre in Chicago, and The Kennedy Center in Washington D.C. He lives and works in Los Angeles.

AUTHOR'S NOTE

About the Dialect: Because the play is set in New Orleans, Louisiana, it is easy to assume that using a Standard Southern accent is appropriate for the characters. This would be inaccurate. The play is written in a specific rhythm indigenous to a certain area of New Orleans.

John Kennedy Toole described it best in his book *A Confederacy of Dunces,* "There is a New Orleans city accent...associated with downtown New Orleans, particularly with the German and Irish Third Ward, that is hard to distinguish from the accent of Hoboken, Jersey City, and Astoria, Long Island, where the Al Smith inflection, extinct in Manhattan, has taken refuge. The reason, as you might expect, is that the same stock that brought the accent to Manhattan imposed it on New Orleans."

The only thing that would throw the rhythm of the play off more than a Standard Southern dialect would be an attempt at a "Cajun" dialect, also associated with the people of Louisiana.

If the dialect gets in the way, don't use it. Or fall back on the Jersey City, Hoboken comparison. It's close enough.

About the Characters: I have seen these characters played by very talented actors who have taken them and owned them each in a different way. I continue to learn new things about them with each interpretation, so I cannot offer any absolute truths about any of them. But because I cannot resist indulging myself, I can tell you what I *believe* to be true about them and you can do what you will with the information.

I do not believe that Sandy is coldhearted and mean. I do not believe it matters whether or not we *like* Sandy by the end of the play. I believe the challenge lies in *understanding* Sandy by the end of the play.

I believe Eddie is certainly cast from a different mold but he's not a buffoon. He is not a hayseed, a clod, or an idiot. I believe he is extraordinarily decent and kind, but can give in to temptation like anyone else.

I believe Perry loves his wife and is just as frightened as she is.

Wil Calhoun

ORIGINAL PRODUCTION

Call it Clover was first presented by the Cactus Theatre at the Chicago Dramatist Workshop November 9, 1991, with the following cast.

Perry............................... Paul Swetland
Sandy............................... Moira Brennan
Eddie............................... William Green

The play was directed by Neil Weiss.

Call it Clover was presented by The Theatre of The Reconstruction in Chicago on February 8, 1992, with the following cast:

Perry............................... James Thoresen
Sandy............................... Hanna Dworkin
Eddie............................... Michael Dalmon

The play was directed by Steve Heller.

Call it Clover was presented by the Company of Angels Theatre in Los Angeles on September 7, 1993, with the following cast:

Perry............................... John Mese
Sandy............................... Suanne Spoke
Eddie............................... Wayne Pere

The play was directed by A.C. Weary.

Call it Clover was produced by Act One in association with Showtime Networks Inc. for Act One: A Festival of New One-Act Plays at the Met Theatre on May 26, 1994, with the following cast.:

Perry............................... John Mese
Sandy............................... Michelle Forbes
Eddie............................... Arliss Howard

The play was directed by Risa Bramon Garcia.

CALL IT CLOVER

The play takes place in a worn out one room apartment in New Orleans. There is a bed, a window looking onto the street, a table with two chairs, a kitchen area that is no more than a hot plate on a counter. There is a small refrigerator. There is a door leading to the tiny bathroom upstage. Street noise bleeds through the open window.

Sandy is lying in bed reading a book. She is a woman in her late twenties to early thirties. She has no movement from her waist down. She is pretty but is showing some wear and tear. This does not diminish her powerful sexual presence.

Perry is at the refrigerator. He stands in his underwear looking inside. There are sandwich makings on the table. Perry is Sandy's husband.

The door buzzer goes off. Perry continues his search without looking up. Sandy looks at him. The door buzzer goes off again.

SANDY: You gonna get that?
PERRY: No.
SANDY: You expectin' somebody?
PERRY: No.
    (*Buzzer goes off again.*)
SANDY: Whoever it is ain't goin' away.

PERRY: (*Frustrated.*) Where's the tomato?

SANDY: What tomato?

PERRY: The one that was in here.

SANDY: I didn't see no tomato.

PERRY: It was in here yesterday. (*Not blaming; just a question.*) Did you eat it?

SANDY: No. I didn't eat no tomato.

PERRY: (*Slamming door.*) Goddamnit!

SANDY: Maybe somebody stole it.

PERRY: Prolly. Prolly that's what happened, Sandy. Somebody broke in here and stole a fuckin' tomato. (*Beat. He sits at table.*) I don't care if you ate it, all right, but you gotta tell me so I know. This fucks up my sandwich.

SANDY: I didn't eat it I said! I don't even like 'em.

(*Buzzer goes off again.*)

PERRY: Jesus! Who the...! (*Goes to intercom.*) What?!!

VOICE: (*Barely audible.*) It's Eddie!

PERRY: (*To Sandy.*) Who?

SANDY: I didn't hear.

PERRY: (*Back to intercom.*) Who?

VOICE: (*Clearly.*) Eddie!

SANDY: Who?

PERRY: Eddie. (*He buzzes the door.*)

SANDY: Don't...! Don't let him up!

PERRY: What? I already buzzed.

SANDY: Damnit, Perry...

PERRY: What?!

SANDY: I can't stand that little shit.

PERRY: When? Since when?

SANDY: You know I don't like him.

(*Perry picks up a pair of jeans by the bed. Starts to put them on.*)

PERRY: What do I know? I know who you like and don't like alla time? I'm a fuckin' mind reader?

SANDY: He's alla time starin' at my tits...

PERRY: Well...Put 'em away! Cover 'em up! Put some clothes on sometimes and maybe he wouldn't do it.

SANDY: It's my house. I can do what I want. (*A knock on the door. Perry moves to answer it.*) Wait, Perry, for God's sake.

PERRY: What?

SANDY: Gimme my robe.

PERRY: Oh for cryin'...(*A knock on the door.*) Hang on a minute, Eddie! (*To Sandy.*) Where is it?

SANDY: Right there. (*She gestures toward a chair. It's no more than three feet away. Perry looks at the robe. Looks back to Sandy. Bites his tongue and retrieves the robe. He helps her put it on. Sandy puts it on, straightens it, ties the waist and looks at Perry.*) All right.

(*Perry opens the door and Eddie, enters. He carries a brown paper bag and a roofer's hammer with him.*)

EDDIE: Perry, where y'at?

PERRY: Whaddaya say, Eddie.

(*Eddie holds up the hammer.*)

EDDIE: You forget somethin'?

PERRY: Oh...damn...

(*Perry takes the hammer and slips it in a nail belt hanging on a coat rack.*)

EDDIE: I thought maybe you wasn't home. I kep' ringin'.

PERRY: No. We home.

EDDIE: I can see that. (*Eddie wanders over to Sandy, who is buried in her book.*) How you doin', Sandy? (*No response.*) That a good book, Sandy? (*No response.*) Sandy?

PERRY: Sandy!

SANDY: (*Wearily, to Eddie.*) What?

EDDIE: I was axin' 'bout the book. It's good?

SANDY: Yeah.

PERRY: (*About the bag.*) What's that?

EDDIE: Some beer.

(*Perry takes the bag and heads for the refrigerator. He takes a couple from the bag and hands one to Eddie.*)

EDDIE: Hey, Sandy? You wanta beer? I brought some beer.

SANDY: No.

PERRY: She don't drink beer.

EDDIE: Sandy, you don't drink beer? I never hearda that, somebody don't drink beer. Whattaya drink, Sandy? Champagne? You want, I'll run over and getcha some champagne. Or one a them coolers? Wine cooler? Lotta ladies drinkin' that now. That what you like...? Sandy...?

SANDY: (*Looking up from book.*) Do you mind?

EDDIE: What?

SANDY: I'm tryna read here.

EDDIE: I'm sorry. I'm just tryna be social. I'm a social person…I thought it'd be nice, you know, come here and see my friends. Have a drink…

SANDY: You're Perry's friend.

(*Beat.*)

EDDIE: (*To Perry.*) Did I…did I say somethin', Perry, to offend her?

PERRY: Don't worry about it. She's havin' a bad day.

EDDIE: Oh. Okay…okay…I know about bad days. I unnerstand that. I'm just gonna…you read! You just read that book, all right, and me and Perry's gonna leave you to yourself. Okay? All right, Perry?

PERRY: Just leave her alone. She'll be all right.

EDDIE: I think that's best. We'll sit down quiet and drink this beer. (*They sit.*) We'll just leave Sandy over there with her book. I know what that's like. You get into a thing, you don't wanna be innerupted. I'm like that with the mornin' paper. You know?

PERRY: Yeah…

EDDIE: Yeah. You're like that too. With the…uh, with things like that, am I right?

PERRY: That's right.

EDDIE: Yeah. (*Pause. They each sip a beer. A long beat.*) It's hot out, you know that? I just took a shower and now I got this. (*Eddie holds up his arm to reveal a huge sweat ring under his armpit.*)

PERRY: Rainin'?

EDDIE: Nah. Looks like it though. *Feels* like it…

(*Quick, overlapping.*)

PERRY: Yeah…

EDDIE: You know what I'm sayin'…

PERRY:…yeah…

EDDIE:…how you can feel it…?

PERRY: Sure, I know…

EDDIE: And on Sunday.

PERRY: Goddamn.

EDDIE: I hate rain on Sunday.

PERRY: I hear ya.

EDDIE: Pisses me off.

PERRY: Me too.

EDDIE: I know. (*Pause. End of overlapping.*) So, what took you so long with the door?

PERRY: What?

EDDIE: I was out there a long time. I didn't innerupt nothin' I hope?
 (*Sandy shoots a look at him over the top of her book.*)

PERRY: No…no. I was makin' a sandwich.

EDDIE: Oh no. Didja eat?

PERRY: No.

EDDIE: Well go ahead, Perry. You gotta eat. Make your sandwich.

PERRY: No point.

EDDIE: No, go ahead and eat.

PERRY: There's no tomato.

EDDIE: What?

PERRY: I hadda tomato, but it's gone.
 (*Small beat.*)

EDDIE: Whattaya mean, Perry? I'm not…I don't…

PERRY: I gotta have tomato on my sandwich. I had one but it's gone so
 now…fuck it.
 (*Eddie takes a beat, considers this.*)

EDDIE: You got cheese?

PERRY: Yeah. I got cheese.

EDDIE: Put that on.

PERRY: Insteada tomato?

EDDIE: Yeah. Put cheese.

PERRY: It ain't the same.
 (*Pause.*)

EDDIE: Perry, are ya hungry?

PERRY: Starvin'.

EDDIE: And you ain't gonna make somethin' to eat 'cause you ain't
 gotta tomato?

PERRY: What's your point?

EDDIE: It's just you must have a big desire for this tomato. If you're not
 gonna eat because…

SANDY: *Shut up about the goddamn tomato!* Jesus Christ!

EDDIE: I'm sorry, Sandy, are we disturbin' you?

PERRY: (*To Sandy.*) It's important!

SANDY: If it's so goddamn important then go out and get your lousy
 tomato.

PERRY: I had one right here! I had one right here inna ice box yesterday
 and now it's gone! Why should I go out inta the hot to get
 somethin' I had already?!

SANDY: If it's not there then…

PERRY: That's not the point! That is not the point! The point is it was there and now it's not. I already had it. I planned ahead for it and now it's fucked up!

SANDY: You don't make sense.

PERRY: You ate it goddamnit!

SANDY: I didn't eat it! I told you I don't like fucking tomatoes!

PERRY: Then you threw it out!

SANDY: Bullshit…

PERRY: On your ass all day long, not doin' a fuckin' thing…
    (*Overlapping.*)

SANDY: Listen, Perry, I gotta idea…

EDDIE: Wait now…

PERRY:…sittin' around in bed…

SANDY: I gotta idea…

EDDIE: Wait…wait now…

PERRY: Breakin' my balls all week, can't keep a lousy fuckin' tomato for my sandwich…

EDDIE: Perry, Perry, Perry…

SANDY: Why don't you take that tomato…

EDDIE: Sandy, wait…

PERRY: And do what?

SANDY: Take that lousy fucking *imaginary* goddamned tomato…

PERRY:…and do what…do what…?

EDDIE:…Uh oh…

SANDY:…and shove it up your fat ass!!

PERRY: Piss off…

SANDY: Tough guy…

PERRY: Tough guy? You wanta see a tough guy…?

EDDIE: Perry, this ain't…

SANDY: That don't scare me, Perry, that bullshit might work someplace else but it don't work here…

PERRY: You think I'm bullshittin'? You don't think I'll come over there and slap your smart ass tomato-eatin' mouth…?

SANDY: Such a tough guy. Eddie, ain't he tough? Look at him. Christ…

PERRY: Watch it, Sandy, you hear me?!

EDDIE: Leave her alone, Perry, let's relax.

PERRY: (*Pummeling the refrigerator.*) Fuck it! Just fuck it! Treatin' me like a fuckin' mutt.

SANDY: (*Taunting.*) There ya go! Show your pal what a big tough swingin' dick you are!

EDDIE: Hey...! Let's calm down...I don't wanta see this...

PERRY: (*To Sandy.*) Fuck you!

SANDY: C'mon, needle dick!

EDDIE: Hey!

(*Simultaneously.*)

PERRY: Shut up, Sandy!	SANDY: Needle dick!
PERRY: Fuck you!	SANDY: Needle dick!
PERRY: Fuck you!	SANDY: Needle dick!

EDDIE: Hey! Hey! Hey! *Shut up!* (*They stop. There is a pause. End overlapping dialogue.*) All right. All right. Perry...Perry...

PERRY: I don't need this shit, Eddie.

EDDIE: I know. Go sit down. All right. Sit down, c'mon. (*Eddie edges Perry toward the table.*)

PERRY: This is bullshit...my own house...

EDDIE: Okay, you know, let's all kinda...Let's not do this. I hate to see this. Okay, Sandy...? Okay?

SANDY: I'm sicka him.

PERRY: I'm sicka *you!*

EDDIE: Don't say them things. That ain't true. The both of you.

SANDY: I'm sick to death of him and his fuckin' tomato...

EDDIE: We all are...we all are...let's leave that alone. That's a bad subject, I can see that.

PERRY: She started the shit.

SANDY: Me? You the one got tomatoes on the brain.

EDDIE: (*Interrupting.*) Hey, hey, hey, that's enough, all right? Let's start over. Whaddaya say? We're gonna start over. I hate to see this between you two. You guys are gonna ruin my...you're gonna ruin it for me here. My favorite couple...don't gimme bad illusions about you two. Terrible. Terrible. And Sandy, it ain't good for you, gettin' upset.

SANDY: What do you know about it?

EDDIE: I don't. I'm just sayin' for your health and all...

SANDY: Fuck do you know about it? You don't know shit about my health.

EDDIE: That's true...that's very true...

PERRY: Don't talk to him like that. You don't have to talk to him like that.

EDDIE: No. It's okay, Per. She's right.

PERRY: He's tryna be nice, Sandy. Don't go bein' rude to the guy, all right?

SANDY: He don't know about it...buttin' in like he...I don't even know this guy!

EDDIE: You're right. (*To Perry.*) She's right.

PERRY: He's my friend in my house. I don't want you talkin' like that.

SANDY: Like what?

PERRY: Puttin' him down...

SANDY: I...

PERRY: Puttin' him down, puttin' him down! Like you do all time.

EDDIE: Ahhhhhh, c'mon now...

SANDY: I can say what I like. I don't want him in my business... Dr....fuckin'...what? Marcus Fuckin' Welby or somethin'?

PERRY: That's what I mean. You and your smart mouth. I don't wanta hear that mouth, all right? About my friends, I don't wanta hear that mouth!

EDDIE: Perry, really, it don't matter. She's right, okay?

PERRY: No. She ain't right! (*Perry picks up shoes and socks. Sits and begins putting them on.*) It ain't right, a person comes here and gets treated like that.

SANDY: (*Suddenly anxious.*) Where you goin'?

EDDIE: It don't matter, Perry.

PERRY: It matters to me, all right?

EDDIE: Sure it does.

SANDY: (*More anxious.*) Where you goin'?

PERRY: It comes to a point, ya know...a little respect. For me. For my friends. I don't ax that much, Eddie.

SANDY: Where you goin', Perry?

EDDIE: Where you goin'?

PERRY: Schwegmann's.

EDDIE: You gonna make some groceries? I'll go with.

PERRY: You stay here.

EDDIE: Tell me what you want. I'll go and you can stay here.

PERRY: No! I gotta get outta here for a minute.

EDDIE: Yeah. You need to cool down. It'll be good for ya. We'll all cool down for awhile. Right, Sandy?

SANDY: (*A bit panicky.*) You leavin' him here? Wait! When you comin' back?

PERRY: (*Going to door.*) When I get back. (*Perry opens the door to leave, gets a foot out.*)

SANDY: (*Pleading.*) Perry, let him go. He said he'd go. Let him go.

PERRY: I'm goin'.

SANDY: Don't leave him here with me! (*Perry exits.*) Perry!

EDDIE: He'll be right back.

SANDY: Perry!

EDDIE: Sandy, he's comin' right back.

SANDY: (*Hurling book at door.*) Perry!

EDDIE: He's just gonna cool off for a...

SANDY: *Shut up! You shut up!*

EDDIE: (*Backing off quickly.*) Okay. All right. (*Alone with Sandy, Eddie doesn't know what to do with himself. He walks over to the door and picks up the book. He brings it over to Sandy and offers it to her. She doesn't react. He drops it on the bed. Looking for something to do, he walks over to the table. He picks up Perry's beer.*)

EDDIE: (*To no one, about Perry's beer.*) Keep this cold.
(*He turns and puts Perry's beer in the refrigerator. He closes the door and leans against it.*)

EDDIE: (*About Sandy's robe.*) That's a good color on you, Sandy. (*Beat. She ignores him.*) What is that? Like, green? Blue. I never seen a color like that, I don't think.
(*No response from Sandy. Eddie opens the refrigerator and rummages around.*)

SANDY: What're you doin'?

EDDIE: Nothin'.

SANDY: What're you rootin' around in there for?

EDDIE: I wasn't rootin'. I was just lookin'.

SANDY: Lookin' for what?

EDDIE: Nothin'.

SANDY: Then quit nosin' around. Ain't none of your business what's in there.

EDDIE: All right. (*He closes the door. Long pause.*) I was lookin' for Perry's tomato.

SANDY: What?

EDDIE: I was just wonderin' if maybe...You know how you can be lookin' right at a thing and don't see it? (*Beat.*) It ain't there.

(*A pause. Sandy begins to cry. There is something very deep in it.*)

SANDY: I didn't take his goddamn tomato.

EDDIE: No. I wasn't sayin' that. (*Sandy cries. Eddie watches, helpless.*) You want some water?

(*Without waiting for a response, he finds a glass and gets water from the bathroom sink. He brings it out to Sandy and she takes it. She drinks it quickly. She sniffles some and wipes her nose with her hand. He rushes back into the bathroom and returns with a roll of toilet paper. It's a new roll and he has difficulty getting the first sheet started. Sandy watches him wordlessly. He tears at the toilet paper and hands a wad to Sandy. Sandy takes care of her nose. A beat then:*)

EDDIE: You really havin' a bad day, huh? (*Sandy shrugs and holds the empty glass out for Eddie. He takes it.*) You want more? (*Sandy shakes her head, "no." Eddie looks at the glass.*) Water. Huh. Funny how when there's trouble that's the first thing ya go for. Am I right? My old lady, when I was a kid, I'd start bawlin', she's right there with the water, skin my knee, somethin'…I don't know. I could be drownin' inna lake, they'll pull me out and she'd be tryna get some more water down me. (*Beat.*) You think it does any good, Sandy, all that water? (*Sandy shrugs.*) I don't know either. (*Pause. Sandy gives a little laugh.*) What?

SANDY: (*Laughing.*) What you just said…

EDDIE: (*Grinning.*) What?

SANDY: About you drownin' and your mother tryna get more water down ya. I just pictured it in my head. Funny.

EDDIE: (*Pleased.*) She would too. I'm tellin' ya. (*Beat.*) You feelin' better? (*A little shrug from Sandy. Eddie takes the empty glass into the kitchen area.*) You know, Sandy…it ain't none of my business whatsoever, but, you gettin' upset like that…that wasn't about no tomato.

SANDY: Don't worry about it.

EDDIE: You and Perry talkin' that way to each other. Sayin' them things.

SANDY: (*Defensive.*) Hey! That don't mean nothin'. People gotta right to be mad at each other sometimes. It's natural. Don't mean nothin'.

EDDIE: Sure, sure. I know that. (*Beat.*) Hey, Sandy?

SANDY: What?

EDDIE: You know I talk a lot, you know I'm always talkin' some bullshit. But one thing about me is sometimes, like at work, somethin', some guy's got a beef, we talk about it. Sometimes I come up with some shit, kinda help 'em out. Just to talk, I don't know...

SANDY: So?

EDDIE: So, I'm just sayin', you know, if...I don't know. You and Perry cooped up in here alla time, you not able to get around...

SANDY: What?! What, what, what?! Jesus, can't you just say a thing without jumpin' around all over it?

EDDIE: No, all's I'm sayin' is, if there's some things you'd like to talk about...

SANDY: To you?

EDDIE: Sure. To me.

SANDY: What could I have to say to you?

EDDIE: I don't know. You're havin' a bad day. Maybe that.

SANDY: I don't know you.

EDDIE: Not that well, I guess, but sometimes that's good too.

SANDY: I ain't talkin' to you.

EDDIE: Okay. I was just axin'.

(*Pause.*)

SANDY: Whadda you know about my problems anyway?

EDDIE: Not a thing, prolly.

SANDY: You couldn't even imagine...

EDDIE: Prolly not...

SANDY: ...even in your dreams, the kinda problems I got to deal with.

EDDIE: ...yeah...

SANDY: ...The things that weigh on me, you'd blow your scrawny little brains out.

EDDIE: I don't think I could deal with it, you're right.

SANDY: Damn right I'm right.

EDDIE: You're right.

SANDY: I know.

(*Pause.*)

EDDIE: Perry's alla time sayin' how much he admires you and all, for what you been goin' through. How you been handlin' it and all.

SANDY: (*Beat. She looks at Eddie.*) He said that?

EDDIE: Yeah. At work, alla time. Talks about how strong you been. How you always talkin' about gettin' well and about your good attitude and all.

SANDY: Yeah. Well. It ain't easy, you know. (*Pause.*) I treat him so bad sometimes. I don't know why, I just…I have these bad days, I start thinkin' about how it was before. You never knew me then, did ya?

EDDIE: Huh uh.

SANDY: That's the hard part, you know? Perry, I don't think he unnerstands that part so good.

EDDIE: Whaddaya mean?

SANDY: Perry looks at me bein' sick. Like that's the whole problem, which it is, kinda, but it's more. I mean, he unnerstands I can't walk and we can't go around like we used to and all them problems. He's real good about that. But he don't unnerstand how it messed up my plans. Things I used to think about, you know? See, it woulda been different if I'da been born like this or somethin'. It's like I coulda included that in my plans. But now the things I thought about my whole life got kinda ruined and I gotta make me a whole new plan.

EDDIE: Perry says this thing you got, he says it could get better.

SANDY: It could maybe, but what if it don't? That's what makes these bad days. I don't feel like makin' me a new plan, I want the old one.

(*Pause.*)

EDDIE: Yeah. You mean like your dreams and shit?

SANDY: Yeah. They wasn't just dreams neither. Before I got sick, they was on their way to comin' true.

EDDIE: What was that?

SANDY: I was on T.V.

EDDIE: For what?

SANDY: A commercial.

EDDIE: You shinin' me.

SANDY: It's true. For A.C.'s Auto Salvage.

EDDIE: When was this?

SANDY: Two years ago. Sometimes I think it still comes on. I seen it on the cable.

EDDIE: Did you talk?

SANDY: Nah. I didn't have to say nothin'.

EDDIE: What was it? Maybe I seen it.

SANDY: You know where there's this old beat up car in front of this house, and there's this girl tryna open the door on it…?

EDDIE: Wait a minute! Wait…and she pulls on the door and it falls off…?

SANDY: Yeah…

EDDIE: And then in the end, they got that guy puttin' that money in her hand?

SANDY: That's me.

EDDIE: That's you?!

SANDY: Uh huh.

EDDIE: I don't believe this! Wait…(*Eddie takes a close look at Sandy.*) Son of a bitch! I seen that commercial maybe a million times, and here I am sittin' with the one that did it! I never knew you was a actress.

SANDY: And a model too. Mostly that's what I wanted to do. I got me some professional pictures made up and everything. I think I coulda done real good. They's a lot of that kind of stuff in New Orleans. For magazines and catalogues and shit. Plus, ya know that commercial?

EDDIE: Yeah.

SANDY: That was the first thing I went out for.

EDDIE: Get outta here.

SANDY: Ask Perry. And they was prolly like a hundred or so girls tried out for it. Beat 'em all the first time out.

EDDIE: That don't surprise me.

SANDY: Whatsa odds of that, you think?

EDDIE: Almost impossible.

SANDY: That's what I'm talkin' about. You have that kinda success right off, you kinda expect things to start goin' your way. It ain't everybody gets a break like that right off.

EDDIE: Hell no.

SANDY: So, right when everything starts lookin' good for me, it all turns to shit.

EDDIE: I know what you mean, Sandy.

SANDY: You do?

EDDIE: Well, only kinda. I never had no plans that big to get spoilt. I'm just one a them guys goes by day to day, you know?

SANDY: What're you talkin' about? Everybody's got their plans. Their dreams.

EDDIE: Yeah, I know. I'm just sayin' some people's got bigger ones than others. I'm just one a them people's got the smaller version.

(*Pause. Sandy checks Eddie out.*)

SANDY: What kinda dreams you got, Eddie?

EDDIE: Who me?

SANDY: You the only one named Eddie.

EDDIE: I don't know, you know, they pretty much the regular stuff.

SANDY: Like what?

EDDIE: (*Small shrug.*) I don't know. I wouldn't mind a unlimited supply of cash.

SANDY: Everybody wants that. If everybody wants it, it don't count. What else you want, Eddie?

EDDIE: (*Beat.*) I usta wanta do some travelin'.

SANDY: Oh yeah?

EDDIE: Yeah. I had this aunt won a trip to Greece. Before she left she was showin' all us kids them pamphlets with them statues and beaches. She was tellin' us how warm and blue that water they got over there is. I thought I wouldn't mind seein' somma that.

SANDY: Don't ya still wanna go?

EDDIE: Nah. Not really. She come back and told me travelin' ain't nothin' but a pain in the ass. She said Greece ain't nothin' but a buncha old ruins and shit. Said she'd just as soon drive to Gulf Shores next time.

SANDY: Oh.

EDDIE: It don't matter.

SANDY: (*Beat.*) Is that it?

EDDIE: Yeah. I guess so. I told you they wasn't much.

SANDY: They ain't shit.

EDDIE: That ain't nice.

SANDY: Well, they ain't.

EDDIE: Well, maybe it ain't bein' on the T.V. but not everybody's like that, Sandy. Not everybody wants dreams like yours, okay? I know, I ain't nothin' but a little French Quarter Dago, all right but it don't bother me.

SANDY: Don't get inna uproar.

EDDIE: I ain't inna uproar. I'm just sayin' some people's satisfied with what they got. Nothin' wrong with that.

SANDY: Nobody's satisfied with what they got. Everybody wants somethin' else.

EDDIE: Maybe so, but a lotta times people just want what comes down the line and they satisfied with that, and when it does come down the line, they damn glad to have it.

SANDY: Bullshit.

EDDIE: Uh uh. It ain't bullshit.

SANDY: What makes you sucha expert?

EDDIE: I ain't a expert, I'm just sayin' for me...

SANDY: Big dream expert when you ain't even got any...

EDDIE: Hey! Hey! That ain't right. I got my dreams, all right. And they ain't any less important than yours or anybody else. Some people's just like that. They don't ask for much...

SANDY: ...and they don't get much...

EDDIE: ...and maybe that's all they want. See what I'm sayin'? Sometimes the only thing I want in the world is to wake up in the mornin' and it's pissin' rain. Thunderin' and lightenin' and I ain't gotta go to work. Don't have to climb up on no roof and sweat my ass off humpin' shingles, all right? Sometimes all I want is enough money in my pocket to buy me a dinner at the Picadilly, read the paper, and drink some coffee. That's all I need. And sometimes, you know, it happens. I get what I want and it's like dreams comin' true. Don't you think? It's like dreams comin' true?

SANDY: That ain't dreams.

EDDIE: You don't think?

SANDY: No. That kinda stuff happens alla time. That's everyday shit.

EDDIE: Well then see? It's like dreams comin' true everyday.

SANDY: Those ain't dreams!

EDDIE: What're you sayin', Sandy? A dream ain't a dream no more if it comes true? A dream is somethin' that don't never come true? (*Pause. Sandy stews.*) I'm just careful is all. I try not to let things get bigger than me. Saves me some heartache. There's lottsa people like that. Different people. Some people want a million bucks, some people just want a tomato inna refrigerator when they makin' a sandwich. Simple as that.

SANDY: Simple as that, huh?

EDDIE: Maybe.

SANDY: Pretty fuckin' sad you ask me.

EDDIE: Maybe so. All's I know is I don't ask for much. I ain't walkin' around disappointed alla time.

(*Pause. Sandy looks at Eddie hard.*)

SANDY: Maybe I should be more like that. That what you're sayin'?

EDDIE: No...

SANDY: That the lesson, Eddie? That the thing being *taught?*

EDDIE: I'm sayin'...no...I'm sayin' for me...

SANDY: Oh, for you. I thought you was tryna...
  (Overlapped dialogue.)
  EDDIE: Oh, no...
  SANDY:...you know...
  EDDIE: No...you gotta...you gotta...
  SANDY: You were just sayin' some people...
  EDDIE: Yeah...*some*...not all...
  SANDY: Oh, I see. At first, I thought maybe this was *advice*...
  EDDIE: Oh, no...
  SANDY:...that I was hearin'.
  EDDIE: Not at all, I would never...
  SANDY: You bein' so good with people's problems. Helpin' people out...
EDDIE: No. We're just talkin'.
SANDY: I see.
EDDIE: This is just talkin'. That's all. Don't mean nothin'.
SANDY: Okay.
EDDIE: Yeah.
  (End of overlapped dialogue. A long pause. Sandy keeps Eddie in the crosshairs. Eddie tries to make himself comfortable beneath her gaze. A very soft roll of thunder sounds in the distance.)
EDDIE: Here it comes. I knew it was gonna...
SANDY: Do you wanta screw me, Eddie?
EDDIE: (*Caught way off.*) What?
SANDY: You wanna screw me?
EDDIE: What the hell kinda question is that?
SANDY: I'm just wonderin'.
EDDIE: What kinda...? How'm I supposed to answer that? That's...that's...
SANDY: Quit squirmin'. It's just a question.
EDDIE: (*Standing.*) I gotta go...
SANDY: No. Wait. Wait a minute...
EDDIE: Nah, really, Sandy. This ain't right. I don't know what you're doin' here...
SANDY: Don't go, Eddie. C'mere, I wanna talk to you.
EDDIE: Nah. I better go. I really gotta go...
SANDY: Wait...
EDDIE: I got...you know...Perry's gonna be here...
SANDY: I wanta ax you somethin.

EDDIE: What?

SANDY: I really wanta know.

EDDIE: What, Sandy...? Jesus...

SANDY: Just stay here and talk to me. Sit down. You were the one wanted to talk...

EDDIE: Yeah, but...

SANDY: Eddie, it ain't no big deal, I'm just wonderin'...I'm axin' you a simple question...

EDDIE: A simple...? That wasn't no simple question. That's the opposite. That's the opposite of a simple question.

SANDY: Just tell me. (*Pause.*) Eddie? (*No response.*) Eddie?

EDDIE: What?

SANDY: I know what's in your head. I can feel it. It's me you come over here for, ain't it?

(*Something like a snort escapes him. Something between a laugh and being punched in the stomach.*)

EDDIE: Yeah. Right.

SANDY: It ain't funny.

EDDIE: You goddamn right it ain't funny.

SANDY: I can smell it, soon as you walk in, Eddie. You sittin' there at that table with Perry, ya'll talkin' bullshit and drinkin' beer, and the whole time you wonderin' about me. That's the truth, ain't it? (*No response.*) Ain't it? (*Pause. Eddie is hooked. Her voice and manner keep him glued to her every word. Everything Sandy says is true and Eddie is caught like a deer in headlights.*) What is it you wonderin', Eddie? (*She loosens her robe and opens it at the top, showing her loose pajama top.*) You wonderin' about my mouth? How it feels, what I taste like? You come over here for a little visit and leave with a head fulla me, ain't that right? When you all by yourself at home, before you go to sleep at night, you think about me? Pretend I'm there in that room with you? (*Sandy unbuttons her pajama top.*) This what you think about? (*She opens her top, revealing her breasts to Eddie. Eddie stares, cannot look away.*) Perry tells stories at work, don't he? 'Bout how I take care of him. He tell you it don't matter I can't feel nothin' down there, I still take care of him. You think about them stories, pretend it's you? I like that you think about me. (*Pause.*) Perry says you like to buy whores, Eddie.

EDDIE: That ain't true!

SANDY: It's all right. That's what they there for.

EDDIE: Perry oughta keep his goddamn mouth shut.

SANDY: You ever take one a them girls, pretend it's me? Them stories Perry tells about us. You get her to do that?

EDDIE: (*Quiet, intense.*) Shut up...

SANDY: It's okay. I like it. I'm glad.

EDDIE: Shut up!

SANDY: C'mere. (*She holds out her hand.*) C'mere. Come sit here a minute. (*She indicates the bed. Eddie shakes his head "no."*) C'mere. Eddie. (*Eddie shoots a look at the door.*)

EDDIE: (*A mumble.*)...Perry...

SANDY: Come see. (*Eddie hesitates, then moves slowly to her. He stands near her but will not sit on the bed.*) Eddie. I'm gonna ask you again, now you tell me. Do you want to screw me? (*Eddie hesitates, he glances nervously at the door again.*) I'm not talkin' about now, sugar. Perry's gonna be home any minute. I was thinkin' maybe one a them rainy days you was talkin' about. Wouldn't that be nice? Me makin' you feel good on one a them rainy days? Would you like that? You want me to make you feel good? (*A beat. Eddie nods his head "yes." The nod is barely perceptible, but a definite yes.*) Okay. (*Sandy smiles, begins buttoning her pajama top.*) I thought so. The only thing is, you make me puke you simple piece of shit. (*Eddie, stunned, backs away from her bed. It dawns on him what she's done. He looks for his keys and hat.*) That's right. Get outta here you "no-problem-easy-to-please" little motherfucker. Talkin' all that bullshit. "Some people don't ax much..." Everybody wants somethin' they ain't never gonna get. You ain't no different from nobody else, you hear me...

EDDIE: Shut up...just...shut the...

SANDY:...so don't go around like you are. *Everybody* is fucked up and *everything* is fucked up and don't pretend it ain't...

EDDIE: You're crazy, Sandy, you know that? Crazy bitch!!
(*Eddie makes for the door.*)

SANDY: Uh huh. At least I know. I know. I ain't the one livin' in shit and callin' it clover!
(*Eddie opens the door and starts out. He stops and moves back into the room quickly. Perry enters the room with a small brown paper bag. He looks at Eddie.*)

PERRY: Where you goin'?

EDDIE: I, uh...I was just...I gotta go.

PERRY: I just got back.

EDDIE: I know, but I gotta meet somebody.

PERRY: Who?

EDDIE: ...Randy. (*Pause. Perry looks at him.*) I gotta go.

PERRY: All right. (*Letting Eddie pass.*) Go get Randy and ya'll come on back here if you want.

EDDIE: Yeah. All right. I'll ax Randy. I'll see ya tomorrow, Per.

SANDY: If it don't rain.

EDDIE: I gotta go.

PERRY: Well, go. Go ahead on.

(*Eddie leaves. Perry walks to the table and sits down. He opens his bag and removes a tomato. He begins the process of rebuilding his sandwich.*)

PERRY: What'd you do?

SANDY: What?

PERRY: What'd you do?

SANDY: Whaddaya mean, what'd I do?

PERRY: What'd you do?

SANDY: What? What, what, what?!

PERRY: To Eddie. I'm axin' what'd you do?

SANDY: I didn't do nothin'.

(*Rapid exchange, overlap dialogue.*)

PERRY: You didn't do nothin?

SANDY: ...no...

PERRY: You didn't say nothin...

SANDY: ...no...

PERRY: ...to offend him...

SANDY: ...no...

PERRY: No?

SANDY: ...No!...

(*Pause. End overlapping dialogue. Perry cuts his tomato. Stops.*)

PERRY: What was them loud voices? Comin' up the stairs, what was that?

SANDY: I don't know.

PERRY: Sounded like you yellin'.

SANDY: Wasn't me.

PERRY: No?

SANDY: No.

PERRY: Sounded like.

SANDY: Maybe it was upstairs.

PERRY: Upstairs you think?

SANDY: Maybe.

PERRY: Maybe. (*Pause. Perry places the tomato slice on his sandwich. Places the top bread slice on. Stops.*) How come he looked like that when I come in? Eddie. How come he looked like that?

SANDY: Always looks the same to me. What'd he look like?

PERRY: Sick. Like he swallowed a turd, somethin'.

SANDY: I don't know. Maybe he remembered some bad news.

PERRY: Bad news you think?

SANDY: Yeah. Or maybe he was just inna hurry to meet somebody, I don't know, Perry, what's the matter with you?

PERRY: Nothin'. I was just wonderin'.

(*Perry turns back to his sandwich. He mashes it down, flattening it just right. He takes a knife and cuts it precisely corner to corner. He picks up a sandwich half and stops.*)

PERRY: You know, I was walkin' to the store and I got almost there and I remembered there never was no tomato. (*Beat.*) I ate it yesterday, but I forgot. (*He turns and looks at Sandy. Sandy looks at Perry. She nods a little nod.*) Anyway…It wasn't you.

SANDY: It's okay, Perry. You was hungry. I know how you get when you're hungry.

PERRY: Yeah. (*Pause.*) Sandy?

SANDY: Huh?

(*Perry moves over to the bed and sits beside her. He begins massaging her legs.*)

PERRY: I'm sorry about yellin' at you, but, I meant what I said about when my friends come here, all right. (*Sandy remains silent.*) I know you're havin' a bad time lately, I know that, but like, Eddie ain't such a bad guy, you know, and the minute he walks in here you freeze him out.

SANDY: He ain't such a bad guy, huh?

PERRY: No. I ain't sayin' you gotta fall all over the man, he comes walkin' in. Just be a little more…you know…

SANDY: Friendly?

PERRY: Yeah. Could ya just do that for me?

SANDY: Sure. If that's what you want.

PERRY: That's what I want. I think things'll be much smoother around here, you know what I'm sayin'?

SANDY: Sure, Perry. (*A beat. Sandy touches Perry's back softly.*) Anything else?

PERRY: What?

SANDY: (*Touches his neck, fingers his hair.*) Anything else you want? (*Perry stiffens a bit. Stops massaging Sandy's legs.*)

PERRY: Um...no. That's...that's all I wanted to tell you. (*Perry moves back to the table, sits, and takes a bite from his sandwich. Sandy, hurt, watches him eat.*)

SANDY: That a good sandwich, Perry?

PERRY: (*Through mouthful.*) Yeah.

SANDY: Been thinkin' about that sandwich all day, huh? And now you got it. Just like you like it. With a nice big tomato. Got just what you wanted, huh baby?

PERRY: I guess so.

SANDY: That's nice. I'm glad. I'm glad somebody got somethin' they wanted today. (*We hold on Sandy and Perry as street noise begins to bleed into the room. Music drifts through.*)

Lights fade to black...

END OF PLAY

Tom And Jerry
by Rick Cleveland

BIOGRAPHY

RICK CLEVELAND earned his MFA from the University of Iowa's Playwrights Workshop and has received play-writing fellowships from the National Endowment for the Arts, the Rockefeller Foundation, and the Illinois Arts Council. His latest play, *Tom and Jerry*, was developed as part of the Minneapolis Playwrights' Center's 1994 PlayLabs, was produced in Los Angeles summer 1994 for Showtime's Act One Festival of One-Act Plays, and is now being developed as a feature film. He has been to the Eugene O'Neill Theater Center's National Playwrights' Conference twice with *Home Grown* in 1991, and with *You Send Me* in 1993. *You Send Me* was recently optioned by Universal Studios. His play, *The Rhino's Policeman*, was commissioned by the Goodman Theatre and won a grant from the Kennedy Center's Fund for New American Plays in 1992. Rick is a Second City-trained actor, a freelance journalist, and a former playwright-in-residence with Victory Gardens Theater in Chicago. He is currently a feature writer for Bungalow 78 Productions at Universal Studios.

AUTHOR'S NOTE

There's this guy tied to a chair with a hood over his head, and he's telling bad jokes to the two other guys who are about to kill him. That's the very first idea I ever had for a play.

When I was still a teenager living in Ohio, I worked in a mob-run comedy club/steakhouse that had dog fights in the basement on weekdays. I was part of the house improv troupe—we were pretty bad —and in between sets, there were these two guys who hung out at the bar who would tell us old barroom jokes in an attempt to help us improve our act. I think their names were something like Tony and Mike, but it's probably better that I don't quite remember. They would tell us an old joke and say, "Feel free to use that one," or "That one would *kill.*" From time to time they would bring their wives into the club and order big porterhouse steaks or prime rib. They lived in the suburbs and would argue about whether or not Sears made the best lawn mower. They were introduced to people by the club's owner as "liquor salesmen," "distributors," or "associates," and to me they were just a couple of regular blue-collar working guys.

A few years later, after I moved to Chicago, the owner of the club and another of his "associates" were tied to chairs with hoods over their heads and executed, gangland style—a shotgun blast to the back of the head for each of them. Not long after that, those two guys who hung out at the bar were implicated, tried, and convicted. The same two guys who used to tell us jokes and sometimes buy us drinks. The same two guys who had families, and lived in the suburbs, and argued about lawn mowers.

The image of the guy tied to a chair with a hood over his head, telling jokes to the two other guys who are about to kill him rattled around in my head for a long, long time. And then in 1992, during a workshop with Maria Irene Fornes at the University of Iowa, it finally hit me (like shovel to the back of the head), and the play just about wrote itself. Those two jamokes really were just a bunch of regular, blue-collar working guys—they just happened to kill people for living. They were hitmen, no doubt about it—but they were hitmen with good, solid, *family values*. And it's probably a good thing that I can't quite, *for the life of me,* remember their names. Those old jokes, however, I'll never forget.

ORIGINAL PRODUCTION

A short one-act version of *Tom and Jerry* was first produced for Showtime's Act One Festival of One-Act Plays at the Met Theatre in Los Angeles, California, on May 28, 1994. The director was Saul Rubinek with the following cast:

Tom . . . . .Sam McMurray
Jerry . . . . .Bruce McVittie
Tony/Karl/Vic/Etc . . . . .Dan Castellaneta

A longer version of *Tom and Jerry* was given a staged reading during the GeVa Theatre's French Roast Festival at the GeVa Theatre in Rochester, New York, on July 5, 1994, with the following cast:

Tom . . . . .Anthony Zerbe
Jerry . . . . .Josh Brolin
Tony/Karl/Vic/Etc. . . . . .Dennis Cockrum

The short full-length version of *Tom and Jerry* was workshopped and presented in a staged reading during the Minneapolis Playwrights' Center's 1994 PlayLabs at the University of Minnesota on August 12, 1994. The director was Mark Hunter. The dramaturg was Tom Poole. The cast was:

Tom . . . . .Joe P. Gilday
Jerry . . . . .Bill Corbett
Tony/Karl/Vic/Etc. . . . . .J.C. Cutler

THE CHARACTERS
Tom, a guy who works for a guy named Billy. In his 40s.
Jerry, another guy who works for a guy named Billy. In his 20s.
Other Characters, all played by the same actor, a Man:
Tony
Karl
Greasy Guy with Elvis sideburns
Fat guy
Vic
Elaine
Woman in bed

THE SETTING
Chicago and Florida.

THE TIME
The mid-1980s to a couple of months from the present.

THE SETTING
Just enough furniture and atmosphere to suggest location. Coat trees and prop tables (for guns and hardware) down left and down right.

TOM AND JERRY

Lights up on a taproom on the south side of Chicago. Mid-afternoon, but a little dark inside. A phone on the bar. Tom and Jerry, and a third guy, Tony, with his hands tied behind his back and a hood over his head. Jerry holds a shotgun. Tom smokes a cigarette.

TOM: You want us to take the hood off for awhile?

TONY: No thanks.

TOM: Could be awhile. Make it easier to breathe.

TONY: I'm okay.

TOM: Suit yourself.
    (*Pause.*)

JERRY: What're we waiting for?

TOM: Phone to ring.

JERRY: Why not just do him?

TOM: Supposed to wait until we get the call.

JERRY: And what, just sit here?

TOM: That's right.

JERRY: All I'm saying is, we could just do him now, get it over with.

TOM: We do him now, the phone rings, there's been a change of plans, there's been a mistake, then what?

JERRY: Too fucking bad, I say.

TOM: You're anxious.

JERRY: So fucking what?

TOM: Hey Tony, are you anxious to get this over with?

TONY: Not especially.

TOM: See, Tony's not anxious.

JERRY: So what I'm anxious, so fucking what.

TOM: Anxious is not good.

JERRY: I just don't want to sit here and dwell on this.

TOM: Go put a couple of quarters in the juke box, clip your nails, I don't care, *something*.

JERRY: Christ.

TOM: Know any good jokes?

JERRY: Not at the moment, no.

TONY: (*Beat.*) I got one.

TOM: You got a joke?

TONY: This grasshopper walks into a bar, the bartender says, "You know, we got a drink named after you." The grasshopper goes, "What, you got a drink named Kevin?"
(*Beat.*)

JERRY: I don't fucking get it.

TOM: (*Starts to laugh.*) Grasshopper named Kevin. That's a good one, Tony.

JERRY: That joke is for shit. I say we do him now.

TONY: (*Quickly.*) I got another one.

TOM: Let's hear it.

TONY: Guy walks into a doctor's office with a duck on his head. Doctor says, "May I help you?" Duck says, "Yeah – any way you can get this *guy* off my ass?"

TOM: (*Beat; he cracks up.*) Guy off my ass...

JERRY: Not even remotely funny. Guy off my ass, my ass.

TOM: Tell us another one, Tony, you crack me up.

TONY: (*Beat.*) Uh – this penguin walks into a bar...

JERRY: A penguin?

TONY: Yeah, a penguin.

JERRY: Why can't it be somethin' else, like a Polack or somethin'?

TONY: Because on this particular day, it happened to be a penguin that walked into the bar.

JERRY: (*Beat.*) Okay. Go ahead.

TONY: Anyway, this penguin walks into a bar and orders a scotch on the rocks. The bartender can't believe his eyes. He goes back to his boss and says, "You're not gonna believe this, but a penguin just walked in here and ordered a scotch on the rocks."

JERRY: How's he gonna drink it...?

TONY: Slowly.

JERRY: Penguins don't have hands. Ducks don't talk. And grasshoppers aren't named Kevin.

TOM: Jerry, it's just a fucking joke.

JERRY: I understand that it's just a joke, Tom. But even a joke has to be remotely possible, am I right?

TONY: (*Beat.*) Maybe he's gonna drink it with his flippers.

JERRY: With his flippers...?

TONY: Yeah.

JERRY: Okay. Go ahead.

TONY: So the bartender goes to his boss, he says, "You're not gonna believe this, but a penguin just walked in here and ordered a scotch on the rocks." The boss goes, "Charge him four bucks." The bartender goes back, pours the penguin his drink, and says, "That'll be four bucks." The penguin pays him.

JERRY: Where's he keep his money...?

TONY: In his wallet like everybody else.

JERRY: Okay, if you say so.

TONY: The penguin sits there drinking his scotch. Slowly, with his flippers. Finally, the bartender says –

TOM: (*Interrupting him.*) I heard this one.

JERRY: You heard this one?

TOM: Yeah, I heard this one.

(*The phone rings.*)

JERRY: There's the phone.

TONY: You want me to finish the joke...?

(*The phone keeps ringing.*)

JERRY: You gonna answer it?

TOM: Yeah.

(*Pause.*)

JERRY: You want me to answer it?

TOM: That's okay, I'll get it.

JERRY: Answer the phone, Tom.

TONY: You want I should finish the joke or not?

JERRY: Forget about the fucking joke, Tony.

TONY: Okay.

(*The phone keeps ringing.*)

JERRY: Answer the phone, Tom. (*Beat.*) Tom. Answer the fucking phone.

(*Tom just sits there, looking old and tired. The phone keeps ringing. Finally, he reaches over and picks it up.*)

TOM: Hello...?

(*Lights fade.*)

SCENE 2

A parked car, about ten years earlier, sometime in the mid-80s. Tom sits in the back seat. Jerry sits behind the wheel, wolfing down a burger. Tony takes the hood off his head, puts on a pair of thick-framed glasses and a windbreaker, grabs a box of fries, and sits in the front seat, on the passenger side – immediately becoming Karl.

KARL: Tom, you remember my nephew, Franky Buddakowski?

JERRY: His brother Chris went to school with me.

KARL: He always liked you, Tom. Used to follow you around when he was a kid.

TOM: Had kind of a temper. Used to get him into trouble. Yeah, I remember Franky.

KARL: He's having some problems with some guys over there in Uptown. So one night they pull him out from behind the bar, take him outside, out front mind you, hold him down on the sidewalk, this big guy, this fucking cocksucker, bites his nose off.

TOM: Jesus.

JERRY: Wait a minute. He bites Franky's nose off?

KARL: Right the fuck off.

JERRY: You can't do that. You can't do that to a guy.

KARL: As you can imagine, this is very upsetting to my family, to my sister. Her boy is maimed. Maimed for life.

JERRY: So what happened to his nose?

KARL: Guy spits it out, the cops hunt around for it, they find it laying there in the street, drive it over to the hospital, they sew it back on.

JERRY: They can do that? Sew it back onto his face?

KARL: Yes. But it doesn't take.

TOM: Christ.

JERRY: What do you mean it doesn't take?

KARL: Nerve endings or something. The thing starts turning green, then black, they have to take it back off.

JERRY: So how's he gonna breathe?

TOM: The holes are still there, Jerry.

JERRY: What holes?

TOM: The what do you call them, the sinus passages.

JERRY: So what, now he's gotta go through life with a couple of holes in his face instead of a nose?

KARL: They're gonna try and build him a new one.

JERRY: Out of what—plastic?

KARL: Out of a piece of his ass.

JERRY: You're fucking kidding me.

KARL: They take a little tissue from his buttocks, make a nose out of it —how? Who the fuck knows. Doctors. They're gonna build him a brand new one.

JERRY: Out of a piece of his ass.

TOM: Jesus H. Christ.

JERRY: Will it be, you know, noticeable?

KARL: At this point in time, how the fuck does anyone know.

JERRY: I mean, there could be scars.

KARL: At the very least.

JERRY: They have to get it exactly right – the shape, the coloring. How's anybody ever gonna look him straight in the face?

TOM: Jerry...

JERRY: He could end up with an unpleasant nickname. I mean, this is his nose we're talking about. You just don't bite a guy's nose off. Spit it out like a piece of bad hotdog. It just isn't done.

KARL: Not to mention out front.

JERRY: Out front?

KARL: Out front of his place.

JERRY: What's that got to do with anything?

TOM: First off, you don't do a thing like this. But if you do, if say you had to, for some unforeseen reason...

KARL: You do it out back.

TOM: That's right. You do it out back.

JERRY: Out front, out back, I would never do a thing like that. To put a guy's nose in my mouth, I don't know where the fuck it's been.

KARL: You know my sister, Tom. She is very upset. Under sedation.

TOM: You want me to look into it?

KARL: Would you?

TOM: Certainly.

KARL: Thank you, Tom.

TOM: Don't mention it.

JERRY: (*Beat; to Karl.*) You gonna eat the rest of those fries...?

KARL: No, go ahead, kid.

TOM: Hey. I thought you said you already ate.

JERRY: I did. (*To Karl, shoving fries in his mouth.*) Thanks.

TOM: You could of stayed back at the office. I could of brought you something.

JERRY: I don't mind. I been cooped up there answering the phone all day.

TOM: Billy ain't gonna like it.

JERRY: Billy ain't gonna like what – that I come with?

TOM: Yeah. That you came with. He ain't gonna like it.

KARL: What's he not gonna like about it, Tom?

TOM: He's moody.

JERRY: Too fuckin' bad. I'll bring him a strawberry shake. He loves those fuckin' strawberry shakes.

(*Pause.*)

TOM: Kid's got a bottomless pit for a stomach.

KARL: So I noticed.

JERRY: What can I say. I'm a growing boy.

KARL: (*Beat.*) I got a funny feeling about this.

JERRY: (*Concentrating on his fries.*) A funny feeling about what?

TOM: Hey, Jerry.

JERRY: What?

TOM: Chew with your mouth closed, would you?

KARL: All of a sudden, I just got this funny feeling, you know, Tom?

TOM: Yeah, Karl, I know.

KARL: (*Beat.*) Can we talk about this, Tom?

TOM: (*Beat.*) No, Karl, I don't think we can.

KARL: We can talk, Tom, we're good friends, we can at least talk this thing through.

TOM: I don't think so, Karl.

KARL: You can at least listen for a minute, to my side of the story, am I right...?

TOM: I'm sorry, Karl.

KARL: We *bowl* together, Tom. Our wives are best friends. We go back. We have history.

TOM: Yes, we do. Hey. What can I say…?

(*Pause.*)

KARL: Oh, Christ. Oh, Jesus, Tom. (*Quietly.*) No…

(*Tom pulls out some wire, wraps it around Karl's neck, and strangles him. It takes a long time. Jerry watches, but tries not to. Finally, Karl stops moving.*)

TOM: I fucking hate it when they know it's coming. (*Beat.*) You okay, kid?

JERRY: Yeah…

TOM: Look at me.

(*Jerry turns around and looks at him.*)

TOM: You're okay with this?

JERRY: (*Beat.*) Yes. Only thing is…

TOM: Only thing is what?

JERRY: I think I'm going to be sick.

TOM: That's perfectly okay with me. Maybe you better get out of the car first.

JERRY: You want me to get out of the car…?

TOM: If you're going to be sick, I would prefer it if you got out of the car, yes.

(*Jerry starts to get out of the car.*)

TOM: Hey, Jerry.

JERRY: Yeah, Tom?

TOM: You need any help – you want me to hold your head or something?

JERRY: No, I'll manage.

TOM: You wanted to come with. This was your idea. I tried to talk you out of it.

JERRY: I know.

TOM: I could of brought you something back.

JERRY: It's okay.

TOM: Billy's gonna be pissed off at me.

JERRY: You tried to talk me out of coming with, Tom. I wouldn't fucking listen.

TOM: (*Beat.*) Go on. Stick your fingers down your throat if you have to. Get it all out.

JERRY: I will, Tom.
TOM: You'll feel better.
JERRY: (*Beat.*) I'm sure I will.
   (*They look at each other. Lights fade.*)

SCENE 3

A darkened movie theater, about a year later. Tom and Jerry sit next to each other, eating popcorn from a tub. Karl pulls off his glasses, puts on a bad Elvis wig, and immediately becomes another guy, Elvis Sideburns. He sits three seats away in the same row, also eating popcorn. Soundtrack of a bad action film in the background.

JERRY: Deb and I had a fight.
TOM: What else is new?
JERRY: This was a bad one.
TOM: How bad?
JERRY: She threw the phone at me.
TOM: She did?
JERRY: From across the room.
TOM: She connect?
JERRY: Missed me. By this much.
TOM: Nothing to worry about. When she *stops* throwing things, start to
   worry.
JERRY: You think?
TOM: I know.
ELVIS SIDEBURNS: Sshh…!
   (*Pause. They watch the screen.*)
TOM: What'd you do?
JERRY: When?
TOM: When she threw the phone at you.
JERRY: Fucking ducked.
TOM: Then what?
JERRY: I took a walk.
TOM: You didn't pop her one?
JERRY: No.
TOM: Good.

JERRY: I got the fuck out of there and went for a walk.

TOM: Good for you.

ELVIS SIDEBURNS: Quiet...!

(*Pause. They watch the movie.*)

TOM: You want my opinion?

JERRY: What.

TOM: Marry her.

JERRY: I don't know.

TOM: You two are suited to each other.

JERRY: You think so?

TOM: She throws the phone. You duck. That's true love. That's passion.

JERRY: It is?

TOM: Fucking Romeo and Juliet threw shit at each other all the time.

JERRY: You think I should ask her to marry me?

TOM: Make an honest woman of her. Start a family. Your whole outlook on life changes.

ELVIS SIDEBURNS: Shut the hell up already, will ya'...?

TOM: I'm truly sorry...

ELVIS SIDEBURNS: (*Beat.*) You see that woman up there?

TOM: Excuse me?

ELVIS SIDEBURNS: You see that woman—up there on the screen?

JERRY: The redhead?

ELVIS SIDEBURNS: The blond. Vicki Torrance.

TOM: Very attractive.

ELVIS SIDEBURNS: That's my Vicki. This next part—watch this...

(*A couple of very loud punches, some gunshots, and an explosion from up on the screen. Things get quiet. Pause.*)

JERRY: Wow.

ELVIS SIDEBURNS: See the way she took those punches? Now that's acting. Did all her own stunts too.

JERRY: You know her?

ELVIS SIDEBURNS: Know her? I loved her more than life itself, friend. She was my fiancé.

JERRY: (*Beat.*) What happened?

ELVIS SIDEBURNS: What happened? I'll tell you what happened. We fell in love. We were gonna get married. But we got mixed up with some fellers. The wrong fellers. We got in over our heads with these fellers. We went to the police. But they got to her anyway. There was an "accident" on the set. "Sudden Extreme Justice 2."

They switched a dummy flamethrower for the real thing, and Vicki had on this flammable beehive hairdo wig. You don't wanna *know*. So they fixed me up with a new identity, a new job—just like they did with Elvis. Yep. He went and got himself mixed up with the wrong fellers just like me and Vicki, and they moved him up to Kalamazoo. And now here we are. A whole brand new life. A life without the King. A life without my Vicki. One of these days they'll find me. You two fellers might even be the ones. But you see, I don't really care anymore. (*Beat.*) Look at her. This was the last thing she did. Seen it 37 times. Sometimes, watching her up there like this, I forget. It's almost like she's still alive. And when she does the trick with the grenade launcher—my heart rolls over sideways and just about quits. This is all I have of her. (*Beat.*) You know what really gets me though? Not the shower scene coming up—and that's no body double, let me tell you in advance. That's her appendix scar, those are her moles. No, what gets me is the scene where she's down in the basement. She's just sitting there, cleaning her Uzi. There's this close up, she wipes the sweat from her face and you can see the little hairs on her arm. That really gets me. Every time. She was the love of my life. I miss her. And I don't give a shit about much of anything anymore.

(*Pause.*)

JERRY: Tom, will you stand up for me?

TOM: You're asking me now?

JERRY: It was your idea.

TOM: I would be honored.

JERRY: You would?

TOM: It would be a fucking honor, yes.

JERRY: I'll ask her tonight.

TOM: (*Beat.*) Let's go.

(*Tom hands Jerry the tub of popcorn, and they get up to go. As he crosses in front of Elvis Sideburns, Tom pulls out a knife and stabs him repeatedly, at least five or six times. Pause. Jerry just stands there.*)

TOM: Is there a problem here, Jerry?

JERRY: I don't know, Tom.

TOM: Look. It's usually not a good idea to make this much conversation with a guy, a guy you don't even know, beforehand. You cannot afford to listen to every guy's sob story. You don't wanna know the particulars. It gives you reason to pause. You end up feeling sympathy. Which has a tendency to get in the way. Something to keep in mind for next time. You okay?

JERRY: I liked him. That's all.

(*Tom wipes the knife off on Elvis Sideburns' shirt, and they exit. Elvis Sideburns sits there, dead, covered with blood. Lights fade.*)

SCENE 4

A Chinese restaurant, about a year later. Tom and Jerry at a booth, finishing dinner. Elvis Sideburns takes off his wig—instantly becoming a different Guy. He sits down at another table, where Tom and Jerry can keep an eye on him.

TOM: The first time is always happenstance. Always. You just happen to be there when it happens. Maybe you happen to be young. A younger man. Billy walks into the office with Vic and another guy, some guy you don't know, some guy you never saw before, and when they go to take this new guy out back, out onto the lot, you naturally get up to go with. And maybe Billy says something like, "No Tom, you stay here, we're just going out back to take a look at a *car*, you stay here and fix those odometers." So now you're curious, right, and you tag along anyway. You watch as they go over an old Chevy—a '65 Impala—black with a red interior, a little rust just starting to pock mark the quarter panels. And Vic looks over at you as the other guy pokes around, and Vic is still looking at you as he pulls out his piece, and then he lets the guy have it, three shots, one after the other, in the back of the head, and then Vic looks back at you, one more time, just to see how well you're taking it. And if you're taking it well, he smiles at you, and just like that the thing is done and over with. Happenstance. You just happened to be there. Second time is coincidence. Third time—is your choice. After that, you are on the job with the other guys, you are watching and listening and learning a thing or two. You are learning a trade.

JERRY: So what was it like?

TOM: My first time on the job?

JERRY: Yes.

TOM: I was along for the ride. You know, the clean up guy. Down by the river. And Vic asks me if I want to do the guy, and I say, "Why not."

JERRY: Did you know the guy?

TOM: No, I did not know him.

JERRY: What did he do?

TOM: Some thing. I don't even fucking know and I never asked.

JERRY: How'd it feel?

TOM: Like I was doing a job.

JERRY: That's it?

TOM: What can I say. I took to it.

JERRY: Just like that?

TOM: It was like a, whatayou call it, an outlet for all my, you know, aggression. Every guy's got that, you know. That male aggression. And every guy needs his outlet. Gotta let it out one way or the other. Can't keep it bottled up. Gives you an ulcer. Or worse. There is a very low incidence, and this is a documented fact, of stomach problems in this line of work. Not just that. Lower risk of heart disease, too. Prostate cancer—almost unheard of. A *dentist* is ten times more likely to get prostate cancer. It's true. (*Beat.*) Hey. My wife and I stopped fighting, we started getting along for the first time maybe ever, and before you know it—bang—we had little Billy. A couple of years later, Suzy. And a few years after that, Tom Junior.

JERRY: And now?

TOM: What else would I do?

JERRY: Real estate.

TOM: Real estate?

JERRY: Why not?

TOM: Too fucking cutthroat for me. Besides, this is what I'm good at.

JERRY: How do you sleep?

TOM: Like a baby. Most nights—like a big, fat baby. (*Beat.*) Here, have some more fried rice.

JERRY: I don't want any more fried rice.

TOM: Have some more fried rice, Jerry.

JERRY: I don't want any more fucking fried rice, okay?

TOM: Then have a fortune cookie.

JERRY: No, thanks.

TOM: Don't you wanna see your fortune?

JERRY: (*Beat.*) No.

TOM: Why not? Afraid it might say, "Today is not a good day to whack a guy out in the parking lot?"

JERRY: I am not afraid of any fucking cookie. My mind is elsewhere right now, that's all.

TOM: Look at me. You look nervous. That is not good. Get your mind off the thing. Now. Or go out and wait in the car.

(*Pause. Jerry cracks open his fortune cookie. He reads it.*)

TOM: What's it say?

JERRY: "Soon you will be lucky in love."

TOM: That's a good one. Put it in your pocket, take it home to Debbie. That should be good for something.

JERRY: (*Looking off.*) That guy over there, does he look like a cop to you?

TOM: What guy—that guy? He's not a cop. He's the busboy.

JERRY: Doesn't look like any busboy to me.

TOM: His name's Jimmy. He's a retard, Jerr. He's retarded.

JERRY: Doesn't look like a retard. Looks smart. Like a cop.

TOM: Dumb as a sack of wet hammers, Jerry. Doesn't know how to tie his own shoes.

JERRY: Still.

TOM: Look at his shoes.

JERRY: So what?

TOM: They're loafers, Jerry. You ever see a cop wearing loafers?

JERRY: Maybe he's undercover. Only acts like a retard. Wears loafers to throw you.

TOM: What are you saying here, Jerry?

JERRY: (*Beat.*) Nothing.

TOM: Would you rather wait out in the car?

JERRY: No.

TOM: You're a little rattled for some reason. You want me to take you home?

JERRY: I didn't say that.

TOM: Maybe you're not up to this.

JERRY: I'm just, you know, a little rattled, that's all.

TOM: You sure?

JERRY: Yeah.

TOM: You're the one said you wanted to do this one.

JERRY: I do.

TOM: Maybe I should do this one. Let you sit this one out.

JERRY: (*Beat.*) I'm doing it.

TOM: It's not a problem for me to do it. You can do the next one.

JERRY: I said I'll do it.

TOM: You sure?

JERRY: (*Beat.*) Yes.

TOM: Okay, then it's settled. Now can we finish our dinner?

JERRY: You go ahead. I'm done.

    (*Jerry's head starts to bob up and down noticeably, as he looks around the restaurant, nervously.*)

TOM: You gonna keep lookin' around like that, doing that thing with your head, or are you going to let me finish my chow mein in peace?

JERRY: What thing with my head?

TOM: You're doing it right now.

JERRY: Doing what?

TOM: Bobbing up and down, bobbing up and fucking down—just like Reagan. You ever watch that guy?

JERRY: It's palsy.

TOM: Palsy?

JERRY: Nervous disorder.

TOM: I know what fucking palsy is, Jerr. I just thought it was nerves. You know, the guy's standing up there lying through his teeth like that, makes his head bob up and down.

JERRY: I'm pretty sure it's palsy.

TOM: You know what his last movie was?

JERRY: Reagan's?

TOM: *The Killers.* Know what he plays?

JERRY: I don't know, a sheriff?

TOM: Hitman.

JERRY: Fuck you.

TOM: I swear. Smacks Angie Dickinson around a little. Pulls an armored car job. Double crosses John Cassavettes, pulls out a pistol, with a fat fucking silencer, gives him a slug in the gut. Then to top it off, he takes out Clu Gulager and Lee Marvin with a deer rifle.

JERRY: He takes out Lee Marvin with a deer rifle?

TOM: Fucking unbelievable, I know.

JERRY: When was this movie?

Tom: Early 60s. right after that, he goes into politics. Is there a connection? Who can say.

Jerry: (*Beat.*) No way I have palsy, Tom.

Tom: You maybe don't have palsy yet, but I would look into it if I were you. That head bobbin' thing's makin' me dizzy. (*Beat.*) You keepin' an eye on him?

(*The guy starts to get up from his table.*)

Jerry: Who?

Tom: The guy. Our guy.

Jerry: (*Pause.*) He's getting up.

Tom: He is?

Jerry: Getting up from the table.

Tom: Heading for the door …?

Jerry: Yes.

(*The Guy exits.*)

Tom: Get up and go to the john. Follow him outside, through the kitchen. Wait until he gets to his car, pulls out his keys, and one shot to the back of the head.

Tom and Jerry: (*Together.*) Take his keys…

Tom: …Slide him into the trunk. Come back in the same way you went out. We'll take care of the car later. (*Beat.*) You're okay to do this?

Jerry: Yeah, I'm fine.

Tom: You're sure?

Jerry: Yes.

Tom: Go do it.

(*Jerry exits. Tom sits there, calmly, eating, for about a minute. He cracks open his fortune cookie, puts on his glasses, and reads it. He smiles to himself, quietly, and puts his glasses back in his pocket. Jerry enters, breathing a little hard.*)

Tom: Everything come out okay?

Jerry: Fine.

Tom: Any problems?

Jerry: None.

Tom: You feel like ordering dessert?

Jerry: Not really.

Tom: You're okay, though?

Jerry: Yeah. I'm good.

Tom: Hold out your hand.

(*Jerry holds out his hand, very still.*)
You're okay, kid.

JERRY: Thanks.

TOM: Should we get out of here? Take care of the car and call it a night?

JERRY: Yeah. Sounds good to me.

TOM: Peggy made an apple pie. You want to come over, have a piece?

JERRY: Not tonight.

TOM: I think you should come over and have a piece. Do you some good.

JERRY: Maybe some other time.

TOM: (*Deliberately.*) Maybe you didn't hear me, Jerry. I said, I think you should come over *and have a piece of pie.*

JERRY: (*Beat.*) Okay.

(*Tom picks up the check.*)

TOM: This one's on me. (*Beat.*) Let's get out of here.

(*They exit. Lights fade.*)

SCENE 5

The basement of a warehouse, about a year later. Afternoon. A Bears or Bulls game on the radio, in the background. The guy from the restaurant comes in and lies down on the floor upstage. He pulls a tarp over his head, leaving one hairy arm sticking out. Jerry puts on safety goggles and a rubber apron, and grabs a brand new chainsaw. He tries to start it a few times, but isn't having any luck. Tom sits nearby, also wearing a rubber apron and heavy-duty rubber gloves. Tom takes out a pack of cigarettes—and although it's awkward because of the gloves— he lights one and smokes. Jerry pulls the starter cord a few times in a row, starting to lose his patience. No luck, the thing won't start.

JERRY: Fuck.

TOM: Gas in it?

JERRY: Yes.

TOM: You check the tank?

JERRY: Tank's half full. (*Jerry pulls the starter cord a couple of times. Nothing.*) Shit.

TOM: Check the tank, Jerry.

JERRY: There's plenty of gas in the thing, Tom.

TOM: You check the oil?

JERRY: The oil's fine.

TOM: You checked it?

JERRY: I checked it.

TOM: Just asking.

> (*Jerry tries to start it a few more times. No luck.*)

JERRY: Shit. Fuck. Black and Decker can both come down here and suck my dick. This piece of shit.

TOM: Black and Decker is not a couple of guys, Jerry. Black and Decker is a corporation.

JERRY: (*Thinking this through.*) I don't give a fuck who they are.

> (*Jerry pushes the goggles up on his head. Throughout this next exchange, Jerry occasionally tries starting the chainsaw. But no matter what, it just won't start.*)

TOM: You still have the receipt?

JERRY: Somewhere, yes. I think so.

TOM: You *think* you have the receipt, or you *do* have the receipt?

JERRY: I might've thrown it out.

TOM: You might've thrown it out?

JERRY: I might've tossed it with the box.

TOM: Should've gone over to Sears, like I told you.

JERRY: I did go to Sears. But the fucking thing was six bucks cheaper at K-Mart.

TOM: One thing about Sears, Jerry—

JERRY: What?

TOM: You never need your receipt.

JERRY: Fuck Sears. Sears can come down here and kiss my ass.

TOM: Sears is not a guy, Jerry. Sears is a corporation, just like Black and Decker, although at one time there *was* a guy named Sears. And another guy named Roebuck. However, Sears and Roebuck did not get along, so Sears tried to buy Roebuck out, but Roebuck wouldn't sell, so Sears hired a couple of guys, and Roebuck had "an accident."

> (*Jerry tries again. Still won't start.*)

JERRY: Fuck.

TOM: Patience, Jerry.

JERRY: Fuck patience. I wanna get this thing done so we can get out of here by halftime.

TOM: This is the same thing I had to go through with Tom Junior and the lawn mower. The same exact thing.

(*Jerry pulls the starter cord a couple of times, and whacks his thumb.*)

JERRY: Fuck. Fuck me.

TOM: Jerry. You are angry. And you are holding a power tool. This is not advisable. Even says so right on the box. Do not operate while under the influence of alcohol. Or while pissed off.

JERRY: It doesn't say that on the box.

TOM: Sure it does. Right on the side. In small print. I'd read it to you if you hadn't thrown it out along with the receipt.

(*Jerry tries again. Nothing.*)

JERRY: Useless piece of shit.

TOM: You check the spark plug?

JERRY: Spark plug?

TOM: Yeah, the spark plug. Check the spark plug. Sometimes the little clip comes loose.

(*Jerry examines the chainsaw and fools around with it.*)

TOM: You have to take your time with these things, Jerry. You can't get all pissed off and fight with the damn thing. You have to follow the instructions. Make sure everything is in proper working order. You must be one with your chainsaw, Jerry.

(*Jerry stops fooling with the saw.*)

JERRY: There.

TOM: And just in case you might have purchased faulty machinery, you should always hang onto your receipt.

(*Jerry pulls the starter cord—and the saw buzzes to life.*)

Spark plug?

JERRY: Little clip came loose.

TOM: Put your goggles on, Jerry.

(*Jerry pulls the goggles down over his eyes.*)

TOM: (*Beat.*) Let's go to work.

(*Tom throws his cigarette onto the floor and stomps on it. He crosses over to the lifeless body under the tarp, and lifts up an arm or a leg. Jerry revs the saw. Lights fade.*)

A bus stop, about a year later. Night. Tom and Jerry, wearing windbreakers, sit on a bench, holding lunchbags. They both pull out sandwiches and begin to eat.

JERRY: Looks like Deb is pregnant.

TOM: You're shitting me.

JERRY: Nope. We did the thing at home, it came out blue, and unless I'm reading the box wrong, she is with child.

TOM: That's great.

JERRY: You think I'll make a good father?

TOM: Are you worried that you won't?

JERRY: Scared shitless.

TOM: That's a good sign.

JERRY: It is?

TOM: Tom Junior turns 13 next year. Fucking *teenager.* I must know something, right?

JERRY: I'd say so.

TOM: You'll be great.

   (*Pause.*)

JERRY: You think Billy will give me a raise?

TOM: If you ask him nice, when Vic's not around, who can say. Billy loves kids.

JERRY: How come Vic don't like me?

TOM: Don't take it personal. Vic doesn't like anybody.

JERRY: Vic the prick.

TOM: Let me tell you something about Vic. In his time, he was the best. The best at what we do. Everything I know, I learned from him. And he had heart, too.

JERRY: So what happened to him?

TOM: He retired. Billy kicked him upstairs, into management. And so he lost his outlet for things. They pulled his teeth, so to speak. (*Beat.*) You know how good he was—in his day?

JERRY: How good?

TOM: Two words. And I ain't ever said them to nobody before tonight. Two little words. Two huge little words.

JERRY: What...?

Tom: *Grassy knoll.*

Jerry: Fuck you.

Tom: Okay, fuck me. He was there, though.

Jerry: You're not fucking with me?

Tom: Dallas. November, 1963. He was there.

Jerry: How do you know?

Tom: You ever seen that Zapruder film?

Jerry: Yeah, so?

Tom: There's a shot of Vic—much younger, but definitely Vic—running across the grass carrying what looks like a box of flowers.

Jerry: No shit.

Tom: You know why he was there?

Jerry: It was a mob hit?

Tom: Revenge. Simple fucking revenge.

Jerry: For what?

Tom: Marilyn Monroe.

Jerry: Marilyn Monroe?

Tom: They had a thing.

Jerry: Vic had a thing with Marilyn Monroe?

Tom: Vic was supposed to do her.

Jerry: He was supposed to "do her," do her?

Tom: But when he got right down to the moment, he couldn't do it. Worse yet, they fell in love.

Jerry: Vic the prick—and Marilyn Monroe?

Tom: So JFK hired someone else, they made it look like suicide, and that sent Vic around the bend.

Jerry: JFK hired Vic.

Tom: Personally. On Frank's boat.

Jerry: Not *the* Frank...?

Tom: How many fuckin' Franks are there?

Jerry: No shit.

Tom: According to Vic, he was gonna marry her. But somebody stuffed her full of pills first. Vic, beyond a doubt, knew who, he took the train to Dallas, and that was that. (*Beat.*) A few years later he did Bobby, too.

Jerry: Vic did Bobby?

Tom: Tried to do Ted, too. Took a shot at him, tire blew out, car went off the bridge and into the river. Vic does not care for that family one bit. Even to this day, you so much as mention the name, just watch the veins stick out in his neck.

JERRY: Jesus.

TOM: He was the best at what we do.

JERRY: Here comes our guy.

TOM: Right on time.

(*Tom and Jerry get up from the bench.*)

JERRY: You want me to do him?

TOM: You *wanna* do him?

JERRY: I'd like to, yes.

TOM: (*Beat.*) Let's flip for it. (*Tom pulls out a coin.*) Call it in the air. (*Tom flips the coin …*)

JERRY: Heads.

(*A Fat Guy, wearing a hat and overcoat and carrying a briefcase, enters and sits on the far end of the bench. Tom looks at the coin.*)

TOM: You win.

(*Jerry smiles, pulls out his gun, screws on a fat silencer, and Tom moves downstage to cover him and block the view. Jerry waits—savoring the moment—just long enough for Tom to shoot him a look.*)

FAT GUY: May I help you?

(*Jerry shoots the Fat Guy once in the chest. He falls to the ground, dead. Jerry leans over and fires two more slugs into him. Jerry looks over at Tom, and smiles. Lights fade.*)

SCENE 7

An Italian restaurant, about a year later. Afternoon. The Fat Guy bounces up off the ground, takes his hat and overcoat off, tossing them on a coat tree—nd immediately becomes Vic—a foul-tempered older guy with a bad silver rug and mustache. Tom and Jerry sit at a table. Vic enters, and sits between them. They are all eating.

TOM: So, Vic. Billy tells me you're gonna write a book.

VIC: Well, I'm not exactly gonna write the damn thing myself, but yeah, I got an agent, and he's gonna fix me up with somebody who's gonna write it for me.

JERRY: You got an agent?

Vice: Some squirrely little Jewish guy.

Tom: This book thing, Vic, I have to tell you, it's making Billy a little nervous.

Vic: Fuck him, he'll get over it. He's got no reason to be nervous about me—I mean, it ain't exactly like I'm turning state's evidence or anything.

Tom: But still.

Vic: I'm not gonna name anybody—not anybody *we* associate with anyway—just a few famous dead people who I may or may not have, over the years, for one reason or another, come into close personal contact with.

Jerry: Tom tells me you took out JFK.

Vic: (*Tossing down his silverware.*) You tell him that?

Tom: I might've mentioned it in passing.

Vic: A thing like that, Tom, it ain't exactly something you mention in passing, not to just anybody.

Tom: I didn't mention it to just anybody. I mentioned it to Jerry.

Jerry: Well, did you…?

Vic: (*Beat.*) I ain't saying I did, and I ain't saying I didn't. I guess you'll just have to wait and read about it in my book. You know what they're gonna call it? *Wet Work: Portrait of a Hitman.* That's a pretty good title, don't you think?

Jerry: I buy a copy, you autograph it for me?

Vic: Fuck no. I'll sign it "Mr. X"—that's the name my agent came up with, you know, just to be safe, sort of like a, what do you call it, a pseudo-name. Me, I came up with Tony Como—on account of I like Perry Como and Tony Bennett so much—but he wouldn't go for it. Too ethnic or some shit.

Tom: I gotta tell you, Vic—Billy doesn't think this is such a good idea, even with the "Mr. X" thing.

Vic: Fuck him *and* his pacemaker! This is my life story we're talking about here. Everybody has a right to tell his fucking life story, am I right or am I right?

Tom: I don't know, Vic.

(*At this point, the door to the restaurant opens a crack.*)

Vic: Hey, we're closed!

Tom: (*Overlapped.*) Get the fuck outta here!

Jerry: (*Overlapped.*) Close the fucking door!

(*The door slams shut, and they resume their conversation.*)

JERRY: So, Vic. You do anybody else famous?

VIC: Maybe two, three people I can think of right off the top of my head.

JERRY: Like who—Jimmy Hoffa?

VIC: No, not Jimmy Hoffa. Although I know a guy…

(*Vic and Tom chuckle, knowingly.*)

JERRY: Like who then—tell me somebody famous you did—besides JFK, I mean.

VIC: (*Beat.*) Four words. Four little words. You still gonna buy the book?

JERRY: Are you kidding? I'll wait in line to get the first copy.

VIC: Four little fuckin' words. "Hunkof, Hunkof, Burning Love."

(*Beat.*)

JERRY: No way, Vic. No fucking way you did Elvis.

VIC: I ain't sayin' I did, and I ain't sayin' I didn't.

JERRY: He died of an overdose in the crapper, fell and hit his head, somethin' like that.

VIC: Could be he did. Could be he might've faked the whole thing, joined the witness protection program on account of he was doing some work for Nixon and the feds and things got a little heated. Could be he just recently resurfaced up near Kalamazoo, living quietly under an assumed name. And maybe I took a little road trip up to Michigan a year or so ago for no good reason. Could be a lot of things, Jerry.

JERRY: You fucking whacked Elvis.

VIC: Could be I did, could be I didn't. I guess you'll just have to wait and read about it in—

TOM: The fucking book.

VIC: Or maybe not. Maybe I'll mention that one on Oprah.

TOM: Excuse me.

VIC: They want me on in two weeks with a bunch of other guys. "Contract Killers Who Write Books." Somethin' like that.

TOM: This is not a good idea, Vic.

VIC: My agent thinks it's a very good idea actually. Could help us land a bigger advance on the book deal. Maybe even the movie rights. We're all gonna be wearin' ski masks—what's the problem?

TOM: It will worry Billy.

VIC: Tell Billy to take a fucking pill already! (*Beat.*) You know who I see playing me in the movie? Ernest Borgnine.

JERRY: Ernest Borgnine is good. He's a good actor. Is he dead?

VIC: I don't know. I hope not. (*Pointedly, a warning to Tom.*) He better fuckin' not be dead, that's all I got to say, because he's playing me in the movie. The movie of my life.

JERRY: Who would play Tom, you think?

TOM: Who would play *me?*

JERRY: Yeah. In the movie. The movie of Vic's life.

TOM: Nobody. I don't wanna be in no movie.

VIC: Kirk Douglas?

JERRY: He's too old.

VIC: Too old? What the fuck do you know about anything?

JERRY: I'd say, if it was up to me, Burt Reynolds.

TOM: (*Beat.*) Burt Reynolds?

JERRY: Yeah.

TOM: (*Beat.*) I like him.

JERRY: He'd be real good as you, I think.

TOM: I could live with that. But this is all hypothetical, mind you, because I'm not gonna be in no movie.

JERRY: What about me?

TOM: Who would play you? I don't know.

VIC: (*To Jerry.*) Who says you're even in this movie, huh? This is my movie.

TOM: Wait a minute. I know. He'd be perfect.

JERRY: Who?

TOM: Don Knotts.

JERRY: Don fucking Knotts?

TOM: He reminds me of you, yeah.

JERRY: You're kidding me, right?

TOM: A *young* Don Knotts.

JERRY: I'm insulted, Tom. I pick somebody good for you, why can't you pick somebody good for me.

TOM: Don Knotts is fucking great.

JERRY: He doesn't have a chin.

TOM: He's still great.

JERRY: Anyway, he's too old. Think of somebody younger. With a chin.

TOM: I don't know any of these young guys, Jerry.

VIC: This is *my* movie we're talking about. (*To Jerry.*) And you're not even in it, so who the fuck cares?

TOM: (*Beat.*) There's no way I can talk you out of this thing, Vic?

VIC: No. No fucking way. (*Beat.*) And don't you get any ideas, Tom. And you know what I mean.

(*Jerry pulls out a medical kit from his jacket, opens it, and removes a larger-than-necessary hypodermic needle and a small bottle.*)

TOM: Jerry…

VIC: What the fuck is this…?

JERRY: My insulin.

VIC: You got diabetes?

JERRY: Yeah.

VIC: Since when?

JERRY: Since I was a kid.

VIC: (*Beat.*) That's a pretty big fuckin' needle, kid.

JERRY: I got a real bad case.

VIC: You have to do that here, right at the table?

JERRY: I'm having a reaction. (*Beat.*) It'll only take a second.

VIC: I can't stand needles.

JERRY: See, you pull the plunger back like this…

(*Jerry rams the needle into Vic's neck and pushes in the plunger.*)

VIC: What the fuck—you asshole…!

JERRY: Uh-oh, I forgot to push the *air* out of the needle first. That's not a good thing.

VIC: (*Pulling out his gun.*) You little fuck…!

(*Vic starts to grasp and convulse at the table, hanging onto his gun the whole time. He collapses face first into his food and stops moving. Jerry puts the needle and the medical kit away.*)

TOM: What the fuck did you do, Jerry?

JERRY: The air travels through his bloodstream, see, down into his heart, his ventricle explodes, it looks pretty much like a heart attack—I saw it in a movie.

TOM: You were supposed to wait until we got him out into the parking lot. Until we got him *out back*.

JERRY: I thought I'd try something different for a change.

TOM: (*Getting angry.*) Next time, you feel like trying out something different, check with me first.

JERRY: Sure, Tom, whatever you say.

TOM: Look at me, Jerry. This was Vic you took out. He was a friend of mine. A close, personal friend. He deserved a little respect, something more respectful than just getting a fucking needle jammed in his neck while he was trying to eat his linguine.

JERRY: (*Beat.*) I'm sorry, Tom.

TOM: (*Beat.*) You're lucky nobody else is in here this time of day. Now go call an ambulance, we gotta make this look good.

(*Jerry wrenches the gun from Vic's hand.*)

JERRY: (*Awestruck.*) You think this is the piece he whacked Elvis with…?

(*Jerry pockets the gun and exits. Tom sits there, looking at Vic. Lights fade.*)

SCENE 8

An office, not quite a year later. A framed photo of Oprah hangs on the wall behind a desk. Tom and Jerry stand on the other side of the desk, looking around the office. They're both wearing sunglasses. While they're waiting, Vic gets up from the table, takes off his wig, switches it for another, kicks off his shoes, rolls up his pant legs—revealing fishnet stocking—puts on a pair of heels, and a skirt—transforming into Elaine, a husky-voiced television producer.

TOM: This is typical.

JERRY: What is?

TOM: This typical waiting around bullshit. We bust our ass to get over here on time, and then what do they do, they make us wait. And if you try and out think them, show up ten minutes late yourself, they make you wait another *fifteen*. It's a power thing. Fuck these people. I hate these people. I hate even the *idea* of doing business with these people.

JERRY: We've only been here ten minutes.

TOM: Still. Who the fuck do these people think they are? Making us wait like this. And do you know *why* they're making us wait like this? They're not doing anything. No, they're making us wait like this just so when they *do* come out they can say, "Sorry to keep you waiting." And then they have us by the shorthairs.

JERRY: They do?

TOM: By the *balls*.

JERRY: Maybe they're just a little busy.

TOM: "Sorry to keep you waiting." Wait and see if I'm wrong.

(*Elaine—middle-aged, maybe smoking a cigarette—enters, and sits behind the desk.*)

ELAINE: Mr. Belefonte. And Mr. Humperdinck…? I'm Elaine Niddry. (*Beat.*) *Sorry* to keep you waiting. (*Beat.*) Which of you is…?

TOM: I'm Mr. Belefonte. And he's—

ELAINE: Mr. Humperdinck. No first names?

TOM: Who needs them.

ELAINE: I like that. Have a seat.

(*Tom and Jerry both sit down. Elaine studies them closely. They both fidget a little in their seats.*)

ELAINE: Don't think of this as an audition. We're just getting to know each other a little first. I had my secretary take an early lunch—just like you asked. (*Beat.*) You work as a team, the two of you?

TOM: That's right.

ELAINE: That's too bad.

TOM: Too bad what?

ELAINE: That one of you isn't African American.

JERRY: I'm half Irish, half German.

ELAINE: (*To Tom.*) And you?

TOM: What's the difference?

ELAINE: Oprah was hoping one of you would be African American, but I like you anyway. You have the right look.

TOM: The right look?

ELAINE: The look of authenticity.

TOM: Thank you.

ELAINE: Let's get down to business, shall we? As you probably already know, we did a segment earlier this year on contract killers— perhaps you saw it?

TOM: We *heard* about it.

ELAINE: Our ratings on that segment told us something, Mr. Belefonte. We touched a nerve. Are you with me on this?

TOM: (*Shooting Jerry a look.*) We're all ears.

ELAINE: Good. Let me tell you a little about me. I've been with Oprah three years. Before that I worked in development, mostly reality-based series. "America's Funniest Accidental Death Video," that was mine.

JERRY: I never saw that one.

ELAINE: Huge hit in Japan. Unfortunately, it never got a green light over here. The networks thought it was too risky. But this is the

90s. A new decade. The dawn of a brand new era. And what this country needs right now, in my opinion, to help usher that new era in, is a good purging.

TOM: A purging?

ELAINE: That's right. And if there's one thing television can do it's purge. That's what we do here on Oprah. We purge. We give people in need a forum for purging.

JERRY: You mean like spilling their guts all over the place?

ELAINE: I prefer the word purging, Mr. Humperdinck. To cleanse or purify, that's what it means. I'm talking about catharsis here. It's a Greek thing. You follow?

JERRY: Uh-huh.

ELAINE: What we have in mind is a series. Reality based. Documentary style. We follow you, during your average workday, so to speak. And maybe we reenact some of your more interesting "jobs" from the past. You're in disguise, whatever makes you comfortable.

(*Tom starts to get up out of his chair.*)

TOM: Okay. I've heard just about all I need to hear. Mr. Humperdinck—are you just about ready?

JERRY: In a minute.

(*Tom shoots Jerry a look, but sits back down.*)

ELAINE: There are certain risks involved, I know. And if you're not interested, I understand perfectly. We have spoken with other people in your profession.

JERRY: (*To Elaine.*) Who said we're not interested? We're *very* interested.

ELAINE: Of course you are, or you wouldn't have come in. I like you two. (*To Tom.*) Let me ask you something. In your line of work, do you ever feel…remorse?

TOM: In your line of work, do you?

ELAINE: I like you Mr. Belefonte. Are you married?

TOM: Believe me lady, that is none of your concern.

ELAINE: Too bad.

TOM: C'mon, Mr. Humperdinck—what do you say we get a move on with this thing…?

ELAINE: I'd like you boys to improvise a scenario for me.

JERRY: A scenario?

ELAINE: A situation gone bad.

TOM: Mr. Humperdinck, don't you think this has gone just about far enough…?

JERRY: Not quite. (*To Elaine.*) You were saying?

ELAINE: Let's say Mr. Belefonte has left his—what do you call it in your line of work—your *piece?*

TOM: My *gun.*

ELAINE: Right. Let's say you've left your gun at home.

TOM: That would never happen.

ELAINE: But let's say, for the sake of argument, that it has. You go to do your job—and for some reason—Mr. Humperdinck's gun jams. What do you do?

TOM: I use a knife or a piece of wire.

ELAINE: A piece of wire?

TOM: Piano wire, rigged with handles at either end.

ELAINE: A "garotte"? I like that. But let's say you've left your "garotte" out in the car.

TOM: For Christ's sake, Jerry.

ELAINE: Your name is Jerry…!

JERRY: (*Taking off his sunglasses.*) Jerry Humperdinck.

ELAINE: Okay, Mr. *Jerry* Humperdinck. You've left your "garotte" out in the car. What do you do?

JERRY: Depends on the situation.

ELAINE: Let's say you were right here in this office. If you'd left all the tools of your trade out in the car, how would you do your job?

JERRY: With what you have right here?

ELAINE: In this office.

JERRY: I'd use the cord from your telephone.

ELAINE: Mr. Belefonte, can you do better than that?

TOM: You must be kidding me.

ELAINE: Not at all.

JERRY: How about a magazine?

ELAINE: A magazine?

JERRY: Sure. You roll it up real tight. Jam it into someone's eye socket nice and hard, that would do it. One of those women's magazines. You know, the thick ones with all the perfume ads.

ELAINE: That's what I call ingenuity.

JERRY: Or.

ELAINE: What?

JERRY: I'd use a sewing needle. Stick it in the ear far enough, it causes the brain to hemorrhage, looks pretty much accidental.

TOM: That's bullshit.

JERRY: How do you know?

TOM: Have you ever tried it?

JERRY: No. But I'd like to. (*To Elaine.*) Someday.

TOM: Mr. Humperdinck—can we quit playing games here and get down to the business at hand?

JERRY: Relax, Mr. Belefonte.

TOM: I would like us to take care of this thing in a professional manner and get the fuck out of here.

ELAINE: I love the way you two banter. It's so real.

(*Pause. Tom looks at Jerry, totally fed up. He takes off his sunglasses.*)

TOM: Okay. You wanna know what I'd use to get the job done?

ELAINE: What?

TOM: The liner from your waste basket.

ELAINE: (*Beat.*) Show me.

TOM: (*Pause.*) You want me to show you?

ELAINE: (*Playfully.*) I'm your victim.

TOM: (*To Jerry.*) You bring any duct tape?

(*Jerry pulls out a roll of duct tape.*)

ELAINE: You boys are resourceful, I'll say that much.

(*Tom takes the roll of duct tape, and goes behind Elaine's desk with it.*)

TOM: May I?

ELAINE: Be my guest.

(*Tom tapes Elaine's wrists together behind her. He pulls the plastic trash liner out of her waste basket and empties it.*)

ELAINE: This is exciting.

TOM: (*To Jerry.*) You wanna play games? You wanna outdo *me*? This is how you get the job *done.*

(*Tom pulls the plastic bag over Elaine's head, and tapes it right around her neck. Pause.*)

ELAINE: Perfect. I love it. I absolutely love it. This is exactly what we're looking for. God, I love this. I have goose bumps. This is going to fly, I can feel it. (*Beat.*) Okay. You can take this thing off my head now. You can untape my wrists. Mr. Belefonte? Mr. Humperdinck? I'm having difficulty breathing. C'mon fellas, this tape is starting to itch.

JERRY: Not bad, Mr. Belefonte but any second she's going to start thrashing around like a fish. Someone might hear her.

TOM: This was your idea.

JERRY: No, the magazine was my idea. And why do I have to be Mr. Humperdinck?

TOM: What the fuck are we doing here, Jerry?

ELAINE: Fellas…?

JERRY: You think we should cut her loose?

(*Tom just looks at him—he's losing heart or stomach for the job. Jerry rips the bag off Elaine's head. She looks at them, her eyes wide with fear. Jerry smiles at her. The tension breaks. They both laugh.*)

JERRY: How'd we do?

ELAINE: (*Very impressed.*) You're hired. Both of you. The network's going to love you guys.

JERRY: (*Beat.*) You want me to finish her?

TOM: If you don't mind.

(*Jerry pulls out a long sewing needle.*)

TOM: What's that?

JERRY: Sewing needle.

TOM: That won't fuckin' work.

JERRY: Only one way to find out.

TOM: Suit yourself.

ELAINE: (*She thinks they're kidding around.*) Guys…?

(*Jerry grabs Elaine by the head, covering her mouth. Tom turns away. Jerry holds up the needle. Looks at it. Elaine looks just a little puzzled.*)

JERRY: Purge this.

(*Lights fade—before the needle strikes home.*)

SCENE 9

A motel room, just about a year later. Elaine pulls the bag off her head, puts on a blond wig, and gets in bed, face down leaving one leg sticking over the side. Jerry pulls a bloody sheet up to her neck, and checks her pulse, still holding onto his gun. Tom watches.

JERRY: Well, She's done.

TOM: Jesus, Jerry.

JERRY: What?

TOM: We weren't here to do the woman.

JERRY: We weren't?

TOM: No.

JERRY: Shit.

TOM: Apparently, the guy we're supposed to do is not here.

JERRY: Shit. She was in the way. What the fuck was I supposed to do?

TOM: You coulda waited. You coulda looked to me. You coulda let me take care of it. We could've gotten out of here, come back later.

JERRY: What do we do now?

TOM: We wait. We wait for the guy. (*Tom lights a cigarette.*)

JERRY: I ain't ever done someone by mistake before, Tom.

TOM: Neither have I.

JERRY: (*Beat.*) She's fucking beautiful, Tom, don't you think?

TOM: So what. You want to fuck her?

JERRY: No.

TOM: Whether or not she is beautiful is, at this point, beside the point.

JERRY: I'm just making an observation is all.

TOM: You think I don't know a beautiful woman when I see one, Jerry?

JERRY: No, I just—

TOM: You think beauty even enters into the equation?

JERRY: No...

TOM: So shut the fuck up about her being beautiful, okay? She wasn't supposed to be here, you got trigger-happy, and here we are. So shut the fuck up.

JERRY: You pissed at me...?

TOM: As a matter of fact, right now, yes, I'm a little pissed at you.

JERRY: I was just doing my job.

TOM: You want to do your job, next time, you look to me, you let me handle these type of situations.

JERRY: She was in the way...

TOM: She's out of the way now.

JERRY: I'm sorry, Tom. I shoulda followed your lead. (*Beat.*) You gonna be okay with this?

TOM: Don't worry about it. The thing is done.

JERRY: (*Pause.*) I always wondered what I'd do if I ever had to—you know—somebody innocent, somebody who just got in the way.

TOM: Now you know.

(*Pause.*)

JERRY: One night, a couple of weeks ago, Deb and I went up to bed. But I couldn't fall asleep. She started snoring, you know, really sawing wood, and then the baby started screaming in his crib. Deb is out like somebody hit her in the head with a shovel. So I got up—it was my turn anyway—I got him a bottle, walked him around the house, *sang* to him—he would not stop screaming, no matter what. So finally, I put him down, went out to the car, in my boxer shorts, got my piece out of the trunk, screwed on the silencer, went back upstairs. Put the muzzle to his head. I stood there for a few seconds, imagined myself actually doing it, actually doing my own son. I mean, everyone has these thoughts at one time or another. You know, "What would it be like to kill my wife and kids?" But those are just thoughts. There's a world of difference between thinking a thing and actually doing it, I know that. But I was standing there, with the muzzle of the gun pointed at my kid's head, stuck in that fucking gray area between the two. Was I only thinking about doing it, or was I actually going to do it? I honestly didn't know. And then, just like that, he fell asleep. I went back down to the car, put the gun away, and went back up to bed.

TOM: Never, never, never point the muzzle of a gun at a loved one. Never. No matter what. Leave your work at the office. Or in this case, in the trunk of your fucking car.

JERRY: Maybe I need a vacation.

TOM: I think maybe you need more than a fucking vacation, Jerry.

JERRY: What's that supposed to mean?

(*The Woman on the bed starts to move and groan.*)

JERRY: Shit.

(*Tom moves over to the bed, takes a pillow, puts it over the Woman's head and holds her down until she quits moving.*)

JERRY: She done?

TOM: (*Beat.*) She is now.

(*Pause. Tom and Jerry look at each other, Tom is tired to the bone.*)

JERRY: (*Beat.*) You okay with this?

TOM: (*Clearly not okay.*) I'm okay.

JERRY: (*Beat.*) I wish this guy would hurry up and come home…

(*Pause. Tom takes the pillow off the Woman's head and looks at her. Jerry just watches the door. Lights fade.*)

SCENE 10

*Tom and Jerry at a table in the clubhouse of a Florida race track,
about a year later. Sunshine and fruity drinks. They both wear short-
sleeved tourist shirts, shorts with dark socks pulled all the way up, and
sunglasses. The Woman in bed gets up and changes into a Guy wearing
a golf cap. He enters and sits at another table.*

TOM: This hot fuckin' weather in December. I love this. (*Beat.*) Is Deb
happy with the motel?
JERRY: She loves it.
TOM: Peg, too.
JERRY: Hangin' out by the pool all day. By tonight they'll both be so
sunburned we won't be able to get within ten feet of them.
TOM: Like a couple of lobsters.
JERRY: I'll bet Tom Junior's pretty excited about going to Disney World,
huh?
TOM: Jesus, are you kidding, he didn't even want to come with. He's at
that age. What about your little one?
JERRY: She's so excited, she's beside herself. But I told her, Business first.
JERRY: That's right.
TOM: You got cable in your room?
JERRY: Sure do.
TOM: I stayed up with Tommy last night, way past midnight, watchin'
that HBO. One of those Arnold Schwarzennegger movies. He's
some kind of killer robot, trying to kill this other killer robot.
JERRY: *Terminator 2.*
TOM: Anyway, this kid tells Arnold not to kill anybody, so he spends
the whole movie shooting people in the kneecap. Walks through
this lobby and kneecaps at least a dozen cops. Now you and I know
how serious kneecapping a guy really is. It's fucking painful.
Cripples you for life. Some guys would rather die than get
kneecapped. But in this movie, it's like he's doing a good thing,
blowing away kneecaps right and left. And Tommy, he was into it.
He has no idea. He loves this movie. (*Beat.*) Me, I found it a little
disturbing. (*Beat.*) I don't know, maybe it's a generational thing.
(*Beat.*) You remember the guy we did a couple of weeks ago up in
Waukegon?

JERRY: The liquor license guy?

TOM: Yeah, him. I was out there in the forest preserve, taking care of the thing, must've been three, four o'clock in the morning. I'm pourin' lime all over the guy, just about done with the thing, and suddenly I look up—and there's this deer standing there, right there in front of me.

JERRY: A deer?

TOM: Fifty feet away. Just a young one. You know, white spots, trembling legs, big wet nose.

JERRY: Fucking Bambi.

TOM: Right. For what seemed like a pretty long time, we just stood there, lookin' at each other.

JERRY: You shoot him?

TOM: No, I didn't shoot him. We were having a moment. And then he took off, into some trees. Just like that, he was gone.

JERRY: At this point was he whole or in sections?

TOM: The guy? I had to take the arms and legs off.

JERRY: That's beautiful, Tom.

TOM: You don't get it, do you?

JERRY: What's not to get? You're out in the woods, dumping lime all over the liquor license guy, who happens to be in sections at the time, and you have a moment with Bambi. That is. That's fucking beautiful.

TOM: I'm trying to tell you something here, Jerry. I'm getting too old for this. I'm starting to lose my appetite for this type of work.

JERRY: You serious?

TOM: I'm just thinking ahead to my retirement.

JERRY: Somehow, Tom, I cannot picture it.

TOM: I'm just mulling it over.

JERRY: If you say so. (*Beat.*) There's our guy.

TOM: He's here...?

JERRY: Right over there.

TOM: The guy with the suit?

JERRY: Behind the guy with the suit and to the left.

TOM: With the sunglasses...?

JERRY: Across from the guy with the sunglasses.

TOM: With the, what is it, a golf cap?

JERRY: That's him.

TOM: You sure?

JERRY: This is the guy.

TOM: He looks older.

JERRY: What do you mean he looks older?

TOM: He looks like a different guy altogether.

JERRY: This is him.

TOM: You're positive?

JERRY: Yes.

TOM: We'll wait for him to get up, go to the john, and then we'll do him in there.

JERRY: (*Beat.*) Let's try something different for a change.

TOM: Different how?

JERRY: Let's do him here and now, in the open.

TOM: There are too many people in the way.

JERRY: Believe me, they'll move.

TOM: Jerry, this is not a good idea. Somebody will I.D. us.

JERRY: Bullshit. They'll say you were fat, that I was skinny, we had on sunglasses. Big deal.

TOM: (*Beat.*) You think I'm getting fat?

JERRY: Maybe a little paunchy around the middle, but that is not what I am saying here, Tom.

TOM: And you are a far cry from skinny.

JERRY: Believe me. No one will I.D. us. I'll make sure of it.

TOM: We wait until he goes to the john.

JERRY: C'mon Tom. Let's do this job right here in broad daylight. Right here in bright Florida sunshine.

TOM: No, Jerry. Read my lips. No fucking way.

JERRY: (*Beat.*) I'm gonna do it, Tom.

TOM: Don't.

JERRY: They'll talk about this for years. It will be legendary.

TOM: Don't, Jerry. I'm too old for this kind of shit.

JERRY: This will make you feel young again, I promise.

TOM: I can't keep up with you anymore, kid. (*Beat.*) Do not take this guy out in this way, Jerry. This is the most serious on-the-job advice I have ever given you. You're a professional. Now act like one.

JERRY: C'mon, Tom. (*Beat.*) Live a little.

(Jerry pulls out a pistol and stands up from the table. He looks at Tom. Tom is none too happy. Jerry raises the gun and takes aim at the Guy with the golf cap. Lights fade.)

A couple of months later—the same taproom as Scene One. The guy with the golf cap gets up, puts on Tony's jacket, pulls the hood back over his head, and sits with his arms behind his back, like before. Jerry holding a shotgun. Tom, just sitting there. The phone on the bar, ringing.

JERRY: Answer the phone, Tom. (*Beat.*) Tom. Answer the fucking phone.
  (*Tom just sits there, looking old and tired. The phone keeps ringing. Finally, he reaches over and picks it up.*)
TOM: Hello…? Yeah. Yeah. Yeah. Uh-huh. He's right here. Yeah. Yeah. Okay. Uh-huh. I understand. Yeah. (*Tom hangs up the phone.*)
JERRY: Was that Billy?
TOM: Yeah, that was Billy.
JERRY: What he say?
TOM: What do you think he said?
JERRY: That's what I thought. Hey, Tony, before we do you, you mind finishing the joke…?
TONY: (*Beat.*) The penguin sits there, drinking his scotch. Finally the bartender says, "You know, we don't get many penguins in here." The penguin looks up and says, "At four bucks a drink, you're not gonna get many more either."
JERRY: (*Beat.*) That's it? That's the punchline?
TONY: That's it.
JERRY: I'm sorry, Tony, but that joke is for shit.
TONY: Shut up and do it.
JERRY: Okay.
  (*Jerry pumps a shell into the shotgun, and starts to raise it. Tony stiffens.*)
TOM: Wait a second, Jerr.
  (*Tom gets up from the bar, goes over the Jerry, and just looks at him.*)
JERRY: (*Not getting it.*) What?
  (*Tom pulls out a knife, rams it into Jerry's stomach, and holds it there.*)
TOM: Sorry, kid. Nothing personal.
  (*Tom pulls out the knife, and Jerry falls to the floor, dead. Pause.*)
TONY: Fucking untie me.

(*Tom wipes off the knife on a hanky and cuts Tony loose. Tony pulls the hood off his head. He fishes around in his jacket pocket and puts on a pair of sunglasses. Tony crosses over to Jerry and picks up his head by the hair.*)

TONY: (*Shouting in Jerry's face.*) Fuck you, you fucking dumb shit.

(*Tony lets Jerry's head thump back to the floor.*)

TOM: I'm sorry about having to tie you up like that, Tony, I had to make it look good.

(*Tony goes behind the bar and pours himself a drink.*)

TONY: Fuck you, too, Tom. This wouldn't have happened if you guys hadn't botched the job in Orlando.

TOM: I know.

(*Tony knocks back his drink.*)

TOM: I'm definitely getting too old for this line of work, Tony.

TONY: You and me both.

TOM: Maybe I'll take Peg up to Lake Geneva, shop around for a condo. Maybe Billy'll kick me upstairs. Into management.

(*Tony pulls a gun out from behind the bar, cocks it, and puts it to the back of Tom's head. Tom doesn't stiffen or flinch.*)

TONY: Sorry, Tom. Orders from Billy. Like you said—

TOM: Nothing personal, Tony.

TONY: (*Beat.*) Know any good jokes…?

(*Tony holds the gun to Tom's head. Long pause. A look of resignation and acceptance washes over Tom's face, and then he smiles.*)

TOM: This gorilla walks into a bar…

(*Lights fade to black.*)

END OF PLAY

Tinkle Time
by Dana Coen

Biography

DANA COEN has extensive experience as an actor, director, and writer. Other produced plays include *Sympathy* (Manhattan Punchline Theatre and Burbank Theatre Guild), *Bunches of Betty* (West End Playhouse), *Ali Baba, Is It You?* (Theatre of Note) and *Speak!* (Theatre Geo and Wooden O Theatre). He is a long-standing member of the Los Angeles Playwrights Group and works often in television, having developed new series for three networks at Walt Disney Studios, and as a member of the writing staffs of *Carol & Company* with Carol Burnett and *Room for Two* with Linda Lavin.

Author's Note

The idea for *Tinkle Time* germinated during the lowest depths of my Reagan-era depression and was an attempt to imagine both karmic and comic satisfaction from the social insensitivity often practiced by our highest elected official. The circumstances suggest many possibilities and, indeed, I've had great fun over a number of drafts. The play was originally read at *Arthur Kopit's Playwriting Workshop* in New York and contained a final scene where Clyde, alone and undressed in a public toilet, was arrested by the police for suspicion of perverse behavior. That ending was later removed. In both versions, Hollander never returned but the sticker remained as proof of his presence. The Act One producers felt strongly that Hollander should reappear, so in a subsequent version he finds himself protecting the "Chief" from Jim, the Student in the beginning, who ends up opening fire on the concourse with an assault rifle. In the final production version, that choice was eschewed for a less satirical idea.

ORIGINAL PRODUCTION

Tinkle Time, which premiered June 18, 1994, was originally directed by Griffin Dunne. The assistant to the director was Gwen Ewart, with the following cast:

Hollander . . . . .James Avery
Student . . . . .Luke Wilson
Clyde . . . . .Christopher Curry
Jack . . . . .Reno Wilson
President . . . . .Howard Hesseman/David Rasche
Charlie . . . . Harry Shearer

TINKLE TIME

A public men's room in a downtown, urban train station. Built during a prouder time, it now reveals indications of overuse and neglect. A toilet stall stands at one side of the room. On the far wall, parallel to the audience, rest two, stained porcelain urinals. A long, open doorway, separating the urinals from two unfortunate-looking sinks, reveals a darkened lounge area. A wall-mounted hand blower rests downstage of the sinks. Only a sliver remains of the long, horizontal mirror that once graced that wall.

At rise a white, college-aged student, his back to the audience, is using the far left urinal. A large piece of luggage rests at his feet. The logo and nickname of a college are emblazoned on the back of his jacket. Leaning against the urinal next to him is Hollander Crawley, a street-wise African-American male in his middle to late 30s.

HOLLANDER: There ain't no excuse for it, dig?! I mean if some sorry-assed-joker in a car cuts you off while you're transversin' the street—keep in mind he's enclosed, right? You can't do shit to him. Your ass is at a disadvantage. So, if he figures he can skin your butt payin' no mind to the fact that you might not dig him doin' that, then it is important, I might even say crucial, for you to let him know that he has committed a severe boo boo. He's gotta know what a shit-for-brains, sheep reamin', pig-faced faggot he is, right?

(*The uncomfortable student nods back weakly.*)

Okay, then, so the next time that happens, you see…(*Reaching into a pocket of his jacket, he removes a yellow, palm-sized paper disc.*) You pull out one of these jobbies…(*He holds it up to view. The sticker reads "I am an asshole!"*) And slap this sticky sucker on his back window. BINGO! And it glows in the dark too! Can you picture that turnip tryin' to scrape this thing off with a razor blade? There *is* justice in this world, Jim, and it ain't gonna cost you more than five Washingtons for a pack of twenty. The name's Hollander, man. What's yours?

STUDENT: Jim.

HOLLANDER: (*Surprised at the coincidence.*) Well, I sincerely hope you are in a mind to be jumpin' on this once in a lifetime offer, Jim. 'Cause if you ain't, you better be askin' yourself some serious questions, like why am I not more interested in standin' up for myself? Why am I not payin' more attention to this very intelligent negro and why am I urinatin' on my casual but elegant loafers?

(*Jim looks down to see that Hollander is correct. He quickly moves his feet out of the way.*)

This one splashes back on ya'. They should put up a sign or somethin'.

(*A nervous Jim quickly zips up his pants and reaches to flush the toilet. Hollander grabs his wrist in an attempt to stop him.*)

Whoa, you don't wanna be doin' that!

(*A concerned Jim yanks his hand away in fear.*)

Chill, friend, I'm just tryin' to help you out here.

(*Jim, deciding to forego washing, prepares to leave. Hollander slips the yellow sticker back into his pocket and pulls out a receipt pad and a pencil.*)

I don't mean you no harm. This is business, a legitimated deal. See, I thought maybe you and me, we could take a leisurely stroll to my office at locker number one-sixty-three whereupon we can enact the transaction and you can check out the rest of my inventory.

JIM/STUDENT: I don't have time.

HOLLANDER: You like fruit rolls?

JIM: I've got a train to catch.

HOLLANDER: When's your train?

JIM: I'm gonna be late.

HOLLANDER: Won't take but a few ticks of the clock.

JIM: (*Anxious.*) Please, I can't.

HOLLANDER: (*Backing off.*) Then be on your way, college boy. I ain't interested in holdin' you against your will.

(*Jim starts to exit. Two men in dark suits enter. Man #1 is white and Man #2 is African-American.*)

Gentlemen! Gentlemen! You both look very well in your similar suits.

(*No response.*)

Your personalities might do with a bit more effervescence, as it were, but if you could give me a moment of your seemingly precious time…

(*To the African-American suit.*)

Hey, bro.

(*Man #2, ignoring Hollander, detains Jim at the door, and begins questioning him softly.*)

MAN #1: (*To Hollander.*) Step over here, please.

HOLLANDER: Can I assume you are addressin' yourself to myself?

(*Man #1 nods his head affirmatively. Hollander takes note of Jim being questioned at the doorway.*)

Wha's up? There be some kind of investigation happenin' here?

(*Man #2 allows Jim to exit. Man #1 beckons to Hollander with one finger as Man #2 comes up behind him.*)

Oh, I see, the strong and silent approach.

(*Man #2 begins to nudge Hollander in the direction of the urinals.*)

Hey, don't go pushin' me, brother. Show some respect?

MAN #1: What's your name?

HOLLANDER: I'll tell you what, we'll do a little exchange here. You tell me yours and I'll reciprocate back to you.

MAN #2: Now, I want you to stay calm. I'm going to search you, okay?

(*Man #2 forces Hollander's arms up in an attempt to frisk him.*)

HOLLANDER: (*Wheeling on Man #2.*) No, it's not okay! You want your face broke, Jack?!

MAN #1: (*To Man #2.*) Hold off, Jack.

HOLLANDER: (*To Man #2.*) Shit! Your name really *is* Jack!

(*Jack removes a leather duo-fold from the inside pocket of his jacket and flashes it for Hollander's benefit.*)

MAN #1: Now, if you choose to be cooperative, this will be easy.

HOLLANDER: Hey, I'm a very cooperative individual. You ain't gonna find too many people around with the cooperativeness of yours truly. I just tend to be less cooperative when I find somebody stickin' their hands in my armpits, you dig?

MAN #1: You're gonna have to tell me your name.

HOLLANDER: Hollander K. Crawley.

JACK/MAN #2: What's the K stand for?

HOLLANDER: Kaptivatin'.

MAN #1: What are you doing here?

HOLLANDER: Lookin' for toadstools.

MAN #1: Hollander, does this look like a patient face?

HOLLANDER: Can't say it does.

MAN #1: Keeping that in mind, I would like you to answer the question again.

HOLLANDER: Alright, I'm gonna be straight with y'all to show you the kind of individual I am. I could say I was performin' my biologicals, but the fact is I was doin' business. See, I got laid off last month and couldn't get work, so I started a retail operation, bought me some goods, even created my own product line. Now, what I have found is that you can meet all kinds of open-minded brothers in a place like this. You see, you just can't walk on by, here. You gotta do what you gotta do. Gives me time to make my pitch.

JACK: And, what would that be?

HOLLANDER: Now, there's a question I would be pleased and proud to answer. I just happen to have on my very person…

(*Hollander reaches into his jacket pocket. Both men react instantly. Jack shoves Hollander over a sink and pins him there, while Man #1 pulls a gun from his inside shoulder holster.*)

Hey, hey, hey!

(*Jack reaches into Hollander's pocket in search of a weapon. He pulls out the yellow sticker and a fruit roll encased in clear plastic. He looks at the items carefully and then reads from the clear plastic package, frowns.*)

JACK: "Honey 'Kist Fruit Roll."

HOLLANDER: Prune Medley, my best seller.

JACK: (*Holding up the yellow sticker.*) What's this?

HOLLANDER: The very thing I've been tryin' to explain to you.

(*Jack shrugs his shoulders with dismay and pats Hollander about the torso and thighs as he continues his search. Finally, he reaches into the other pocket, pulls out a small locker key and hands it to Man #1.*)

JACK: This is all.

(*Man #1 inspects it and then gives Jack the all-clear-nod. They back off.*)

MAN #1: Can't be too careful, Hollander. Where's your identification?

HOLLANDER: You're starin' at it. You know anyone else looks like this, Clyde?

MAN #1: My name isn't Clyde.

HOLLANDER: That's a relief.

MAN #1: (*Nodding to the items Jack is holding.*) Those you can have back.

(*Jack hands Hollander back the fruit roll and the yellow sticker. Man #1 shows Hollander the key.*)

But, what am I holding here?

HOLLANDER: The key to my Testosterosa.

JACK: (*Irritated.*) Alright, let's take a walk.

HOLLANDER: Hold it, wait a minute! (*To Man #1.*) Can I ask *you* a stupid question?

MAN #1: (*Pause.*) Go ahead.

HOLLANDER: How come he didn't search the college boy?

MAN #1: You know the answer to that.

HOLLANDER: (*Leveling Jack a look.*) I'd like to hear it from *his* ever so pink lips.

JACK: (*To Hollander.*) I don't have to explain shit to you, pal.

MAN #1: (*To Hollander.*) *I'll* tell you. He's not a suspicious-looking weird-apple like you, Hollander.

HOLLANDER: So what you're sayin' is, if I bought my clothes at Sears...

MAN #1: Shut up and pay attention.

(*Jack grips one of Hollander's arms.*)

Jack is going to accompany you to this locker.

(*Clyde tosses Jack the key. Jack starts to lead him out.*)

HOLLANDER: You wanna loosen your grip a little, bro?

MAN #1: Now, while he's doing that I want you to keep this in mind. There are other people around this place that look like us, watching people that look like you.

HOLLANDER: (*Insulted.*) Hey, I look like America, friend and don't you forget it.

(*Jack hurries Hollander out the door. Man #1 looks the place over one more time, checking it carefully. Finally satisfied, he speaks into the collar of his jacket.)*

MAN #1: Alright, Marty, send him in.

(A moment passes. Suddenly, a well-groomed, older man in an expensive suit enters hurriedly. He seems quite uncomfortable.)

Sorry for the delay, Mr. President.

PRESIDENT: Not your fault, Clyde. *(Dashing over to the nearest urinal, he unzips his pants.)* Do you know what it's like traveling through life with an undersized bladder, Clyde?

CLYDE/MAN #1: No sir, I don't.

PRESIDENT: It's like carrying around a bowling ball in a paper bag. Christ it stinks in here!

CLYDE: This is not a previously secured area, sir. The sooner we can leave, the better it will make me feel.

PRESIDENT: I understand but this detour was essential. There was no way in Hades I was going to last through a forty-five minute motorcade.

(Charlie, the President's overtaxed Chief of Staff, enters.)

CHARLIE: *(Looking around in amazement.)* Jesus! Ever thought of doing the East Room like this?

PRESIDENT: Think The First Lady would go for it?

CHARLIE: You could do a whole motif. Costume the staff. Special functions would be great—winos serving cocktails...

PRESIDENT: *(Picking it up.)* Junkies taking coats...

CHARLIE: And on the way out everyone would get a free social disease.

PRESIDENT: What do you think of this guy, huh Clyde?

CLYDE: Pretty funny, sir.

PRESIDENT: That's why he's my number one man. *(Then, aggravated.)* Shit!

CHARLIE: What's wrong?

PRESIDENT: I can't go.

CHARLIE: What are you talking about?! The whole city just stopped so you could drain your dragon.

PRESIDENT: I want to but I can't.

CHARLIE: Good Christ!

PRESIDENT: *(To himself.)* C'mon, c'mon, c'mon! *(Giving up.)* It's not happening.

CHARLIE: Give it a minute. You're going to have to let go at some point and I'd prefer it not be in front of the NATO delegation.

PRESIDENT: (*Zipping up his fly.*) No, I've completely lost the urge. The hell with it.

CLYDE: (*To Charlie.*) We *are* behind schedule, sir.

CHARLIE: (*To the President.*) You sure you're okay?

PRESIDENT: Yeah, false alarm. Let's go.

CHARLIE: (*To Clyde.*) Let 'em know.

CLYDE: (*Into his collar.*) We're on our way out, Marty.

(*The President strides confidently from the room with Charlie and Clyde close behind. A few moments pass and the President, zipping down his fly, frantically rushes back into the room and over to the same urinal. Clyde and an aggravated Charlie follow.*)

CHARLIE: (*Exasperated.*) It's this kind of flip-flopping that's killing us in the polls!

PRESIDENT: (*Frustrated.*) What the hell do you want from me?

(*Clyde waits patiently as Charlie checks his watch. A moment passes. Then...*)

Shit!

CHARLIE: You know, there should have been something in your oath of office. (*An example.*) "And I promise to exercise good bladder control for the sake of my country."

PRESIDENT: Goddamn it!

CLYDE: You're probably just tense, sir. Maybe if I ran some water. (*Clyde turns the knob on one of the sinks. The knob comes off. He tries the other one, nothing.*) Alright, imagine standing by a waterfall and...

PRESIDENT: (*With self-pity.*) I appreciate the effort, Clyde, but I'm blocked.

CHARLIE: (*Last resort.*) Okay, pay attention. I'm going to take a shot here. My Dad used to recite this to me when I was being toilet trained. It never failed. You listening?

(*The President nods.*)

Let me see...okay..."See the toidy. See it shine. Feel it tinkle down the line..."

(*The President gives him a look of utter contempt.*)

"See the toidy..."

(*Pointing to the President's urinal.*)

See it!

(*The President, up for anything at this point, gazes at his urinal.*)

"Feel it tinkle down the line. As it sparkles in the sun, I am having tinkly fun."

PRESIDENT: (*Suddenly moaning with relief.*) Ohhhhhhhhhhhhh!...
Oh!...Oh, God!...Oh, boy!

CLYDE: (*Into his collar.*) The canary is free. I repeat, the canary is free.

CHARLIE: (*To the President.*) I want Attorney General in your next term.
(*Pointing at the President's feet.*)
Watch it!
(*The President quickly moves his feet out of the way.*)
Listen, I was wrong about the press. The barricades are fifty yards
closer than instructed. You'll be within shouting distance.

PRESIDENT: What are they on to?

CHARLIE: You know, standard beefs...reduced aid to cities, urban decay,
teens with guns...uhm, what else...oh, black unemployment is
through the roof here. If you get that question, tell them...what?
Tell them you've already spent eight percent more than your
predecessor on job assistance.

PRESIDENT: They've got to know that's an inflation-adjusted figure.

CHARLIE: They'll be no time to probe. Just head for the car. The public
doesn't know from inflation-adjusted figures.

PRESIDENT: What if I just say we're refunding the program?

CHARLIE: You're dumping the program.

PRESIDENT: (*Zipping up his fly.*) This is true.

CHARLIE: See, that's why I keep telling you to watch what you say off
the cuff. We'll never survive another "flying fetus" remark.

PRESIDENT: Am I the only the one who thought that was funny? (*The
President flushes the toilet. Quite suddenly, a torrent of water splashes
up from the urinal and directly back on to the President's suit.*)
Holy...!

CHARLIE: Jesus Christ!
(*A terrible shaking and unearthly roar follows, then slowly calms.
Suddenly, the blue disinfectant cake pops from the bottom of the urinal
and shoots across the room. Clyde, ever the ready, pulls his gun, and
blocks the President from any possible harm.*)

CLYDE: (*Alarmed.*) You all right, sir?

PRESIDENT: Judge for yourself. (*The entire front of his suit from his crotch
to his chest is soaked.*)

CHARLIE: I don't believe it! (*He begins kicking the sink in an uncontrolled
burst of anger.*) GOD DAMN IT! (*Calming down, Charlie consults
his watch.*) Shit!

PRESIDENT: How much time do we have?

CHARLIE: We're supposed to be there twenty-two minutes ago.

PRESIDENT: I'm going to have to change.

CHARLIE: Can't do it. The bags have already left the hotel. God knows where they are.

PRESIDENT: Well, let's buy something.

CHARLIE: Where?

PRESIDENT: I don't know. Is there a clothing store on the concourse?

CHARLIE: I'm not picturing you in a stocking cap and high tops.

PRESIDENT: Well, what then?!

CLYDE: May I make a suggestion?

PRESIDENT: Go ahead.

CLYDE: We could try and dry you off under the hand blower.

(Pause. Charlie looks to the President for approval.)

PRESIDENT: Let's do it.

(They rush over to the hand blower. Charlie presses the switch. He and Clyde then try to position the President so that the nozzle is blowing hot air onto his midsection. The President responds with growing panic.)

Uh…uhm…wait a minute! WAIT A MINUTE! (*He twists away and steps out of range.*) I'm gonna fry my frijole under that thing! (*He removes his jacket and hands it to Clyde, begins taking off his tie.*) You can start on that, Clyde.

CLYDE: Right away, sir. (*Clyde begins drying the suit jacket under the nozzle of the blower.*)

CHARLIE: What are you doing?

(The President hands Charlie his tie and begins unbuttoning his shirt.)

PRESIDENT: Get to work, Charlie.

(Charlie, sharing the blower with Clyde, attempts to dry the tie.)

I'm completely soaked through. Unbelievable!

CLYDE: (*Into his transmitter.*) It's gonna be about five minutes, Marty.

CHARLIE: (*Suddenly not feeling well.*) Clyde, do I look pale to you?

CLYDE: Always, sir.

PRESIDENT: (*Removing his shirt.*) Charlie! (*The President tosses Charlie his shirt.*) Any progress, Clyde?

CLYDE: Yes, sir.

(The hand blower shuts off. A moment passes. Clyde presses the switch to reactivate it. They wait. They watch. Nothing happens. He presses it again. Still nothing.)

I don't think it's working, sir.

PRESIDENT: Clyde?

CLYDE: Yes, sir?

PRESIDENT: Would you mind telling me what I'm standing in? Frankly, I'm afraid to look.

(*Both Clyde and Charlie look.*)

CLYDE: Oh...uh...well, sir it's...

PRESIDENT: Never mind. I don't really want to know. What size suit do you wear?

CLYDE: Forty-two long.

PRESIDENT: Do you know what I'm about to ask you?

CLYDE: Will it fit, sir?

PRESIDENT: I think so.

CLYDE: Then, by all means.

(*Clyde quickly disrobes as the President kicks off his shoes.*)

CHARLIE: (*Apprehensive.*) Is this smart? Are we thinking clearly here?

(*The President begins removing his pants.*)

He's taking his pants off, Clyde. The President of the largest country in the free world is dropping his trousers in a public bathroom.

PRESIDENT: Don't start falling apart on me, Clyde.

CHARLIE: You don't have any hair on your legs.

PRESIDENT: What?

CHARLIE: Why don't you have hair on your legs?

PRESIDENT: Who cares!

CHARLIE: (*To himself as he enters the toilet stall.*) Nixon was covered. He was like a shag carpet.

PRESIDENT: Charlie, how 'bout some help here?! (*As he turns back to Clyde, he notices Clyde standing in his underwear and bulletproof vest. Embarrassed, he turns his eyes away.*) Charlie?!

(*No response.*)

Sorry I'm asking you to wear wet clothes Clyde but you'll look a lot less conspicuous in them than I will. (*The President jumps into Clyde's clothing.*)

CLYDE: Don't worry about it, sir.

(*Clyde slips his tie over the President's head and adjusts it.*)

PRESIDENT: (*To Clyde.*) I'm going to need the shoes too.

CLYDE: I take a ten-D.

PRESIDENT: A little small but we'll make it work.

(*Clyde removes his shoes and the President slips into them.*)

CHARLIE: (*Reappearing from the stall.*) I don't think that toilet's ever been flushed. (*Checking out the President's new neckwear.*) Do you like this tie?

PRESIDENT: It'll do.

CHARLIE: (*Peering more closely.*) What are those figures?

CLYDE: Fairy Winkles, sir.

CHARLIE: Excuse me?

CLYDE: They're little Fairy Winkles, cartoon characters. My girls gave it to me. It's my lucky tie.

PRESIDENT: Can only help.

CHARLIE: You're going to address NATO with Fairy Winkles on your tie?

PRESIDENT: This is no time to nitpick, Charlie.

CHARLIE: Wait a minute. (*Charlie crosses to the exit and calls out.*) Marty, what do you have on your tie?

MARTY: (*Shouting back from offstage.*) Spaghetti sauce, sir.

CHARLIE: Never mind. (*To the President.*) We'll go with what we've got. (*Looking him over.*) Your zipper's down.
(*The President tries to zip it up. It's stuck. He tries with more effort. No luck.*)

PRESIDENT: I'm at a loss for words.

CHARLIE: (*With an Excedrin headache.*) Clyde, do you know how to work that thing?

CLYDE: Usually, sir.

CHARLIE: Would you help him out, please?
(*Clyde kneels in front of the President. Charlie watches as he fiddles with the zipper.*)

CLYDE: I think it's jammed, sir.
(*Without warning, Hollander Crawley enters alone, sees Clyde, without clothes, kneeling in front of the President's crotch, holding onto his zipper. He stops, looks on with curiosity. Clyde, Charlie, and the President look over at him. A moment passes.*)

HOLLANDER: (*To the President.*) Are you the leader of my country?
(*Suddenly, Jack rushes in, gun drawn.*)

JACK: HIT THE DECK!
(*Charlie and the President duck for cover as Clyde pulls out his gun and positions himself in front of them. In an instant, Jack backs Hollander against the wall.*)

HOLLANDER: (*Frightened.*) Whoa! Chill! I'm not armed, remember?

CLYDE: (*To Jack.*) What happened?!

JACK: (*To Clyde.*) This is one slippery son of a bitch. (*To the President.*) Sorry, sir. I was checking him out and he got away from me. (*Noticing Clyde's undressed state.*) What's going on?

HOLLANDER: *My* lips are sealed.

CLYDE: Shutup! (*To Jack.*) I exchanged clothing with the President. (*Jack is confused.*) He wet his suit. (*This doesn't help.*) Does the zipper on your pants work? (*Neither does this.*)

CHARLIE: Screw the explanation! Get this character out of here.

HOLLANDER: Someone got a problem with their zipper, I can fix it.

CHARLIE: I think not.

HOLLANDER: No, really, before they laid me off, I repaired tuxedos for nine years. Is it stuck?

PRESIDENT: Yeah, it's stuck.

HOLLANDER: Plastic or metal?

PRESIDENT: Plastic.

HOLLANDER: No, problem. You got a Sears Easy-glide—small teeth, can't take much action. See, the girls on the street all wear metal. They hip to that shit.

PRESIDENT: Well, what do I do?

HOLLANDER: Try the double yank.

PRESIDENT: What's that?

HOLLANDER: Twist one way, pull the other.

(*The President follows Hollander's instructions and, to everyone's amazement, pulls the zipper free.*)

PRESIDENT: (*Delighted.*) I don't believe it! Ease off him, boys. He's not a problem.

(*Jack and Clyde cautiously give Hollander room as the President quickly begins to pull his outfit together, tucking in his shirt, tying his shoes, etc.*)

What's your name?

HOLLANDER: Hollander K. Crawley.

PRESIDENT: Thanks, Hollander. You're okay.

HOLLANDER: Are you really the man?!

PRESIDENT: I'm him.

HOLLANDER: (*Delighted.*) Well, ain't this a serindipfluous thing! I'm with the Chief! Listen, since I helped and all, would it be alright to ask you 'bout some things that have been on my mind?

PRESIDENT: (*The benevolent leader.*) Sure. What do you want to know?

HOLLANDER: Do you do it with your dog?

PRESIDENT: (*Outraged.*) What?!

HOLLANDER: (*Pointing.*)It's written on the wall here.

JACK: (*To Hollander.*) This is the President. Don't fuck it up!

HOLLANDER: Okay, then tell me what you plan to do 'bout puttin' brothers back to work?

CHARLIE: (*To the President.*) Do you really want to deal with this?

HOLLANDER: See, Chief, people like me, we're just lookin' for a reason to get up in the morning, you dig?

PRESIDENT: (*Sincere.*) I do dig, Hollander. I hear you. I'm not happy about the unemployment figures. They stink. I can smell them from the Oval Office. All I can tell you is I'm working on it. I'm sorry you got laid off. I wish I could do something for you.

HOLLANDER: Maybe you can. (*Hollander pulls out the plastic-wrapped fruit roll.*) Costs sixty-five cents.

(*The President looks at him with confusion.*)

It's how I been makin' my livin'.

PRESIDENT: (*With a nod of understanding.*) Let's see it.

(*The President cues Clyde, who takes the fruit roll from Hollander and hands it to the President. He reads the wrapper information.*)

Prune medley. I can use this. I have a regularity problem.

(*The President removes a roll from his pocket and hands Clyde a fifty dollar bill.*)

PRESIDENT: Here you go, Hollander.

CLYDE: (*Realizing that it's his money.*) Excuse me, sir, but that's my...

PRESIDENT: (*Interrupting.*) Clyde, I would like to personally help the man.

CLYDE: I know, sir, but you have my...

PRESIDENT: (*Firm.*) Give it to him.

(*Clyde, in deference to his leader, tries to hand Hollander the money but he refuses it.*)

HOLLANDER: This is too much.

PRESIDENT: Hollander, keep the change.

HOLLANDER: I charge sixty-five cents, no more, no less.

CHARLIE: Jesus H!

JACK: I have it, sir.

(*Jack digs into a pocket, scoops out some change, counts out sixty-five cents and hands it to Hollander, who pockets it.*)

HOLLANDER: Much appreciated. You help us out now, okay Chief?

PRESIDENT: We'll take care of it, Hollander. Keep the faith. Charlie, help me with the jacket.

(*Charlie picks Clyde's jacket off the floor.*)

HOLLANDER: (*Like a little kid.*) Hey, would it be okay if I...you know...?

(*The President, enjoying Hollander's infatuation, nods to Charlie.*)

PRESIDENT: (*To Charlie.*) Let him do it.

(*Charlie reluctantly hands the jacket to Hollander, while Clyde and Jack stand at the ready. During the following exchange of lines, Hollander eases the President into the jacket, carefully straightens it out and completely dusts it off.*)

HOLLANDER: So, Chief when you say you'll take care of it, how do you mean? What you got goin' on?

PRESIDENT: A lot. All kinds of things.

HOLLANDER: Programs and shit?

PRESIDENT: Right, programs and...shit, these shoes!

CHARLIE: C'mon, let's get out of here.

PRESIDENT: I'm almost ready.

HOLLANDER: (*Continuing his thought.*) So, what kind of programs?

PRESIDENT: Huh?

HOLLANDER: What's the deal? What's happenin' now?

PRESIDENT: (*Checking his outfit.*) Well...uh...this year I've already spent eight percent more on job assistance then my predecessor and I've got plans to fatten the whole program.

HOLLANDER: That so?

PRESIDENT: Absolutely, we've also been huddling over increased aid to cities.

HOLLANDER: I thought eight percent was an inflation-adjusted figure.

CHARLIE: (*Impatient, to President.*) Thirty-four minutes and counting!

HOLLANDER: And, all *I* read about is *decreased* aid to cities.

PRESIDENT: (*To Clyde.*) Make sure The First Lady knows I'm on the way.

CLYDE: Yes, sir.

HOLLANDER: (*To the President, irritated.*) What you givin' me that Washington-fried-shit for?! You think you can lie to Hollander Crawley?!

JACK: (*To Hollander.*) Didn't you hear what he said?

HOLLANDER: (*Surly.*) Back out of my face, chocolate drop. Don't you dig what's going down?!

CHARLIE: (*To Hollander.*) Alright you're gone!
(*Charlie nods to Jack, who grabs Hollander by the back of the collar and starts to yank him out of the room.*)
HOLLANDER: (*Resisting.*) You go ahead, Chief. You invade my privacy, push my ass around, put guns to my head, but let me tell you something, no matter what your rap is, you can't hide the truth about yourself. It's gonna follow you wherever you go, you understand? You hear what I'm sayin'?!
(*Jack drags Hollander out the door. They're gone.*)
CHARLIE: (*Sarcastic.*) I haven't had this much fun since the Mid East Peace talks.
PRESIDENT: The guy was a prize, huh? Who does he think he is, the voice of the people? So, how do I look?
(*The President pivots upstage, revealing the back of Clyde's suit jacket to the audience. Positioned squarely in the middle of his shoulder blades sits a palm-sized, yellow sticker that reads, "I am an asshole!"*)
CHARLIE: It works. It's you. Ready to carry on?
PRESIDENT: Are we having lunch?
CHARLIE: But, of course.
PRESIDENT: (*Pleased.*) Then, lead the way.
(*Clyde turns to gather up the clothing on the floor. The President, limping in his tight shoes, follows Charlie out the door. Clyde, dressed in his underwear is left holding a pile of wet, dirty clothing. Shortly, the urinal begins to vibrate and rumble ominously. Clyde glances back with concern. Blackout.*)

END OF PLAY

The Other Five Percent
by Bryan Goluboff

BIOGRAPHY

BRYAN GOLUBOFF was born in Brooklyn and has lived in New York all his life. His plays include *Big Al, My Side of the Story,* and *In-Betweens.* Bryan also wrote the screenplay for the film *The Basketball Diaries.* He went to N.Y.U. and is a member of the Ensemble Studio Theatre.

AUTHOR'S NOTE

This play leaves room for a wide variety of interpretations. Have fun with it. Experiment with music, lights, and setting. It doen't necessarily have to be "realistic".

ORIGINAL PRODUCTION

The original production, directed by David Cammon, was held in the Pearl Theatre in New York.

Hughie ....Richard Paul
Jimmy ....Shane Blodgett
Amy ....Dana Barron

THE OTHER FIVE
PERCENT

Darkness. Sinister music sounds in the night.
Lights come up slowly to reveal a dark, dirty street in Manhattan,
decorated for Halloween with ghosts and jack o'lanterns on their doors.
This street is something out of a nightmare.
Amy, a teenage girl, sits on a stoop. She is a pretty, large-eyed blond
who wears cat's ears, drawn on whiskers and a cat's tail attached to her
white miniskirt. She holds an umbrella and a pocketbook. She is
putting on make-up.
Suddenly, a man in a skeleton suit with a black leather bomber jacket
over it, leaps out of the shadows. His name is Hughie.

HUGHIE: Boo! (*Amy jumps up, startled. Hughie lifts up the skeleton mask*
    to reveal what once was a shockingly handsome face. His overall
    appearance is wild, unkempt, a young man who has hit bottom.) Hey,
    Happy Halloween, how ya doin'? (*Amy smiles.*) Yeah, I'm just
    prowlin' around. You know how it is, New York at night. Didn't
    mean to scare ya.
AMY: You didn't scare me, don't worry.
HUGHIE: I've been watching you.
AMY: Is that right?
HUGHIE: Yeah. I'm trying to figure out what the hell you're doing here.

AMY: What do you mean?

HUGHIE: This isn't exactly the greatest place for little kittens. Are you lost?

AMY: Why do you wanna know?

HUGHIE: Curious.

AMY: I guess I am kinda lost. I went from the parade to 14th Street and just kept walking.

HUGHIE: You've been alone all night?

AMY: No, my friends totally fagged out. I couldn't believe it.

HUGHIE: What do you mean?

AMY: Me, my friend, Marnie, and her boyfriend, Jesse, came in. We were on Sixth Avenue, it was so crowded at the parade we actually had to go underground in the subway just to get across the street. Well, somebody pinched Marnie's ass or something and Jesse freaked out. He's such an infant. Then, somebody threw a bottle, missed him by like an inch. He said, "We're going home. Are you coming?" I said, "Adios."

HUGHIE: They left you out here?

AMY: Well, they tried to drag me into the cab, but I slammed the door on Jesse's leg. Marnie'll probably never talk to me again, like I really care, my one night in the city.

HUGHIE: Heavy turmoil.

AMY: There's so many things I still wanna do, I…I wanna go dancing. I wanna dance all night! I need music and people. There's no way I'm going home yet.

HUGHIE: Where's home?

AMY: Brooklyn. Can't you tell?

HUGHIE: What part?

AMY: Uh, Bensonhurst…

HUGHIE: No way…No way you're from Brooklyn. I know Brooklyn girls inside out, top to bottom. No way—

AMY: Yeah, I—

HUGHIE: Long Island. (*Pause.*) Five towns, specifically.

AMY: Oh, my God, how could you tell? I am so ashamed.

HUGHIE: The Island and Jersey invade our borough at the slightest excuse for a Holiday. Holiday. That's my last name. My full name is Hubert Allen Holiday. Friends and lovers—isn't that a song?— call me Hughie.

AMY: Hi, Hughie. I'm Amy. (*They shake hands, she holds on for a lingering moment.*) You're cute.

HUGHIE: What?

AMY: You heard me...Now come on, Hughie, take me dancing, I bet you know all the cool places.

HUGHIE: Wanna do me a favor?

AMY: Anything...(*Hughie takes off his coat and offers it to her.*)

HUGHIE: Put on my jacket.

AMY: I'm not cold.

HUGHIE: Just put it on...

AMY: Something wrong with my shoulders? (*Hughie looks at her shoulders a moment.*)

HUGHIE: Nothing. That's the problem. Here...(*She still doesn't take the jacket.*) Put on the jacket. I'm not gonna tell you again.

AMY: Are you kidding me?

HUGHIE: It's time we got you back to civilization.

AMY: Who do you think you are?

HUGHIE: Someone who knows trouble when he sees it—

AMY: Trouble? Hey, look, I have a father and he works overtime at it, O.K.? I knew you weren't taking me seriously, I knew it—

HUGHIE: I'm doing you a big favor—

AMY: Just because I'm cute, everyone thinks it's their natural right to protect me—

HUGHIE: Put your hand in—

AMY: No! The last thing I wanted tonight was to be treated like this. You don't understand, my brothers walk me to the bathroom in restaurants. You wouldn't even believe my father. Last week, I was forty-five minutes late, he called the police. They went around with my photograph and wound up pulling me out of a bar. I almost died right there. I told about 7,000 lies to get here tonight and I am gonna do everything! You can take that jacket and...(*She throws the jacket on the ground. Hughie stares at her a moment.*)

HUGHIE: Look all the way West, O.K.? (*Amy looks.*) Nobody. No cops. They're all at the parade. Look all the way East. (*Amy looks.*) Like miles down. The only sign of the men in blue is a little horseshit on 28th Street. If I felt like hurting you, you'd be bleeding on the ground with an empty purse. Don't you understand that?

AMY: You wouldn't hurt me. I can tell. You have nice eyes.

HUGHIE: I'm a stranger out in the street! You don't have a clue. No instincts. I don't wanna pick up the *Post* tomorrow and find you in four pieces on the front page. That could wear on a man's conscience. Now, c'mon, let's get you on a train home...(*He offers her the jacket again.*)

AMY: I told you I'm not going home. Not tonight.

HUGHIE: So don't go home, there must be a party out on Long Island or something.

AMY: No way. Boring.

HUGHIE: What if I came with you?

AMY: You mean if you went to the party with me? (*She laughs.*) You and Woodmere won't work, Hughie.

HUGHIE: Think of what your friends would say if you showed up with me?

AMY: Oh, God—

HUGHIE: I'm cute. You'd be a smash hit.

AMY: I'm sorry, I have a boyfriend.

HUGHIE: We can make him jealous. I'm good at that.

AMY: Well, he's not really my boyfriend. I like him. I just like him that's all.

HUGHIE: Oh...What's his name?

AMY: Paul

HUGHIE: (*Suddenly furious.*) Paul? Paul? You know how many girlfriends I've lost to guys named Paul? Hundreds! Fuckin' sharks! I'll take care of him for ya—

AMY: No, no, he's shy—

HUGHIE: Paul?

AMY: He's very shy—

HUGHIE: I bet he's got another girl out in the car by now, fucking Paul.

AMY: He's not like that.

HUGHIE: I will not let some fucking shark put his hands on your little body. Not after I took the time to get you home safe.

AMY: He's never even kissed me—

HUGHIE: Sure—

AMY: He goes to a Yeshiva in West Hempstead. I think I'm the first girl he ever even talked to. You better not do anything to him...Oh, I can't believe this...

(*Pause.*)

HUGHIE: He's really never kissed you?

AMY: No.

HUGHIE: Well what happens at the end of a typical date?

AMY: He just says goodnight. I don't know.

HUGHIE: You do know, stop saying that. Now he sounds like a nice guy, let me help you out...Is there tension at the door? Do you linger there with nothing to say, just mumbling? Maybe he's got one of your hands.

AMY: Yes.

HUGHIE: But no kiss?

AMY: He...He acts like we're just friends.

HUGHIE: All right, come here...

AMY: Why?

HUGHIE: I wanna show you a trick...C'mere...(*She walks to him, still keeping some distance.*) Here we are at the door of your colossal mansion at the end of a typical evening...(*Becomes "Paul."*) What a great night at the movies as friends. Boy, yeah...(*He puts out his hand to Amy. She doesn't take it.*) If Paul puts out his hand, you take it...(*She still doesn't move.*) Aren't I here? Aren't I talking to you? (*She takes his hand.*)

AMY: I'm uncomfortable when I hold his hand. So I was trying to make it real.

HUGHIE: Right, good. Good. Here we are, Paul and Amy. Holding hands. Let me show you a little magic. (*They are holding hands.*) He says, "Shalom" mumble mumble, and you give my hand just a little tug. (*She gives his hand a tug.*) No. No, subtle just a little tiny pull. Just enough of a hint. (*She pulls his hand slightly. Hughie flows gracefully toward her, in position to kiss.*) Amazing, right? One little pull, a kiss of true love. Try it again. (*She does it again. Hughie is very close to her face. He moves away.*) One more time. (*Amy does it again. Hughie is an inch from her lips.*) Any man who wouldn't kiss you now is either crazy or homosexual. (*They stay that way for a moment. Amy has her eyes closed. She tries to kiss him. Hughie turns his face away.*)

AMY: Kiss me, Hughie...(*She kisses his face. Hughie caresses her hair and then touches her shoulders. She kisses his face again, closer to his mouth. Hughie breaks away from her.*)

HUGHIE: I can't kiss you. I can never kiss another girl again. See, I got the killer's kiss.

AMY: What do you mean?

HUGHIE: This is my last Halloween...(*Pause.*) So you think it'll work with him, our little tug? Of course it'll work. That kiss can't miss. That kiss can't miss.

AMY: Thank you.

HUGHIE: Hey, I know how important every victory of love can be. I was in love once. Rachel. (*Hughie takes a snapshot out of his pocket.*) There's me and her in high school.

AMY: She's very pretty.

HUGHIE: Yes, she was...I miss her a lot, Amy. A lot. When you're kissing Paul tonight remember how lucky you are. (*Hughie closes his eyes, rubs his head.*) It feels so good to just be talking to someone. I think that's why I'm talking so much—

AMY: It's O.K.—

HUGHIE: Amy, can I crash at your place after the party? I won't wanna come back so late...

AMY: Hughie...

HUGHIE: What?

AMY: You can't go to the party or stay in my house.

HUGHIE: Yes, I can.

AMY: No, my father will freak if he finds out I was even in the city. At the party all the parents will see you. He'll find out. You don't know him, Hughie. You can walk me to the train, O.K.? I'll go home...

HUGHIE: It's not enough.

AMY: Hughie, this isn't funny.

HUGHIE: I'm glad you realize that.

AMY: Why do we have to do this? I'll be O.K. If I went to any other bus stop in the city, I would've been on my own.

HUGHIE: I have a confession to make, Amy. Our meeting was not a chance occurrence. I saw you leave your friends. I followed you here.

AMY: You followed me?

HUGHIE: Yes.

AMY: Why me? Thousands of girls at the parade. Why?

HUGHIE: You don't know? I saw it happen. It wasn't your night. (*Hughie drops to his knees and picks up her right leg.*)

AMY: What are you doing?

HUGHIE: This, I saw this happen to you—(*He is pointing to a gash on her shin.*)

AMY: I don't want you to touch me! (*She kicks her leg at him. He takes the blow on his neck, but holds tight to her leg.*)

HUGHIE: You were standing on the curb, in the crowds on Sixth Avenue—

AMY: Get off me, Hughie, I mean it—

HUGHIE: There was this circle of monsters in the street sharing a fifth of bourbon. Dracula was opening his mouth showing his fangs.

AMY: Please let go—

HUGHIE: They were so drunk. The Bride of Frankenstein's dress was ripped and she was laughing a ghoul's laugh. The fifth was finally dry and Drac threw it high in the sky. It seemed to hang in the streetlights for a long time. I watched it fall out of the night and shatter at your feet. Glass leaped off the ground and—"Ouch," you said, just like that.

AMY: It's just a little cut, it's nothing—

HUGHIE: You were surprised when the blood came right out. It comes out so easy. (*Hughie is caressing her leg.*) The bottle could've landed anywhere. Someone once said, "Chance is a strange arithmetic." I believe it's true. The math is against you tonight.

AMY: Help! (*Hughie clasps his hand over her mouth.*)

HUGHIE: Stop it! Will you stop it? It hurts my feelings! (*He takes his hand away.*)

AMY: Leave me alone! Please! (*He covers her mouth harshly.*)

HUGHIE: Shut up, please...Please. I wouldn't hurt anyone else. (*He holds her face in his hands.*) I've done enough damage. Rachel...I killed the girl I loved. I put her in the ground. Something broke inside of me, don't you understand that? Something broke off...I feel like tearing the hair outta my head!

AMY: I'm sorry.

HUGHIE: You think I wanted to hurt her? All I wanted was for her to be happy. If I was killing her like that something is very wrong here. You see, something is very, very wrong here...(*He touches Amy's hair.*) I see you tonight...A pussy cat...A little pussy cat with a wounded paw...Defenseless...I have to help you. (*He holds Amy's face.*) I look in your eyes, I see tragedies. I see your face collapsed with crying.

AMY: I'm O.K.—

HUGHIE: I can't let you go...(*He hugs Amy. She is terrified.*) Any time you're in trouble, in school, at home, in the street, in the store, I'll be there. I'll be there till I die. I'll be there. (*He collapses to his knees. She sits on the stoop. His head is on her lap.*) Oh…

AMY: Shhh…

HUGHIE: I'll never let you go…(*Amy reaches into her pocketbook.*) I'm sorry I scared you. I'm sorry.

AMY: It's O.K.…

HUGHIE: I need…(*Hughie pushes his head against her hand like a dog.*)

AMY: It's O.K.…

HUGHIE: I'm gonna take you home.

(*Amy takes a bottle out of her purse.*)

AMY: Thank you…

(*Hughie looks up at her. Amy sprays the bottle into his eyes. Hughie screams and falls down with his hands over his eyes. Amy tries to run away, but Hughie grabs her legs and knocks her down. She screams.*)

HUGHIE: No! No!

(*Hughie holds onto her blindly. She is trying to get away, but he is too strong. Slowly, slowly his eyes start clearing. A Policeman walks aggressively toward them from stage right. He is young, strong looking, with a cruel face. Even though it is the middle of the night he wears mirror sunglasses. He has his gun belt hanging low like a cowboy. His name is Jimmy Witteck.*)

JIMMY: Hey hey hey! Get off her, scumbag! Now!

(*Hughie looks up and sees him. He slowly lets Amy go. She runs to Jimmy and hugs him tightly, crying. She is safe.*)

HUGHIE: Oh, God, it was only perfume! It was only lovely perfume. I smell beautiful. Beautiful tootiful ha ha!

JIMMY: Shut up and don't move! (*Hughie rubs the scent into his neck and face. Jimmy turns to Amy.*) What did he do to you, Ma'am?

AMY: He was talking crazy and touching me, he wouldn't let me go—

JIMMY: O.K., O.K., calm down…(*He points offstage right.*) Go sit in my car and wait for me. I'm gonna talk to this gentleman for a minute, O.K.? (*Amy nods.*) I'll be right there. Lock the door. (*She walks off stage right.*)

HUGHIE: Officer, listen—

JIMMY: Stand up and face the wall.

HUGHIE: Come on, man, I—

JIMMY: Stand up and face the wall. (*Hughie stands up and faces the wall.*) Put your hands behind your head.

HUGHIE: This is a big mistake—

JIMMY: I don't wanna tell you again…Behind your head. (*Hughie puts his hands behind his head.*) Knuckles and thumbs together. Come on…(*Jimmy puts Hughie's hands in the right position.*) Spread your legs.

HUGHIE: Pardon me—(*Jimmy kicks Hughie's legs apart.*) Come on, I gotta bad toe.

JIMMY: Then spread your fucking legs. We can do this the easy way or we can do this the hard way—(*Jimmy starts frisking Hughie.*)

HUGHIE: I didn't do anything. She sprayed me in the eyes with perfume. Smell me. Smell me.

(*Jimmy looks at him like he's crazy. Hughie starts to turn around to plead his case.*)

JIMMY: Face the fuckin' wall before I crack you in the head. (*Jimmy picks up Hughie's bomber jacket and starts looking through the pockets. There are a few tissues and two empty bullet casings.*) Where did you get these bullet shells? Do you have a gun?

HUGHIE: No. I found them in Little Italy. They're good luck. (*Jimmy tosses them onto the garbage pile.*) Hey, c'mon officer…(*Jimmy goes through another pocket. He finds the pictures. He looks through them with mounting interest.*) Can I put my hands down?

JIMMY: Where did you get these pictures?

HUGHIE: They're mine. They're me.

JIMMY: That's not you.

HUGHIE: Yes, it is.

JIMMY: Turn around. Slowly. (*Hughie turns slowly around. Jimmy studies his face.*) Hughie Holiday, is that you?

HUGHIE: Yeah, of course it's me. Is that good?

JIMMY: I don't believe this. Put your hands down. Shit.

HUGHIE: You know me?

JIMMY: Stuyvescent High School Class of '85. (*He slaps hands with Hughie.*) I haven't seen you since Graduation.

HUGHIE: Are you sure we know each other?

(*Jimmy laughs.*)

JIMMY: Of course we know each other. I can still remember the "Three things Hughie Holiday knows in this world—How to seduce a woman, how to hit a baseball and never to eat Italian food in a Greek diner."

HUGHIE: Did I really say that?

JIMMY: You used to talk all kinds of shit...What happened tonight, Hughie? Were you trying to pick her up?

HUGHIE: Me? No—

JIMMY: C'mon, I know you better than that—

HUGHIE: No, we just had a misunderstanding—

JIMMY: Must have been more than that, she was cryin'.

HUGHIE: I took an interest in her, Officer. She was out here alone. A young girl. You know how it is—

JIMMY: Sure.

HUGHIE: I was worried about her.

JIMMY: Right.

HUGHIE: You'll take care of her now?

JIMMY: I'll take real good care of her, don't you worry...Now, you put me in a bad position here, Hughie. Usually, with the riff-raff, I put my nightstick up their ass a bit before I even question 'em, but—

HUGHIE: Officer—

JIMMY: But you're a friend of mine and that has to count for something.

HUGHIE: I didn't do anything to her. I swear.

JIMMY: The oath of a friend has got to count for something...She is the first girl I ever saw run away from Hughie Holiday...(*Jimmy laughs.*) In High School she would've melted right there on the street—

HUGHIE: I don't know about that—

JIMMY: If she saw you playing baseball, c'mon...I remember how the girls went crazy after you hit that home run—

HUGHIE: You were at the championship game?

JIMMY: Yeah. There were two out in the 9th, down one, man on. Every kid's wet dream. You went into that stance of yours, with your hands held high. Guy came in with a curveball, a wicked curveball on three and two and you jerk it outta the park. I said to myself, "That man's gonna be on a box of cereal someday."

HUGHIE: It was a nice shot.

JIMMY: This girl woulda been right there with the others that day. Don't deny it. You had your pick.

HUGHIE: Things change.

JIMMY: Obviously. You're supposed to be in Shea Stadium by now, not on the street, in trouble with the N.Y.P.D.

HUGHIE: That's how it worked out. What can I tell you?

JIMMY: You just cost me $75—

HUGHIE: How?

JIMMY: I had a bet with Gino Bova that you'd be playing with the Mets by 1994.

HUGHIE: I hope you don't hold it against me, Officer.

JIMMY: You remember Gino?

HUGHIE: I'm not sure—

JIMMY: Dark hair? Skinny? He was working on my Plymouth Grand Fury in shop senior year.

HUGHIE: Can't place him.

JIMMY: Everybody called him Digga Hooplai—

HUGHIE: Digga Hooplai! (*Hughie laughs.*) Digga Hooplai. Of course I remember Digga. He had his name tattooed to his forearm. Did you hang around with him?

JIMMY: Not that much in high school.

HUGHIE: How is old Digga doing?

JIMMY: He's fine. He's a mechanic. We were wondering what happened to you. I mean, I heard you went to Spring training—

HUGHIE: I even played a year—

JIMMY: Where?

HUGHIE: Out in Virginia, Double A ball—

JIMMY: How'd you do?

HUGHIE: Good. .309. 63 ribbies. Stole a bunch of bases—

JIMMY: .309…You never struck out, Hughie. With the girls either, you know what I mean? (*Jimmy puts his hand out for Hughie to slap it. He does.*) .309? Did your knee blow out? (*Hughie shakes his head "no."*) You quit? What happened?

HUGHIE: They released me. I couldn't pass the physical.

JIMMY: Why?

HUGHIE: Doctor wouldn't let me play.

JIMMY: I know that. Why?

(*Pause.*)

HUGHIE: That's none of your business.

JIMMY: Come on, Hughie, we're friends here. Gino's gonna ask.

HUGHIE: It didn't work out, O.K.?

JIMMY: Wait a minute, wait a minute, wait a minute here. (*He looks very closely at Hughie.*) No offense, but you look like shit.

HUGHIE: Thank you—

(*Jimmy keeps staring at Hughie.*)

JIMMY: You failed the drug test, right? They're cracking down on that—

HUGHIE: No...

JIMMY: You're not a drinker, if I remember right, although that's one way to end up out here...(*Jimmy keeps staring at Hughie.*)

HUGHIE: What are you lookin' at?

JIMMY: I can't fucking believe it! You...You got it, right? The Magic Johnson thing? I know I'm right...I'm sorry, I'm sorry, man. Wait till I tell Gino. You don't mind if I tell Gino, do you? They're gonna freak at the class reunion.

HUGHIE: You don't know what you're talking about.

JIMMY: You got a place to sleep?

HUGHIE: A different place every night. That's what I want—

JIMMY: Listen, you can stay with me. I don't care what you got—

HUGHIE: It's O.K.—

JIMMY: You sure? I got a new place. You need some money? How about a shower even? I'm so sorry, Hughie, man—

HUGHIE: Can you stop for a second, please?

JIMMY: Do you know how you got it, Hughie? You get into guys? Oh man, did you get into guys or something?

HUGHIE: No. Take it easy...

JIMMY: Well, you never were too smart about things...

HUGHIE: Whaddya mean?

JIMMY: Third floor bathroom. "Hughie Holiday fucks 'em 8 to 80 blind, deaf, dumb, and crazy."

HUGHIE: You got a good memory.

JIMMY: I don't forget nothin'. You used to go to 42nd every weekend. That coulda done it, too.

HUGHIE: How did you know about that?

JIMMY: I went with you one night—

HUGHIE: What? When was this?

JIMMY: Junior year. You played a joke on me.

HUGHIE: I don't remember this.

JIMMY: We were downstairs in one of the peep joints. Come on, you remember this—

HUGHIE: What joke did I play on you?

JIMMY: A hot lady was dancin' and showin' herself. You had to put a quarter in the slot to watch. You guys kept coming outta the booths saying you got blow jobs from the girl. All you hadda do was stick a dollar in the hole at the top of the booth and she'd come over, then you stick your dick in the hole and she'd do her thing. That's what you told me. Well, the hole was all the way at the top of the booth. I kept climbing up on the change counter. No matter what I did I couldn't get my dick in the hole. I didn't realize it was a joke until I saw all you guys hysterical when I came out. I was really mad at you, Hughie.

HUGHIE: You sure it was me?

JIMMY: Positive. We wound up at Billy's Topless that night. You left me downstairs with the free buffet while you guys were fucking those shanky whores. I guess the joke was really on you.

HUGHIE: I don't remember any of this, Officer.

JIMMY: You don't haveta call me Officer.

HUGHIE: I can't place your name.

JIMMY: This should help. (*Jimmy takes off his sunglasses.*) I shouldn't wear these at night anyway, but I like 'em. (*Hughie doesn't say anything. Jimmy takes off his police cap.*) It's me, Jimmy Witteck. (*Hughie shrugs.*) James Witteck. I look different. I got bigger, a lot bigger. My face smoothed out. I had pimples on my forehead. You know me.

HUGHIE: I'm sure I do.

JIMMY: Are you pulling my leg, Hughie? It's me, Jimmy Witteck. James Witteck. J.W. You called me "Chief" sometimes, Jimmy Witteck. Come on!

HUGHIE: I've been trying to place you. What classes did we have together?

JIMMY: I used to sit with you every day at lunch.

HUGHIE: At lunch?

JIMMY: You used to tell me, "Chief, 95% of life is waiting in lines, small talk, bullshit. You gotta find the other five percent, You gotta fly, Chief, you gotta burn." You remember the other five percent, don't you? I been lookin' for it all my life.

HUGHIE: I remember talking about that—

JIMMY: Good—

HUGHIE: I'm not gonna lie to you, I don't—

JIMMY: This is very funny. Very, very very fucking funny.

HUGHIE: I don't mean to—

JIMMY: No, I didn't have no trademark then, that's all. You just figure you spend some time with a person...It's not that big a deal, it's not that big a deal. I'm offering you a place to stay and you don't know who the fuck I am—

HUGHIE: I got a lot on my mind, Jimmy. That's all it is.

JIMMY: No. I could never get...in there, you know? In with the crowd—

HUGHIE: Jimmy—

JIMMY: It's true. I was a doorman at the Drake Hotel for a couple of months. I figured doormen get involved with people's lives, they're trusted, they banter with everybody. Right? Doormen?

HUGHIE: Some do, I guess.

JIMMY: I tried to have routines with people. Like every morning guy comes out I say, "Rain or shine today, Mr. Thomas?" Like a bit, you know. Except first day I tried it, it was pouring out. He looked at me like I was crazy. I couldn't get it going.

HUGHIE: I'm sorry.

JIMMY: It's not that big a deal. Forget it. You forget everything else.

HUGHIE: Listen—

JIMMY: How can you be with someone for four years, talk with them and not remember? I didn't even make a dent with you, did I? That's fucking crazy!

HUGHIE: I think your face is coming back to me—

JIMMY: Don't you fucking lie to me! That's it, that's it, that's the power of the ugly duckling, my friend, you don't remember him, but he remembers you. (*Jimmy puts on his mirror sunglasses and his police cap. Silence.*)

HUGHIE: What's gonna happen, Jimmy? You gonna take me down to the station or what? I really didn't do anything to the girl. I just wanted to help her.

JIMMY: I don't give a shit what you did.

HUGHIE: You don't?

JIMMY: I'm not really a Police Officer.

HUGHIE: What?

JIMMY: You heard me.

HUGHIE: You're bullshitting.

JIMMY: Happy Halloween. I bought the whole uniform at Don Alvaro's on 14th Street. The gun is mine.

HUGHIE: Are you serious?

JIMMY: Remember when I said, "We can do this the easy way or we can do this the hard way"?

HUGHIE: Yes—

JIMMY: That was straight outta *Kojak*. People get very tense.

HUGHIE: Then what the fuck are you throwing me against the bench and frisking me for? (*Hughie grabs his pictures back and puts them back in his jacket.*)

JIMMY: I been taking things off people all night, that's why. I took $400, two AK-47's and 500 vials of crack off a guy on Ave A. Just showed him my badge. The power is awesome. I broke some little Puerto Rican's face on the subway. Took his chains. Three women in the back of the car. Whoever meets me now remembers me forever.

HUGHIE: This isn't cool, Jimmy.

JIMMY: This has been the greatest night of my life. Nothing can stop me. The other 5%. I'm gonna enroll in the Police Academy. I mean it. Whatta job...

HUGHIE: What about Amy?

JIMMY: What about her?

HUGHIE: What are you gonna do with her, Jimmy?

JIMMY: Don't call me Jimmy all the time to make up for it—

HUGHIE: O.K., O.K., what are you gonna do?

JIMMY: I don't know.

HUGHIE: You don't know? Are you gonna take her to Penn Station like she wants?

JIMMY: Maybe later. Much later.

HUGHIE: What are you thinking about. (*Jimmy just smiles.*) She wants to go home.

JIMMY: Maybe that's not what I want.

HUGHIE: You're blowing off some steam tonight, that's your business. But as a personal favor to me, don't do anything to her, she's just a little girl.

JIMMY: I only do personal favors for friends.

HUGHIE: I'm sorry. What do you want me to say? (*Jimmy is silent.*) Are you gonna...hurt her? You wanna ruin her life?

JIMMY: Did it ever cross your mind that she might like me?

HUGHIE: Jimmy—

JIMMY: Don't call me that. I know to you I'm nothing. I don't even show up on the radar. But to her, tonight, I'm the man. Did you ever think of that?

HUGHIE: I talked to the girl, she's scared. She just wants to get home to her boyfriend.

JIMMY: You saw how she hugged me when she was cryin'. She wants me—

HUGHIE: She thought you were a cop! She thought you were gonna help her, that's all it was.

JIMMY: Let's say I try to kiss her later and she turns away saying, "No, Jimmy, you're ugly" or "Jimmy, you're a creep." Before I'd probably just cry. But now I take that no and I—(*He makes a magic motion with his hands.*) Turn it into a yes. I'm a ladies' man just like you were. I break hearts.

HUGHIE: But I never forced anybody—

JIMMY: Bullshit, that's bullshit. I seen so many girls crying over you. Joking around with your fast lines, putting your hands on their bodies when you dance. With that smile you got. Give me a fuckin' break! You'd make 'em do things they didn't wanna do.

HUGHIE: That was in High School!

JIMMY: I gotta different style, that's all. Like in the movies, there's this big violent clash. The man's holding the woman's hands down and she's screaming and slapping at him. Then he kisses her savage on the lips and she melts away into hot love. Instant. Don't fucking look at me that way! It works. I done it. You don't think I done it?

HUGHIE: I don't want you to do it to her...

JIMMY: Flyin'. I can't help myself.

HUGHIE: Are you crazy?

JIMMY: That's the world. You can't stop the world.

HUGHIE: It's a life, Jimmy. A person. You got no right to—

JIMMY: What about my life? What about me?

HUGHIE: It's gonna come back. All the pain you cause will come back at you.

JIMMY: Shut up—

HUGHIE: You wanna be like me? Take a look, I'm gonna die out here. Is this how you wanna end up?

JIMMY: You had your time. I never had no naked curvy girls slithering all over me, never stood in the batter's box three and two. When's my time, huh? When's my time?

HUGHIE: There's nothing wrong with you. You're nice looking, find someone. Fall in love. Save yourself.

JIMMY: Fall in love? Is that what you're telling me?

HUGHIE: Yes—

JIMMY: I was in love, motherfucker. She wasn't a glamour queen like Amy in the car. She was fat, obese—

HUGHIE: It doesn't matter what she looks like—

JIMMY: Oh, I didn't care about that. I was crazy for her. It was her who did it to me.

HUGHIE: What happened?

JIMMY: I don't know what happened. She didn't like how I snored, I was boring. Who knows. But we're trapped in this closet on 11th Avenue and 54th Street we co-signed the fucking lease and she won't even talk to me. I still cared for this fat sow. So when she brings in these men off the street and fucks 'em on the bed, I gotta sleep on the floor. I didn't have the money to move out. I had a fury building, a fury. I kept pushing it down in me. She was taking my balls away, Hughie, my heart...This fucking whip lean Puerto Rican, he's got the thin mustache, swaggers over my sleeping body, still getting his clothes on, like I'm not even there. I see the cow spread out on the bed through the open door and she's laughing like she can't control it and I'm the joke. He leaves. I could feel myself...Oh, Hughie, I went into the bedroom. It was my moment...I came in that bedroom and I grabbed her fat face. I saw her eyes go scared. I felt full for the first time. Full with power. And I...I...

(*Jimmy sees Amy entering stage right and stops talking. Long pause.*)

HUGHIE: Finish the story, Jimmy?

AMY: What is going on here? I thought you were taking me home.

JIMMY: I told you to stay in the car.

AMY: I got scared in the car. I called my neighbor and she said to stay with the Police. I...wanna go home. I feel sick.

JIMMY: Let's go, let's go, I'll drive you...

AMY: What were you talking about?

HUGHIE: This man is not a Police Officer, Amy.

AMY: What do you mean? What's going on?

HUGHIE: He's going to take you back to the car and hurt you. He's done it before. I'm begging you to believe me.

AMY: Are you kidding me?

JIMMY: You're gonna believe him?

AMY: (*To Jimmy.*) Are you a cop?

JIMMY: Of course I'm a cop. Come with me to the car. I'll take you home. He's crazy, like you said.

(*Jimmy tries to take her arm. She pulls it away.*)

AMY: Get away from me! My father will kill anyone who touches me! I want you to know that. I want you both to know that!

JIMMY: I thought you liked me, Amy. (*Hughie moves between Amy and Jimmy.*) Whatsamatter?

AMY: Are you all fucking maniacs?

HUGHIE: Don't worry, I made a vow to you. You will get home safe tonight.

JIMMY: I got the car—

AMY: Wait a second, wait a second, this is what I'm going to do. I'm going to get in a cab and drive it all the way to Long Island. Alone. My neighbor will pay whatever it costs when I get home.

HUGHIE: That's a great idea. I'll help you hail a cab. We'll go to 7th Avenue.

JIMMY: She's not going anywhere.

HUGHIE: The night's over, Jimmy. Come on—

JIMMY: Don't call me Jimmy! (*To Amy.*) You're going to the car with me. The Grand Fury.

HUGHIE: No, she's not.

AMY: I can talk for myself. I wanna get a cab with Hughie, O.K.?

JIMMY: (*To Amy.*) What about the hug? What about the hug, Amy?

(*He makes a move for Amy. Hughie stops him physically.*)

JIMMY: Don't fuck with me tonight. I'm warning you.

HUGHIE: You heard the girl.

JIMMY: I don't wanna hurt you, Hughie.

HUGHIE: Do anything to me you want, I told you that. But let Amy go home.

JIMMY: You might be more handsome than me, smarter, but tonight I get the girl. Tell him, Amy! (*Jimmy holds up his nightstick. Hughie quickly picks up Amy's umbrella.*) I'm gonna tell you once. Get outta my way…(*Hughie stands firm. Jimmy undoes his holster. He puts his hand on the gun.*)

HUGHIE: Jimmy, there's no need for this. Let's all sit down somewhere and talk. The three of us. All right? What are you gonna do? Kill somebody now?

JIMMY: I wanna be alone with Amy.

HUGHIE: I'm sorry. That's not gonna happen.

(*Jimmy takes the gun out of the holster.*)

JIMMY: Is this what you want?

AMY: Stop! Stop this—

JIMMY: Is it?

HUGHIE: Let's just talk it out—

JIMMY: Step away from the girl, Hughie. You can't stop the world.

HUGHIE: I can't let you do it—

(*Hughie makes a sudden move toward Jimmy. Boom! Jimmy fires a single shot into Hughie's head. Hughie slumps to the floor. Amy holds her head in disbelief.*)

AMY: Oh, my God...

JIMMY: I never fired this gun before. It works. (*Jimmy fires another shot into Hughie's prone body.*) I like it! (*Jimmy fires a shot into the air.*) See where that comes down...(*Amy screams.*) You...You sit on the stoop there...While I—Whoa...(*Amy hurries to the stoop.*) Sit right down—

AMY: O.K., O.K....

JIMMY: What should I do? What should I do? (*He walks to Amy at the stoop.*) Put your hands like this...Behind your head...Yes...(*He handcuffs her to a pole.*) You just...Just sit there while I...Don't make a peep...I gotta...The gun was loud, wasn't it? (*He walks to Hughie's body.*) Oh, shit...His crazy blood is all over everything... Oh, shit...What did I do? No, it's O.K., it's O.K.:...I'm a cop, cops...(*Jimmy lifts Hughie's body over his shoulders and carries him over to the garbage pile. He dumps him on top and buries him with the debris. He wipes his bloody hands on his pants.*) This crazy blood...(*He holds his head in anguish for a moment.*) Walk tall brother, c'mon...(*He walks over to Amy at the stoop. He kneels in front of her.*) It was like a rocket ship in my hand...It shot right out...(*He rubs Amy's knee.*) You have no idea how that man hurt me...

AMY: Don't do that to me. I'll do anything you want.

JIMMY: You like me, don't you?

AMY: Yes, yes...

JIMMY: I knew it how you hugged me. It was...(*Jimmy kisses her on the lips.*) Can we hug like that now for awhile?

AMY: Anything you want.

JIMMY: I'm gonna take off the cuffs. Do I have to warn you?

AMY: No...

(*Jimmy uncuffs her. She hugs him, tentatively at first, then they hold onto each other tightly. We see her face over his shoulder, she's holding* back tears. *Jimmy sighs in pleasure. He kisses her neck, then her mouth.*) Can't we just hug?

JIMMY: Don't you wanna make love to me?

(*Jimmy stands up.*)

AMY: Here? I thought we were going back to the car, I—

JIMMY: Right here.

AMY: Won't people see?

JIMMY: What people.

(*Jimmy drops his gun belt to the floor.*)

AMY: Wait, wait, wait, wait...I'll give you anything you want. Here, take my ring! Take it! Anything you want...Here...(*She takes off her ring and hands it to him. He throws it into the garbage pile.*)

JIMMY: All I want is you...

AMY: Please...(*Amy starts crying.*)

JIMMY: What are you doing? That makes your face ugly.

AMY: I'm sorry, I can't help it...

JIMMY: What can I do...? (*He picks up Hughie's skeleton mask from the floor and gently puts it over Amy's face.*) I don't wanna see your face like that...(*Jimmy unbuttons Amy's shirt and pulls it off. She is wearing a flimsy black tank top underneath.*) I'm gonna be good, don't worry...(*He kisses her shoulder.*) I'm hot...(*He starts unbuttoning his own shirt.*) I'm a hot knife through butter...(*He takes off the shirt. He has a T-shirt underneath.*) I'm a burning house... (*He takes off his police cap.*) I'm an irresistible force...(*He puts it on her head over the skeleton mask.*) I'm a pretty bird making sounds...(*He takes off his t-shirt. His back is very broad.*) I'm a human cannonball, I'm a fucking bullet! (*He kneels down in front of her and reaches under her skirt.*) I'm the man...(*He slides her panties down to her ankles as the lights slowly fade. The last thing we see is the white glow of the skeleton mask under the Police Cap.*)

(*Blackout.*)

END OF PLAY

Dice And Cards
by Sam Henry Kass

for John Gotti

Biography

SAM HENRY KASS was born and raised in Brooklyn. Previously produced plays include *Side Street Scenes, Family Snapshots, Lusting After Pipino's Wife, Lefty and Squinty* and *What's It all Mean, Hah?*

He is the Writer/Director of the feature film *The Search For One-Eye Jimmy*, starring John Turturro, Samuel Jackson, Steve Buscemi, and Jennifer Beales. Currently he is the Executive Consultant on *Seinfeld*. Mr. Kass is a 1994 Dramalogue winner for *Dice & Cards*.

Characters

Sal and Richie, two "Wise Guys" in their thirties.

Scene

The back room of a social club. An afternoon in spring.

Original Production

Dice & Cards was originally produced in 1992, at the Trocadero Cafe in New York City. The part of Sal was played by Holt McCallany, and the part of Richie was played by Nicholas Turturro. The play was directed by the author.

DICE AND CARDS

The Back Room of a Social Club. Sal and Richie are seated at a table.

SAL: Gonna ask you somethin' now...Ask you now and not later, and it's honesty that I'm after.

RICHIE: Okay.

SAL: Wha'?

RICHIE: Honesty, yea...Sure, I heard you.

SAL: 'Cause you ain't deaf, right?

RICHIE: No.

SAL: 'Cause that ain't one of your problems, right?

RICHIE: No, I ain't deaf.

SAL: Wha'?

RICHIE: I said I ain't deaf, Sal.

SAL: Are you fuckin' stupid?

RICHIE: Is this a new subject? Sometimes I think you just like to fuck around—Try to confuse me, or somethin'. Am I stupid?...Lemme just say...

SAL: (*Cutting him off.*) Somethin' almost happened last night, on your account—Because of you, right here in this room.

RICHIE: What happened?

SAL: Did you work the crap game, last night?

RICHIE: Yes I did. This is what you told me to do, and so that is what I did. I worked the crap game.

SAL: Wha'?

RICHIE: I worked the crap game.

SAL: So you worked the game?

RICHIE: Lemme just think…Yea, I worked the game. Sure, that was me.

SAL: Fucking, motherfucking, big mouth cocksucker, shut up.

RICHIE: I think I know what you're talking about here…You're talking in fuckin' tongues, but I can decipher your logic. Somethin' happened and…

SAL: I want to ask you something. How much do you think you know, 'bout running this type of game? Organizational fuckin' expertise, that is needed for this type of procedure. How much do you know?

RICHIE: Could you be more specific…It's like you're all over the fuckin' map, here. I mean, I ain't even had a cup of coffee yet.

SAL: On account of you, last night three fuckin' guys—Three fuckin' guys almost got killed on your account. And I mean crippled, not just dead. Now you tell me 'bout the dice, that was used in the game.

RICHIE: Last night's game?

SAL: No…The fuckin' last game Jesus Christ played, sittin' on the fuckin' grass, waitin' for 'em to nail his ass to the fuckin' cross.

RICHIE: On the basis of validity here…Lemme just explain somethin', Sal.

SAL: What do you know about the dice, that are used in these particular games? Mister fuckin' expert—Now watch how you answer me.

RICHIE: I think…

SAL: (*Cutting him off.*) Wrong…Wrong fuckin' answer already.

RICHIE: What's wrong? What did I say?

SAL: If I were ever again, stupid enough to put you in charge of another fuckin' game—If I was ever that fuckin' stupid twice in one lifetime…Explain to me, what would be the first and only thing you would do to that table, each and every night. Assuming I was to get hit in the fuckin' head with a steel girder, and then walk around the rest of my remaining days with a plate, in my fuckin' skull—Assuming that should happen, and because of my loss of common sense and brain power, I was to put you in charge of another game…What would you do, each and every time to that table?

RICHIE: I would…

SAL: You would what?…You would serve fish 'n chips? Explain to me, why there was old dice on that table last night. I'd like to hear this answer…

RICHIE: Are you gonna listen to me, Sal?

SAL: No, you motherfucker. Now shut up! Lemme tell you something, huh. I've been in the crap business all my life, and before that too . . . Don't you ever let a pair of dice, that's been used two, two and a half hours, stay on the fuckin' table. You understand me? One fuckin' hour goes by, you take the dice, you replace it with a brand new set—And that old set goes in your pocket, and then you throw 'em down the fuckin' sewer. Do you understand that? That's a fuckin' order, because you're a fuckin' idiot.

RICHIE: In my defense…

SAL: Don't say another word…I swear to God, I'll hit you in the head with a fuckin' bottle.

RICHIE: Let me tell you something here…There was this asshole there last night—

SAL: You were the asshole, Buster Brown.

RICHIE: I ain't gonna take this personally…This guy last night, he wouldn't get off the table.

SAL: What guy?

RICHIE: A guy I'd seen before, but have never heard…At least prior to last night, he'd never made a sound. However last night—Last night he decided to speak up.

SAL: And who is he to me, that you should be listening to him, and not to yourself, regarding what I told you…In simpleton layman terms, who the fuck is he?

RICHIE: I understand completely, Sal…

SAL: You understand what, completely? What do you understand completely?

RICHIE: All the do's and don't's that should have been followed…All the ramifications that have probably yet to be felt…But Sal, to err is human—to forgive is…

SAL: (*Cutting him off.*) Now for the one hundred and first time, I will explain this protocol…I will once again take the time, to bang my fuckin' head against the wall—Because in reality, that's what's happening here. The words, they don't sink in. What has to happen, is noise has to be created...Because without hysteria, without the fuckin' rockets red glare, you don't catch on.

RICHIE: In all fairness here...

SAL: You stupid bastard...Why do you think I got that other retard, backing up the truck once a week, bringing me dice by the thousands? Because I like to stock up? Because it's my fuckin' avocation, my calling in life? Because I'm some kind of collector?

RICHIE: I always wondered about that.

SAL: Wha'?

RICHIE: I gotta be honest here, Sal...I never understood, what's with all the dice in the back room. I mean, the whole room—up to the fuckin' ceiling...These little cubes...I'd be afraid to take one. What do I do, grab from the top, from the bottom? One false move, forget about it—The whole thing comes tumbling down. Don't you think, there's gotta be a better way? Maybe build some shelves or somethin'...Perhaps an empty refrigerator, huh? You get a couple of those General Electric, forty-five inch jobs, you stick the dice in there—With all the compartments and everything, you got good room. And not only are they stored nice and neat, they also come out cold. Cold dice, Sal...A guy feels ice in his hands, he's gonna feel lucky. This sounds logical to me, no?

SAL: Let's pretend I didn't hear any of that. Let's just pretend I'm fuckin' deaf, my hearing aid don't work, and I also got wax build-up to boot...And on top of that, and just for good measure, let's also say I'm fuckin' blind as well...Now, not only didn't I hear what you said—I also didn't see it. Okay? You understand?

RICHIE: Absolutely.

SAL: And now I will do the math for you...I will break it down to the most common fuckin' denomination possible—For your lack of edification here, and everything that goes with it. Follow me here closely, Einstein...You are our average patron—The customer who comes on a regular basis. This is your gambling night, and you are prepared to come to our game. So far, are you with me?

RICHIE: I am your average patron?

SAL: "You," as in him...Or as in anyone...This here is an example I'm trying to make. And you are an example of a fuckin' mongoloid. If I have to repeat myself again, I'm gonna make you dig your own grave—You hear me, Richie? Not only will you dig it, you'll climb in after, and then I'll kick the fuckin' dirt into the hole!

RICHIE: I'm the average patron...I got it.

SAL: You will go to the gambling affair, expecting to spend perhaps an average of five to six hours there...You also expect an atmosphere, conducive to the fuckin' element of which you've grown accustomed—As a regular at this sort of thing, a person who returns on a basis more often than not...You come to expect certain givens. Things that are to be there, be available, be constant.

RICHIE: Coffee, danish...

SAL: Don't interrupt me...You understand? Don't jump in with "coffee, danish..." Like you're some kind of fuckin' expert. I can't tell you how angry that gets me—That after we've established the fact, that you're hatched from fuckin' birth...That possibly with some kind of act of God, you could be upgraded to the status of a fuckin' cretin—Don't matter of factly, finish off my sentences. Especially after we've already established the obvious.

RICHIE: The obvious what?

SAL: Are you a comedian?

RICHIE: No, no...It's just that sometimes...

SAL: (*Cutting him off.*) Are you a fuckin' comedian? Or did someone put you up to this? Where's the fuckin' hidden camera?...It's like a set-up, right?

RICHIE: No, Sal...There's no set-up. I just like to be clear on issues. I just like to be sure and exact...Because I consider myself a professional, Sal...And despite the names you offer me, I believe you too think the same.

SAL: Oh, is that right?

RICHIE: I believe so...Now, if that's a problem—If there's a problem with being too thorough, too complete—Then I'll relinquish my professional demeanor. And I'll become one of these average flunkies...Just another fuckin' "yes" man. If that's what you want, Sal, then that's what I'll be. Just another buffoon.

SAL: Don't do me any favors here...What are you kiddin' me, or wha'? You're gonna relinquish your professional demeanor? Who are you, fuckin' Blake Carrington? You some kind of nut job, or what?...Let's just set the record straight; Okay? You're already just another fuckin' buffoon. On your best day, with the sun shining, church bells ringing, and gutters devoid of any fuckin' dog shit— You're still just another buffoon. That's what you are. (*Pause.*) Now you listen carefully—No set of dice will ever stay on a table, for more than fifteen minutes. That's the new rule, because anything longer obviously confuses you, to the point of mental madness...Fifteen minutes, and the dice get taken off the table. Do you understand?

RICHIE: Yes...Now what about playing cards?

SAL: What about them? I sense another can of worms, about to be opened here—And I swear to God, they're gonna stink to high heaven. Like the most fuckin' rotten pussy imaginable, you're about to say somethin' here, the stinkin stupidity of it, is gonna raise the roof. I just know it...Lemme hear it.

RICHIE: Never mind, Sal.

SAL: Lemme hear it.

RICHIE: Never mind, Sal...

SAL: Lemme hear it, because by the grace of fuckin' god almighty, maybe I'll find some humor in it...Possibly I'll get one little chuckle, for whatever reason...And then I can walk away with a heart still beating...'Cause I'm telling you, Richie—You're gonna kill me. My heart is going to just jump out of my fuckin' chest, and run down the boulevard fleeing for its life. That's what's gonna happen here. You and your logic are a medical liability—If I stay here any longer, I'm gonna have a heart attack of major proportions...

RICHIE: Okay...

SAL: Okay, what?

RICHIE: Concerning the playing cards...

SAL: Go 'head—My fuckin' breath is bated.

RICHIE: Can I just assume, the playing cards should be clean...That they should be changed on some sort of regular basis?

SAL: I'm gonna drop dead...I can feel it coming.

RICHIE: I thought it was a fair question, Sal.

SAL: Are you using dirty cards? Is this the implication I'm smelling now? Dirty cards are being used in my game?

RICHIE: We've never really discussed cards—You know, when to change a deck...That sort of thing.

SAL: We've also never discussed, when you should change your fuckin' underwears—But there are some things, people are just able to figure out by themselves...What am I faced with here? You're like a walking, talking billboard, advocating some kind of fuckin' suicide!

Like the most painful of deaths. Dealing with you, is like dying so painfully slow—They wouldn't put a fuckin' laboratory rat through this...And yet, here I am. Who would believe this?

RICHIE: Alright...So from now on, the cards get changed. It's taken care of Sal. That's it. That's all you had to say.

SAL: That's all I had to say? Now why do you think, this game is so popular? This never crossed your mind?...You think it's the fuckin' danish? If I played in this game last week, and now I come back the following week—I'd know every fuckin' card in that fuckin' deck, you fuckin' motherfucker fuckhead! Why don't you just give the money away? It's easier that way. Mark the cards, give the money away, save on the danish. You let them steal from me, and then you feed 'em too? What are you, the Salvation Army?

RICHIE: Sal...I'm gonna tell you why, we haven't been changing the cards. Let me just explain this here, and then I think you'll understand.

SAL: The only thing I'll fuckin' understand is, I should check into a mental hospital. That's what I understand...It's perfectly clear. Thanks to my relationship with you, that's perfectly clear. Now go find me a copy of the Yellow Pages—The first nuthouse that answers the phone, I'm checkin' in...

RICHIE: You see, we ran out of cards a few weeks ago...

SAL: (*Cutting him off.*) I ain't interested, you hear me...On behalf of my rapidly fuckin' dwindling sanity, I ain't interested Richie. Take pity on a sick man, okay?

RICHIE: Once explained, it's highly understandable...

SAL: Please, please...Don't explain it. What difference is it going to make? This cross is full of nails already—I ain't got room for no more holes.

RICHIE: You see, we couldn't change the cards, because some guy spilled some drinks all over the table...Those cards got all soiled, and couldn't be used no more. So we were down to the last available decks, Sal. There was no surplus, so we couldn't dip into the reserve. We had to stay with the original cards. Really, that's what happened here.

SAL: This happened several weeks ago?

RICHIE: Yea.

SAL: And all the extra decks got ruined?

RICHIE: Yea...I mean, they were all sticky and smelled like booze too.

SAL: And you never thought of asking for some new cards? You never thought of going into that back room, that room where I got ten thousand fuckin' pieces of dice—You never thought of going back there, and taking a couple of decks from the ten thousand or so, fuckin' decks of cards that are also stacked in that back room? This is something you never considered, huh?

RICHIE: I considered it.

SAL: Oh, you considered it...

RICHIE: Yes.

SAL: But you did not act on this consideration.

RICHIE: No...No I did not.

SAL: Why not?

RICHIE: It was a choice, Sal...Just a choice. People make 'em every day. You decide to act on something, or you decide not to—What's life but a choice? Right or wrong, good or bad...It's part of the human experience. I never live in the past, Sal. There's no point to the madness. My mind is here today, and my eyes are on tomorrow.

SAL: Your mind is up your ass, you fuckin' idiot you. Now consider this possibility here—Consider this, Mr. fuckin' Socrates...the asshole who dropped the drinks—Could it have been done on purpose?

RICHIE: What do you mean?

SAL: What am I talking, Swahili? I said, "could it have been done on purpose?"

RICHIE: I don't think so.

SAL: Oh, you don't think so?

RICHIE: I don't think so, Sal.

SAL: Why not? Why couldn't it have been deliberate? Why couldn't some fuckin' asshole, come into this game, with the deliberate and predetermined plan, to damage the cards? Why couldn't that have been done?...You think we're the only crooked minds, around here?

RICHIE: But how would he know, we would let the game continue?...How could he possibly think, we wouldn't change the deck upon seeing the dirty cards?

SAL: Excuse me...Excuse me...Who's "we," white man? Who's "we"? You and I are in this together? Under the heading of fuckin' stupidity, you and I are partners? No, I don't think so. The reason he knew the cards weren't goin' to be changed, is because he came back every week, and saw that you never changed the cards. This is what he saw. And it took him a few weeks, before he could actually believe what he was seeing...And then just to verify this madness—he probably brought several other pair of eyeballs, down to the game—Just so they could also witness the retardation of this fuckin' situation.

RICHIE: Could I just jump in here, for a moment?

SAL: No, you can't just jump in here...You wanna jump, go jump off the fuckin' building—Right now, I'm just trying to figure out, what percentage of the fuckin' gambling public is laughing at me...That's what I'm trying to compute right now. A reputation that has taken years to build, is shot down in a matter of days—How is this possible? How is this fuckin' possible? That one creature such as yourself, can be responsible for so much damage. I've created a fuckin' monster, and now I don't have the combination to kill it. Isn't that something?

RICHIE: (*Losing control.*) The fuckin' shit you are spouting, Sal...The flood of shinola comin' from your side over here—This is not fair! Even in the most fuckin' unfair of fuckin' worlds, this is just not heard of. Things go bad, I get blamed—Things go wrong, where's Richie? Let's piss on Richie. And I accept that role, Sal...I accept that role up to a point; up to a limit, up to the edge of the fuckin' mountain—But then wha'? Then I gotta push myself over? For what? With every fuckin' reason in the world not to continue, I always go on. And this is because of you. Because of you, Sal...Loyalty counts for somethin' here. It must count for somethin', Sal! You can't collect on it, down at unemployment...And it doesn't mean jack doo squat, most anywhere else. But it must count for something here, Sal. It just fuckin' must! 'Cause the other benefits are null and void. 'Cause the things I should be receiving in return, are so non-existent, that I won't even bother to mention them...My loyalty to this situation here, overrides any lack of balancing your ledgers may show; Fiscal or otherwise, Sal. That is just a fact of basic life. It is something you have blinders to, and I'm fuckin' sorry I have to make you aware of it...I'm fuckin' sorry for myself, on this issue—Because I'm a fuckin' chump once too often. Once too often, Sal...Once too often, and now never no more. I quit, I'm gone, kill me, hang me, put my fuckin' photo on the post office wall—I'm outta here. Get someone else, to mop up the mess. I don't do it anymore. Okay?... And now I'm finished. You may have the floor.

SAL: (*Pause.*) I may have the floor?

RICHIE: I think it's only fair.

SAL: You think it's only fair?

RICHIE: To be honest, fairness isn't really the issue...I was finished talking, you know...caught up in the emotional peak of the moment, and...

SAL: Yea?

RICHIE: I just thought it was a very, you know...Theatrical thing to say.

SAL: Oh, that's what you thought...

RICHIE: Like, I give you the floor...I give you your moment...I give you a chance to say, what words can't come close to saying...I give you...

SAL: You give me a thousand and one, fuckin' excellent reasons to kill you. That's what you give me...Now, should I count the ways?

RICHIE: Let's forget it, Sal...Deaf ears all around. Let's just wax the entire moment here, save it for a busload of fuckin' tourists, somewhere in the distant future. This conversation is squash. Really...Like vegetables I just won't fuckin' touch. Now, about the cards. One final time, please; the point of extra decks...Or lack of...

SAL: Brand new cards, every fifteen minutes. That's it, for the future and every day after.

RICHIE: Every fifteen minutes...

SAL: That's right.

RICHIE: The cards should be changed, every fifteen minutes...

SAL: From this point on...

RICHIE: That's the way you want it...New cards, every fifteen minutes. (*Pause.*) You're talking each table, right?

SAL: Every table, every fifteen minutes, Like fuckin' clockwork...Tick, tick, tick, new cards...Tick, tick, tick, new fuckin' cards. Like there should be some sort of revolving door, with the cards comin' and going...It should be so fast, fuckin' heads should be spinning.

RICHIE: I got it...No problem. (*Pause.*) We got twenty tables...The room back there has twenty tables, Sal.

SAL: So what does that mean to me? Twenty tables, twenty decks...A hundred tables, a fuckin' hundred decks...This is the directive being handed down to you—No dirty cards any more. I don't wanna hear about 'em, I don't wanna smell 'em, I don't wanna see them around.

RICHIE: Okay…

SAL: Okay?

RICHIE: Yea…

SAL: What do you mean, "okay"?

RICHIE: What do you mean, "what do I mean"? Just what I said…My answer to your question is okay…I said yes. I mean, what else is there?

SAL: Ah, you see…I didn't ask a question. See, that's where you don't quite understand—I gave a fuckin' order; I did not ask a question, or make a request, or some kind of fuckin' bended knee plea…You hear me here, Richie? I gave an order. New cards every fifteen minutes, is not a question—You understand the difference?

RICHIE: Sure.

SAL: Okay…

RICHIE: I understand…

SAL: Good.

RICHIE: New cards, the whole bit…You want them changed, whatever —

SAL: What do you mean, "whatever."

RICHIE: Huh?

SAL: Now tell me, what the fuck does "whatever" mean.

RICHIE: Figure of speech, Sal.

SAL: Figure of speech?

RICHIE: That's all.

SAL: You're sure?

RICHIE: 'Course…

SAL: Why do I feel, you're not quite finished…I have this lingering feeling, that perhaps you have something else to say…On this issue here, why do I feel you're like the fuckin' mother-in-law, that just won't leave.

RICHIE: I don't know, Sal. I can't help you with these feelings. I put a period at the end of my sentences, and that should be that…If I'm not saying anything beyond, what's already been said—Then what's the static here?

SAL: That's it…No more.

RICHIE: Okay. (*They stare at each other silently, for the longest of moments. And then…*) These are brand new decks, right?

SAL: I beg your pardon?

RICHIE: These are brand new decks, as opposed to slightly used cards, as opposed to the type of cards we were originally talking about...

SAL: (*Pause.*) I don't want you to talk anymore, Richie...No more fuckin' talking. I can't take that no more. You wanna communicate with me, you gotta find another way—No more talking, that's it. Let me hear you sing...You want to say something, ask something, you do it musically—You hear me? From now on, you must sing.

RICHIE: What are you talking about, Sal? I'm just clearing up loose ends—What's the problem?

SAL: Sing...Don't say nothing else, Richie—Just sing. I'm losing my fuckin' mind here.

RICHIE: You should take a vacation, Sal—A cruise or somethin'... fuckin' salt water, maybe it'll help you relax. Go to the Bahamas; drink a little, swim a little, get laid. There's a nice hotel right...
(*Sal pulls out a gun, and points it at Richie.*)

SAL: I said sing!

RICHIE: Sal...what are you doing? I can't ask a few questions here? A fuckin' few questions, and you go off the deep end...

SAL: Sing it...

RICHIE: (*Confused and scared.*) Sing it? I should sing it? (*Sal fires the gun...Richie ducks for cover. Richie, singing.*) "SAL...WHAT THE FUCK ARE YOU DO-ING???"

SAL: You're off-key...Sing it right.

RICHIE: (*Singing.*) "SAL...WHAT THE FUCK ARE YOU DO-ING???"

SAL: Louder!!!

RICHIE: (*Singing louder.*) "WHAT THE FUCK ARE YOU DO-ING???" "WHY ARE YOU POINTING THAT GUN AT ME???" "OH, PLEASE...POINT IT AT THE SEA..." "BABY, BABY, BABY, OH, BABY..." (*In plain talk.*) How was that?

SAL: Terrible...That was fuckin' terrible.

RICHIE: I can do better.

SAL: (*Puts the gun away.*) Forget it...

RICHIE: Alright...

SAL: Lemme give you some advice, Richie...From a customer's view point, gambling is a very simple thing—You win some, you lose some, and you walk around smoking cigarettes...That's from the customer's point of view—From the operator; a whole different story. You understand?

RICHIE: Responsibility.

SAL: Yes.

RICHIE: I understand.

SAL: Sure you do...You think I need tough guys, Richie? You think that's all I'm looking for? No—I need intelligent tough guys. Intelligent, Richie.

RICHIE: I understand, Sal...

SAL: Sure you do...Learn from me, Richie—Don't be afraid to learn from me. I'm a very sharp guy, and I know what I'm talking about ...Believe me. Even the President, Richie...Even the fuckin' President of the United States—If he's smart, if he needed help, he'd come to me. I could do a favor for the President, and nobody would be shortchanged...Believe me, Richie.

RICHIE: I believe you, Sal.

SAL: 'Course you do...

RICHIE: Okay.

SAL: That's it...

RICHIE: That's it...

SAL: And the things I say to you, I always say them for a reason... There's always some method to the madness.

RICHIE: I know that, Sal...Deep down, I believe I know that.

SAL: Because if something goes wrong, it's all on me—God forbid something happens over here, we'll be right in the fucking soup. You understand?

RICHIE: Sure.

SAL: And this is not just paranoia talking...This is real here—Things have to be answered for, etcetera...

RICHIE: But you gotta realize, this ain't second nature to me, Sal...Under the pretense of not understanding—Believe me, there's a lot being understood.

SAL: Let's move on, now...I got a fuckin' headache, larger than my skull. Just my luck, huh?

RICHIE: Enough is enough...

SAL: I swear on my mother—I'd like to forget about the whole thing.

RICHIE: Believe me, Sal...I got cast iron balls. All this shit, this abuse— it rolls right off me. That's just part of my make up.

SAL: Alright, fine...

RICHIE: I better get ready to set up, no?

SAL: (*Checking his watch.*) Yea...Everything is in order, back there?

RICHIE: I took care of it myself.

SAL: That's very comforting…

RICHIE: And that thing we talked about—You want me to start it, tonight?

SAL: What thing?

RICHIE: What we were discussing…I should start doing it, at tonight's game?

SAL: What are you asking me, Richie? God, I'd rather be dead, than listen to what you're about to say…(*Pause.*) You're goin' to ask me about the fuckin' dice, aren't you? The dice and the cards, that's what this is all about, right?

RICHIE: (*Hesitating.*) (*Pause.*) No.

SAL: No?

RICHIE: Not really…

SAL: Not really?

RICHIE: Whatever…

SAL: (*Getting up.*) I'm goin' do the set-up…

RICHIE: (*Starting to get up.*) No, no…Sal—I'll do it. Really, there's no problem concerning…

(*Sal pulls the gun again…Points it at Richie.*)

SAL: I said, I'm going do the set-up, Richie. Don't fuckin' move one inch, you hear me? I'm goin' do the set-up, and if you move from that seat—I'll fuckin' kill you.

RICHIE: Okay Sal.

SAL: (*Still holding the gun on him.*) I'm going do the set-up, and I'm going to run the fuckin' game, serve the danish, pour the coffee, sweep the floor, and then turn off the lights…And don't you move during any of that time…

RICHIE: I ain't gonna move, Sal…I'm goin' to stay right here.

SAL: That's right, Richie. It's not that I don't like you…Don't take it personally. It's just a situation of mental fuckin' salvation.

RICHIE: Fine…No problem. I can use a day off, anyways.

SAL: (*Slowly starting to back away.*) I'm going now, Richie.

RICHIE: Alright, Sal.

SAL: Don't even think of moving…

RICHIE: I'm not. (*Sal exits the room. Richie is left alone, seated in his chair. He stares off into the distance…*) (*Richie, calling out to no one.*) I ain't movin', Sal!!! Don't worry about a thing!!! (*Pauses; to self.*) I ain't movin'…

The Dying Gaul
by Craig Lucas

The play is dedicated to Tony Kushner—
with love and deepest gratitude.

BIOGRAPHY

CRAIG LUCAS is the author of *Missing Persons, Reckless, Blue Window, Three Postcards* (with composer/lyricist Craig Carnelia) and *Prelude to a Kiss.* With his frequent collaborator, director Norman René, he conceived *Marry Me a Little,* a bookless musical fashioned from seventeen previously unpublished songs by Stephen Sondheim. The two also worked together on four films—an adaptation of *Blue Window,* which premiered on American Playhouse in 1987, *Longtime Companion, Prelude to a Kiss* and *Reckless.* Mr. Lucas has received the George and Elisabeth Marton Award, the L.A. Drama Critics Award, the Drama Logue Award, Guggenheim and Rockefeller Grants, the Outer Critics Circle Award, the Obie Award and three Drama Desk nominations. *Three Postcards* was selected as Best Musical of 1986–1987 by the *Burns Mantel Theatre Yearbook* and by *Time Magazine* as one of its ten best. *Longtime Companion* received the Audience Award at the 1990 Sundance U.S. Film Festival. *Prelude to a Kiss* received a Tony Nomination for Best Play during the 1989–1990 season. Mr. Lucas has written two opera texts with composer Gerald Busby, *Breedlove* and *Orpheus in Love,* which were done at Circle Repertory. His work has been preformed at South Coast Repertory, Playwrights Horizons, Circle Repertory, The Production Company, Naked Angels, Ensemble Studio Theater, the Long Wharf, Berkeley Repertory, Steppenwolf, American Repertory Theatre, San Diego Old Globe, Atlanta Alliance, Trinity Repertory and numerous other regional and resident theatres. He lives in New York State.

ORIGINAL PRODUCTION

The Dying Gaul is the first scene of a longer play. It received its first performance at Circle Repertory Theatre, directed by Gloria Muzio; the actors were Robert Sean Leonard (Robert) and Giancarto Esposito (Roger).

The Dying Gaul

Roger is gesturing for Robert to take a seat. Roger is wearing very expensive casual clothes. Robert is dressed as well as he can manage.

ROGER: So, Robert...do people call you Robert or Bob?
ROBERT: Both.
ROGER: Which do you prefer?
ROGER: I don't...I sort of like to see which they prefer and then that tells them something, tells me something about them.
ROGER: I gotcha. Interesting. You're a very good writer.
ROBERT: Thank you.
  (*Pause.*)
ROGER: What kinds of movies do you like? You like movies?
ROBERT: Oh yeah.
ROGER: You do. What are some of your favorite movies?
ROBERT: Oh, you know, I like all kinds of movies.
ROGER: You do.
ROBERT: Oh yeah, I like, you know, movie movies, and I like old movies and foreign movies.
  (*Pause.*)
ROGER: What was your favorite movie last year?
ROBERT: Last year? I don't really go in for favorites, you know, I sort of think each movie, like each painting or book or...national park ...is actually unique and to be appreciated as such, God I sound

like an English professor, I like...I liked very much...um...I thought that, uh...

ROGER: That's okay.

ROBERT: No, I liked that English—*The Remains of the Day*—and I loved the dinosaur movie. I mean I like all uh...everything along the continuum.

(*Short pause.*)

ROGER: Well, Disney is interested in your script.

ROBERT: What?

ROGER: We're interested in *The Dying Gaul.*

(*Little beat.*)

ROBERT: Okay.

ROGER: So. That's that...

(*He looks for the script on his desk.*)

ROGER: Your agent is...?

ROBERT: Dead.

ROGER: Oh.

ROBERT: Yeah. Malcolm Cartonis.

ROGER: I'm sorry.

(*Pause.*)

ROBERT: Yeah.

ROGER: Who's...?...taken over for him?

ROBERT: Well, nobody, unfortunately, he was kind of a one–man band...

ROGER: Well, a good one, obviously, because he got us the script and I read it and Katzenberg's read it.

ROBERT: He has?

ROGER: Yes. We don't greenlight anything without his approval.

ROBERT: Greenlight?

ROGER: No, I'm not saying we're making your script, I'm saying we've all read it and we all think it's good...and that's why I'm talking to you.

(*Intercom buzzes. Roger talks to the phone without picking up a receiver.*)

ROGER: Yes?

WOMAN'S VOICE: Your wife.

ROGER: All right. (*Roger moves to the phone, glancing this off of Robert.*) Excuse me. (*He picks up the receiver.*)

Hi...Sure...Sure...Sure...(*Pause.*) Sure...(*Pause.*) Okay. (*Pause.*) Love you too. (*He hangs up.*)

ROGER: Where do you think you want to go with the script?

ROBERT: I'm sorry?

ROGER: Where else do you want to go with the script?

ROBERT: Well, I...I guess I could take it to some of the independents.

ROGER: No, no, no...what a doll you are. What kind of work do you want to do on it?

ROBERT: Oh. Oh, sorry...

ROGER: That's okay. That was just so sweet. From acceptance to total rejection, you took it all in stride. What kinds of things have you thought about, or do you think it's finished as it is?

ROBERT: Well, it's as far as I could take it without some sort of input from a director.

ROGER: Uh-huh. And who's your dream director?

ROBERT: Oh, Gus Van Sant, I guess. Since Truffaut's dead.

ROGER: Good. He's very good. Would you like me to show him the script?

ROBERT: Yeah, sure, why not?

ROGER: Good. 'Cause I already have. And he likes it.

ROBERT: Do you have any smelling salts?

ROGER: You're really very charming. He likes it very much, and he has some questions as we all do, and...who knows if he's the right person or not, but I wanted to talk to you first before we set up a meeting. What's the title, explain the title to me.

ROBERT: Well, you know, they go to that museum in Rome...

ROGER: Ken and Maurice.

ROBERT:...and they see the sculpture...

ROGER: Yeah, yeah, yeah, but why is that the name of the movie?

ROBERT: Because. Oh, I see, because they feel that the statue in depicting the, like, the defeated, the vanquished—

ROGER: Uh-huh.

ROBERT:...and dying soldier, and being, the statue is *by* a Roman, by one of those whose side was responsible for all the slaughter, for the death of the soldier in the statue, I mean, it would be like an American making a statue honoring the suffering of...one of the countries we've fought, a person from...

ROGER: From where?

ROBERT: One of, whatever countries we've invaded, not invaded. You know what I'm saying. Like Vietnam or something.

ROGER: (*or:*) Iraq.

(*Pause. Robert has tipped his head as if to say "Well, not quite, but okay."*)

ROGER: Okay, so, Ken and Maurice see this sculpture of this...Gaul. Who is dying...And?

ROBERT: And they identify with the Gaul in a way because they're gay and so many of their friends are dying and they keep looking for some kind of response from the enemy...

ROGER: Right?

ROBERT: And then you remember where they talk about the sculpture and say..."Well, what good did this sculpture do for the poor guy who bled to death, the guy in the sculpture?"

ROGER: Right.

ROBERT: But at least...maybe...some kind of compassion was awakened in the Romans, in the people who defeated him and overran his country, and maybe at some time in the future as a result of somebody *seeing* the sculpture, maybe some other...

ROGER: Gaul.

ROBERT:...was, somebody took pity or spared some other French peasant from...

ROGER: Yeah, I get it. That's very...

ROBERT: It's kind of oblique.

ROGER: No, I understand, and it has a political overtone.

ROBERT: That's right. Which I imagine...

ROGER: No, no, we're not afraid of that, we're not afraid of anything, the idea, obviously, is to reach as many people as possible and to have the broadest appeal, so that we can make money, but also so that...to whatever degree the movie affects people, it can also serve as a kind of dying Gaul for the viewers. I mean, if you even look at a movie like...well, say, just to pick something, *Tootsie,* which we didn't make but which is a very good movie—

Robert: It's a great comedy.

ROGER: It says something...in a small, but totally amusing way...and you don't see it coming: about men and women. The guy is an arrogant...you know, chauvinist, and he, for his own reasons, dresses up, feels he has to dress up as a woman, and as a result, he learns something about what it means to be a man. He finds, it's so obvious, if you know it's there, but he finds a feminine side to himself and vows: you don't actually see it happen, but you know he does it—

ROBERT: Uh-huh.

ROGER:—he vows not to be such an asshole, and you feel good for him.

ROBERT: Yeah.

ROGER: So that's the kind of political statement you can slip an audience without their feeling they've been had or they're being lectured.

ROBERT: Right.

ROGER: And...Well, *The Dying Gaul* isn't a comedy, it's a weepie, what I call—Like *Terms of Endearment*. And these movies are VERY. HARD. TO SELL.

(*Pause.*)

ROBERT: Uh-huh.

ROGER: They're VERY. HARD. (*Pause.*) And they're my favorite kind of movie. They just have to be made with care. And... *The Silence of the Lambs* is another one which touches on feminist ideology without...Did you like that movie?

ROBERT: Yes and no.

(*Tiny pause.*)

ROGER: Okay. (*Pause.*) So.

ROBERT: Did you make it?

ROGER: No, no. No, no. No. (*Little pause.*) But...Why didn't you like it?

ROBERT: The, uh, faggy portrayal of the killer.

ROGER: He's not gay. Jamie Gumm is not gay.

ROBERT: Yeah, that's what I heard, but I think that's a bunch of bullshit. Because he has the poodle...

ROGER: I have a poodle. My wife and I have a poodle.

ROBERT: Yeah, but I bet you don't wear nipple rings and put on eyeliner and, you probably don't cut up women because you want to be one.

(*Pause.*)

ROGER: You never know.

ROBERT: True.

ROGER: Okay, so never mind. What are we gonna do, do you want to sell this script?

ROBERT: Sure.

ROGER: And…do you want to do the re-writes?

ROBERT: Well…what do you mean?

ROGER: I mean…are you interested in doing the re-writes or do you want to sell the script outright?

ROBERT: I don't…*Of course*. I don't want somebody else…

ROGER: Okay.

ROBERT:…mucking around with this script.

ROGER: Good. Great. I'm glad you're…I'm sorry you don't have an agent, though. Are you going to sign with somebody else?

ROBERT: Oh, I don't know, Malcolm was a really close friend and…I really loved him. I was thinking…I haven't been able to find another agent. Nobody's really been…

ROGER: We can deal directly with you. Or recommend a lawyer. Or whatever. We'll…Do you want to talk—?…(*He leaves off before saying the word "numbers."*)

ROBERT: Sure.

ROGER: I'd say…Oh, I'll let business affairs call you, but…we should stick to the artistic discussion.

ROBERT: Great.

ROGER: They'll offer you more than minimum, so, with the re–writes, you know, this could be a couple hundred thousand, but…(*Winking*.) don't let that sway you.

ROBERT: Oooo, I feel the lubrication.

ROGER: What?

ROBERT: I feel my butt getting lubed up.

ROGER: (*Laughing along*.) Oh. Right. Okay, so…I understand your reasons for wanting the men to be men, because of the political dimension, but…Ken and Maurice.

ROBERT: I'm not making them heterosexual.

ROGER: No, no. *Please*.

ROBERT: I'm sorry.

ROGER: No, I mean, I understand…I read your script, Robert, I know what kind of person you are.

ROBERT: I'm sorry.

ROGER: I'm not asking you to jettison any of your principles.
(*Pause*.)

ROBERT: Sorry.

ROGER: We like. Your script.

ROGER: Okay, okay, okay.

(*Intercom buzzes.*)

Hold all my calls. (*Silence.*) What…Presumably you are looking for something universal…in the experience of two gay men…which a wider audience can identify with.

ROBERT: You could say that.

ROGER: Would that be a true statement?

ROBERT: Yes.

ROGER: Okay. You want to reach as many people as possible with the universal human…*truth* about these two characters.

ROBERT: Yes.

ROGER: One of whom is a Person With AIDS.

ROBERT: That's correct.

ROGER: Now. Don't. Say. Anything…until—

ROBERT: Okay.

ROGER:—I've had a chance. Okay. Most Americans. Hate. Gay people.

ROBERT: What about *Philadelphia?*

ROGER: *Philadelphia* is about a man who hates gay people. Period. And it's been done. To get people into the theater, the movie theater, they have to think it's going to be fun. Or sensational. Or…some kind of dynamite. Or make them feel good about themselves. No one. Goes to the movies. To have a bad time. Or to learn anything. To be improved. Do we agree with this?

(*Pause.*)

ROBERT: Yes.

ROGER: What is important is what they leave the theater with. Yes? (*A nod.*) And if they don't…*enterrrrrr*…the theater, they don't get a chance to leave it. Is this all acceptable to you…as a thesis?

(*Pause. A nod from Robert.*)

No one is going to see *The Dying Gaul.* If you make it with Tom Cruise—who wouldn't go near it for a hundred million dollars, oh fuck, he'd blow me and you for a hundred million dollars, but you know what I'm saying, and with…Clint Eastwood…and got Steven Spielberg to direct it and released it in two hundred million screens…No one. Is going. To see. *The Dying. Gaul.* (*Pause.*) I am sorry. Now. If we make Maurice a woman dying of AIDS, and let's face it, heterosexuals are also getting AIDS, in disastrous numbers.

ROBERT: (*Rises.*) I want nothing to do with this.

ROGER: We'll write our own script based loosely on *The Dying Gaul—*

ROBERT: (*Moving toward the door.*) Fine.

ROGER: Or we'll give you one million dollars for your script.

ROBERT: You are the devil incarnate. (*Robert does not leave the room.*) A million dollars?

ROGER: With which you can go out and write four hundred new screenplays about men with, gay men with AIDS, without AIDS, a gay love story, whatever is the most important to you.

ROBERT: If you want the script so much—

ROGER: We think it is good. Robert. We want to make your script, and we will pay you for it. We will not make *The Dying Gaul* with two men in bed, falling in love, surviving pain and all the blah blah blah, it's not going to happen. Ever. Ever. Ever. I will guarantee you the first re-write, *twice* scale, because you are a wonderful writer, with a beautiful visual sense, and a realistic understanding of forward action, which is not nothing, and an appreciation of the innate laws of storytelling as it directly relates to movie–making, and there are about mmmmmaybe twenty of you. In the world. We want your script. We want you to re-write it.

ROBERT: This is so...

ROGER: I know. Sit down. (*Pause.*) Please? You don't have to stay, or agree, you just, you could listen.

ROBERT: (*An unvoiced sigh.*) Ohhh...

(*Pause.*)

ROGER: There can be minor characters who are gay. They don't have to be gags.

ROBERT: Oh, they can be noble, right?

ROGER: They don't have to be noble. They can be whatever you want. They cannot be the center of the story, because the center of the country is not gay and the center of the country is what pays for the movies to be made.

ROBERT: The center of the country isn't black, either, but they made *Malcolm X.*

ROGER: Yes. In fifty or twenty-five or maybe even who knows how many years we can make the gay version of *Malcolm X,* and people will go, but they will not go now, and how we know this is empirical observation.

(*Pause.*)

ROBERT: Were you serious about the million dollars?

ROGER: Are we having a conversation, Robert—

ROBERT: I'm going to take the script to Paramount—

ROGER: Yes, we are serious about the million dollars.

ROBERT: Somebody wants to be in my movie. Who wants to be in my movie?

ROGER: I told you that Gus Van Sant is interested, he has not committed—

ROBERT: Oh come on, you're not gonna let Gus Van Sant direct this movie, not until he makes a blockbuster which he will *never* do, because Gus Van Sant doesn't have a commercial bone in his body and you would fire him from this movie before it ever went into production and bring in Joel Fucking Schumacher.

ROGER: It's not a bad idea, you know, and he's gay!

ROBERT: *Who wants to be in the movie?* Tell me now or it's a million and a half.

ROGER: Tom Cruise and Michelle Pfeiffer. And Denzel Washington, Martin Sheen, Jim Carrey and Winona Rider, Meg Ryan, Daniel Day Lewis, Debra Winger and Johnny Depp...among others. I wish you would sit.

ROBERT: (*Not bitter.*) Word travels fast. Who wants to play Maurice?

ROGER: They all want to play Maurice, but we can work that out.
(*Pause.*)

ROBERT: (*Evenly.*) You have virtually no idea how much one million dollars would mean in my life. I live in a basement apartment which floods when it rains, because I am still paying off my college loan. I have a son for whom I pay child support, and Malcolm who just died, my agent, was also my lover.
(*Pause.*)

ROGER: I'm sorry.

ROBERT: I can't in good conscience...take this money from you.

ROGER: You are an amazing and lovely person, Robert, and you have succeeded in making me feel like a total scumbag.
(*Pause.*)

ROBERT: Well, good, I'm glad.

ROGER: How's your health?

ROBERT: It's okay. I'm negative.

ROGER: Good.

ROBERT: Yeah, I check it every two seconds, Maurice and—I mean Malcolm, God oh God, Malcolm and I always had safe sex. Can't I write you a new script, something altogether—

ROGER: We want *The Dying Gaul,* and we want you to write it. Take the million and write something else.

(*Pause.*)

ROBERT: (*A silent:*) Oh Jesus…

ROGER: Yes?

(*Pause. Robert slowly nods. Roger leans into the intercom.*)

ROGER: Liz, would you call Albert in business affairs and ask him to come on down here, please, give me two minutes. (*Pause.*) Congratulations. You are a millionaire. (*Pause.*) Do you want to see the brand new Mike Leigh? Have you seen it?

ROBERT: No.

ROGER: Are you interested?

ROBERT: Sure:

ROGER: (*Into the intercom.*) Liz, would you arrange a private screening for this evening with Robert Isaacson and me for the Mike Leigh film, and then book a table at Spago for ten-thirty—(*He glances at Robert.*) You have plans?

ROBERT: No. No.

ROGER: (*Into the intercom.*) And call my wife and tell her I have to work late, please, tell her I'll call her from the restaurant.

(*Pause. Roger and Robert look at one another.*)

ROGER: You're very talented, and very lucky, and so are we. I feel good about this, Robert…I want you to feel good.

(*He has risen, and puts his arm around Robert.*)

Yes?

(*Pause. Robert shakes his head slightly.*)

What's wrong?

ROBERT: I can't really…I can't say.

ROGER: What? Tell me?

(*Robert covers one of his eyes with the palm of one hand: he is about to cry.*)

ROGER: Hey. Hey. Hey. Hey. It's going to be a beautiful movie, and you are going to write more movies, and some day…you are going to be able to write your own. Ticket. Do you…Look at me. I mean that…I mean that, Robert. You can write your own ticket. Look at Spike Lee. He makes movies he cares about…About his own people. And they make money. And that will happen. For you. I want that for you. Come here…Give me a hug.

(*They hug.*)

Okay?

(*Robert nods.*)

You are very very handsome...And I'm getting...a little turned on...Are you?

(*He grabs Robert's face with both hands, and speaks directly into Robert's eyes.*)

You can do anything you want. As long as you don't call it what it is. You understand?

(*Robert stares back.*)

END OF PLAY

Waltzing De Niro
by Lynn Martin

Biography

LYNN MARTIN, a graduate of Georgetown University, received her M.F.A. in Playwriting from Columbia University's Oscar Hammerstein II School of Theatre Arts. Her plays have been produced at Columbia University, Case Western Reserve, Off-Broadway at the Samuel French/Double Image Short Play Contest, Contemporary American Theatre Festival, Arena Stage, Lincoln Center Theatre, Zebra Crossing Theatre, and George Street Playhouse. Her plays include: *Still Waters, Babes in Boyland, Summer Feet Hearts, The Problem of God, The Bodhisattva Locksmith, Cops and Fathers,* and *The Evil That Friends Do.* She is the recipient of a W. Alton Jones Grant for her play *Psyche Was Here,* a Mark A. Klein Award, the New York Foundation for the Arts Fellowship for Playwriting, New Dramatists' Van Lier Fellowship, as well as a Playwriting Fellowship from the Juilliard School. She is a member of the Playwrights Horizons' African-American Playwrights Unit.

Ms. Martin is a member of the Dramatists Guild.

Author's Note

A couple of years ago, after sharing a particularly depressing birthday with friends, I returned home alone to my empty apartment. Oh, there had been music. And laughter. And kisses and champagne. There was one wish, only one wish I'd made of my friends—"Bring me De Niro." And as real life would have it, he never showed. So as the music played in my empty apartment, I wrote this play. For me, *Waltzing De Niro* is about friendship, dreaming, and love. So it is with much love that I dedicate this play to my family, John Guare, Kathleen Drohan, and all my friends who gave me the courage and support that allowed my dreams to live.

...To dreamers everywhere...

Original Production

Waltzing DeNiro was originally directed by Stephanie Shroyer with Jennifer Butt as Clara, Vanessa Williams as Joanna and Scott Alan Campbell as Bobby.

CHARACTERS
Joanna, twenty-nine year old Administrative Assistant
Clara, Joanna's best friend. A little more "together" than her friend.
A little more "street-smart".
Bobby, Robert De Niro

SETTING
A New York apartment. Neither messy nor clean, neither upscale nor downtrodden. A few obviously expensive doodads and a huge stereo. Also an old, box-style turntable.

MUSIC
The song that brings Bobby on stage should be "Perfidia" as sung by Nat King Cole, or "Embraceable You" as sung by Billie Holiday. Something in that line—bluesy and slow.

WALTZING DE NIRO by Lynn Martin. ©1992 by Lynn Martin. All rights reserved. Reprinted by permission of the author. All inquires should be sent to International Creative Management Inc., 40 W57th Street, New York, NY 10019, attention Brad Kalos. For caution notice, please refer to copyright page.

WALTZING DE NIRO

*A knock on the door. Joanna runs from the bedroom to the door,
carrying several outfits on hangers. She is wearing a robe. She looks
through the peephole and opens the door.*

CLARA: I'm sorry I took so long. What's wrong?

JOANNA: (*Pulls her in, shuts door.*) Get in here!

CLARA: What happened?

JOANNA: You're not going to believe this one.

CLARA: It better be good, whatever it is, because I was in the middle
of—

JOANNA: Just don't get mad at me. Okay?

CLARA: Why should I? What's wrong, Jo?

JOANNA: Okay. Now I *know* I'm using up all my friendship points on
this one, but could you do me a favor?

CLARA: (*Opens purse.*) How much do you need?

JOANNA: Not money. I need two weeks of your life.

CLARA: Two weeks? For what?

JOANNA: Now, do you think "pack light" means one suitcase and a
carry-on? Or his gold card and a smile?

CLARA: "He"? Who's he? What's two weeks?

JOANNA: Vacation! He's taking me on vacation, Clara! For two weeks!
Two weeks out of here, away from my job—Which is where you
come in. Can you water anything green and watch my mail?

CLARA: Sure, but—

JOANNA: He said he would hire somebody, if I really thought there was anything worth stealing, which there isn't, except what he's bought.

CLARA: Who's he?

JOANNA: (*Examining clothes.*) Do you think this is my color? I never really thought this was my color, but—

CLARA: He. Who is this he?

JOANNA: He?

CLARA: The "he" who's taking you on vacation. Who do you know who can afford to take you on vacation? For two weeks? And hire someone to watch your place?

JOANNA: Robert. Bobby.

CLARA: Robert Bobby? Who's Robert Bobby?

JOANNA: Not "Robert Bobby." His name is Robert. I call him Bobby.

CLARA: Right.

JOANNA: So you'll do it?

CLARA: Sure. Sure.

JOANNA: Thanks. You're the best. (*She sits.*) Oh, God. I'm so nervous. I actually have butterflies! I can't believe this! I can't believe I'm actually doing this!

CLARA: What are you doing?

JOANNA: I'm falling in love! Well, I've actually been in love for a while, but—

(*Clara picks up an expensive doodad, holds it up to Joanna.*)

A gift. From Bobby.

CLARA: Interesting. And where'd this come from?

JOANNA: What?

CLARA: The stereo. The stack of CDs. Did you get a raise?

JOANNA: Bobby.

CLARA: Does this Bobby have any brothers?

JOANNA: He's an only.

CLARA: Just my luck.

JOANNA: Do you remember when I found out about Patrick?

CLARA: Yeah.

JOANNA: Ever since that night, it's been him. Bobby. At first, I thought I was just on the rebound, and I let it go at that, but—I don't think I'm speeding down any one-way streets here, this time.

CLARA: Come on, Jo. You do this all the time. You decide you're in love and damn the world!

JOANNA: But I am! Meet him! Sit, relax, and—

CLARA: What's wrong with him?

JOANNA: Oh! That's the best part! NOTHING! He's not married, he's not bisexual, he's not cheap. Obviously. And look. (*Pulls very expensive cosmetic traveling case into view.*) He had his personal assistant leave this at my door this morning. Along with an orange juicer, a crate of oranges he had flown in from California, and bagels from the bagel store on ninety-second. And this note.
(*Hands note to Clara, mouths the words while Clara reads.*)

CLARA: "This is your last New York breakfast for two weeks. Eat, drink, and be merry, for tomorrow, we fly. Call me when you're ready to dance." This worries me.

JOANNA: I know. You think it's too much too soon. That's what I was thinking. But it's been a year since the Patrick incident, and I've been seeing Bobby since then—whenever he's in town, of course.

CLARA: Of course.

JOANNA: So what do you think?

CLARA: Me?

JOANNA: Yeah.

CLARA: I think you emptied out your savings and went shopping for all this.

JOANNA: What?

CLARA: I think you feel bad about being twenty-nine and alone. It's not a curse, Jo. Plenty of women our age haven't gotten married yet. But that doesn't mean—

JOANNA: Do you really imagine that even if I *did* lose my mind and go on a shopping spree that I would buy *this*? (*Holds up expensive doodad.*)

CLARA: Well...

JOANNA: After I bought this—if I could afford it in the first place on the fifteen dollars and twenty-seven cents I've managed to keep in savings over the last five years—I'd barely be able to afford two weeks away from work.

CLARA: Who *is* this guy?

JOANNA: I already told you. Robert. Bobby.

CLARA: Did he come with a last name?

JOANNA: You won't believe me.

CLARA: I barely believe you now.

JOANNA: (*Opens wallet.*) I've got his picture in here somewhere.

CLARA: Nice wallet.

JOANNA: Thanks.

CLARA: You have a thing for leather now?

JOANNA: It matches the purse. Which matches the traveling case.

CLARA: I didn't think your tastes ran along these lines.

JOANNA: Neither did I. Till I got everything. It's so heavy, you know? It's got weight to it. Like it's really real.

CLARA: Heavy luggage? How are you supposed to carry it?

JOANNA: (*Still searching bag, emptying contents onto coffee table.*) Red caps! He can afford red caps at the airports! I've *never* been able to afford red caps! I can't find it.

CLARA: Awww.

JOANNA: I swear I had one.

CLARA: Sure you did.

JOANNA: I did. I had his picture, and on the back, it said, "To the girl I love and her goofy smile, much love, Bob."

CLARA: (*Disbelieving.*) Really.

JOANNA: He took it at one of those little photo booths? Out at JFK.

CLARA: What's he do?

JOANNA: He's an actor.

CLARA: Not an actor! Don't you know that actors are the worst the absolute worst people to get mixed up with? I bet he bought all of this on credit and some nice young men in overalls are going to come up and take it all back.

JOANNA: That's what I keep thinking. That someone's going to just shake me awake and say, it's all over, Joanna.

CLARA: An actor?

JOANNA: An actor slash director slash producer.

CLARA: Great. You've just sent an engraved invitation to trouble, and he's about to RSVP.

JOANNA: He wouldn't do anything to hurt me.

CLARA: How do you know?

JOANNA: I can just tell.

CLARA: Great. "And that's when he killed her, officer." How's he feel about you?

JOANNA: With his hands, mostly. I don't know. We're at *least* really good friends.

CLARA: Un-huh. Okay.

JOANNA: Do you want to meet him?

CLARA: Sure. Unless he's at an audition, or something.

JOANNA: He doesn't audition anymore.

CLARA: Even better. An out-of-work actor. That's new.

JOANNA: He'll be home in a little while.

CLARA: You two moved in together!? Oh, please tell me you haven't moved in with him.

JOANNA: He lives across the hall. I have to go jump in the shower so— You know where the fridge is. There's nothing in it, of course, but—

CLARA: Jo, I hate to see you do this to yourself.

JOANNA: You don't believe me, do you?

CLARA: I believe you've been under a lot of stress at work, and I believe you deserve two weeks off, paid vacation, but—

JOANNA: (*In wallet again.*) Here it is. It got stuck to a coupon. (*Hands Clara picture.*)

CLARA: (*Hands picture back.*) Show me the real one.

JOANNA: That *is* the real picture.

CLARA: But this is—

JOANNA: He is.

CLARA: De Niro.

JOANNA: Robert. Bobby.

CLARA: De Niro.

JOANNA: Yes.

CLARA: You're in love with Robert Bobby De Niro. The actor.

JOANNA: Actor slash director slash blah blah blah.

CLARA: Can you set me up with Pacino?

JOANNA: I'll ask him. I'm sure he'll do what he can, but—

CLARA: Do you remember when you got drunk and you'd tell everybody that De Niro was leaving messages on your answering machine?

JOANNA: Yeah, but—

CLARA: And that Eric Clapton wrote "Bell Bottom Blues" for you when you two were together in the shower?

JOANNA: But that was—

CLARA: And Denzel Washington was supposedly in your bed on New Year's Eve last year, and that's why you weren't going to any parties? Because he couldn't bear to have you away from his side?

JOANNA: I was just—

CLARA: And Andy Garcia stopped by a couple of years ago to help you cook?

JOANNA: That was kid stuff. That was joking around.

CLARA: And what is this?

JOANNA: Proof that dreams come true.

CLARA: You've changed your real life to fit inside your dream life. That's all. What are you looking for?

JOANNA: This is his favorite album.

CLARA: He's got a favorite album now?

JOANNA: Well, it's not his very favorite. He likes others, too. But this is what I was listening to the night we met.

CLARA: You and—

JOANNA: The night I found out about Patrick, I was sitting here in the candlelight, playing this album, and Bobby—

CLARA: If he's got so much money, why doesn't he buy you the CD?

JOANNA: He did. But he says it's to convenient to be romantic. He likes the skips. In the songs.

CLARA: He lives downtown, Jo.

JOANNA: You read that in an interview?

(*Clara nods.*)

He hates interviews, and interviewers are sometimes mistaken. He lives right there. He also has a place downtown. But when he's uptown, and he's uptown an *awful* lot lately…

CLARA: He just happens to live across the hall.

JOANNA: Yup.

CLARA: But how—

JOANNA: I just happen to have one of his most favorite albums in the whole wide world. (*Sits with Clara.*) I've danced with him. We dance. He moves like silk. He thinks I'm pretty. He says—

CLARA: Joanna, things like this…like De Niro living next door—

JOANNA: Across the hall.

CLARA: Whatever. These things are reserved for other people.

JOANNA: That's what I keep thinking. I need you to anchor me. I'm afraid I'll just float up up and away. And what if it's a soap bubble instead of the Goodyear blimp?

CLARA: What if there's not even a soap bubble there at all? What if it's the Hindenburg.

JOANNA: You still don't believe me, do you?

CLARA: Honestly?

JOANNA: Honestly?

CLARA: Not for a second.

JOANNA: Out of everyone I know, I thought you would believe me.

CLARA: I need proof.

JOANNA: (*Finds picture in wallet.*) This is his picture.

CLARA: Anybody could get a picture of him.

JOANNA: He wrote on the back.

CLARA: It could be anyone's signature.

JOANNA: And all the gifts?

CLARA: Jo! Don't go crazy on me!

JOANNA: I'm not! Just—just let me shower and make myself beautiful. He's getting back from the coast tonight.

CLARA: "From the coast"!?

JOANNA: From L.A. Meet him.

CLARA: A little fantasy once in a while is fine. Good for the brain. But this—Why didn't you say something? I would've gotten you help.

JOANNA: I don't *need* help!

CLARA: You do! Look at yourself! You're just still confused about Patrick.

JOANNA: The last thing I'm confused about is Patrick. Turn on the tube, make yourself a drink or read or whatever. Soon as I get out of the shower, I'll get him here and if you don't think he's De Niro, then fine. He's not De Niro. And if you don't think he's great— You'll think he's great! He's wonderful! He's a dream! (*She exits with clothes.*)

CLARA: That's what I'm afraid of. (*Goes to stereo.*) Let's see what kind of taste he has. (*She puts the album on the turntable, turns it on, and begins snooping around the apartment—out of boredom and curiosity. The shower is turned on. There is a knock at the door. Clara looks toward the shower and back at the door. She yells to bathroom.*) Joanna!? There's someone—

(*A key in the lock. Bobby enters, smiling and ready to dance. Stops himself and looks at the number on the apartment door.*)

BOBBY: Who are—

CLARA: I'm Clara.

BOBBY: Where is Joanna?

CLARA: Shower.

BOBBY: Oh. *Clara.* Well. (*Takes needle off record.*) Good to finally meet you. I was starting to wonder if you really existed. I'm Bobby.

CLARA: She—She—

BOBBY: She said you might be by tonight. You want something to eat? You like Chinese?

CLARA: Yeah, but—

BOBBY: I'm starving. I get hungry about two in the morning. I'm Take-Out and Delivery King. Though I do love the art of cooking. It's very relaxing. But not as relaxing as a good dance. No. There's nothing better than a good dance. Well... Yeah. So I'm still on California time. California clothes, too, so please forgive me. (*Phone in hand.*) What would you like?

CLARA: I'm not very—

BOBBY: Hi. Put this on the Bennett account. I want an order of the regular plus... (*Covers mouthpiece.*) Plus?

CLARA: I'm not very—

BOBBY: (*Into phone.*) Uhhh— (*Points to her.*) Diced chicken with cashews and— (*Opens hand, questioning.*) Shrimp lo mein? (*Cocks head.*)

CLARA: How did you know?

BOBBY: Two Diet Cokes, a black cherry Soho and no fruit. No oranges. No plums. No apples. No. I always tell you "No oranges." Please. I'm paying you not to put oranges in . . . You want to make me happy? You know what makes me happy? Opening the bag and finding no fruit. NO oranges. NO plums. No apples. I know it's good for me. So are enemas, but—What? Yeah. Extra fortune cookies. Maybe a few almond—Yeah. And good fortunes. Only good fortunes. Okay? Okay. I'm hanging up! I'm hanging up! (*Hangs up. To Clara.*) Takes them no time. I'm famished. You'd think on the plane? No. First-class even and still. I know. I know. It's late to eat, two o'clock. And something a man my age can ill-afford to do, but—Were you trying to tell me something?

CLARA: I'm not very hungry.

BOBBY: Oh, Clara, please do not deny me the pleasure of eating one of my greatest pleasures in the home of one of my greatest pleasures. I'm Italian. We eat. You'll eat, too. End of discussion.

CLARA: How did you know what I like?

BOBBY: (*Motions with head.*) She told me.

CLARA: And you remembered?

BOBBY: (*Going to kitchen.*) You don't mind if I imbibe a little, do you?

CLARA: No. Go ahead.

BOBBY: Can I get something for you?

CLARA: Tequila with a—

BOBBY: Rolling Rock back. Coming right up.

CLARA: She told you that, too?

BOBBY: (*Motions to his head.*) Steel trap. I'll tell you something, Clara. Nothing like New York water. It's polluted. It's rusty. It's not fit for a dog. But for a mixer? I don't think it can be beat. Are you okay? I mean you seem—

CLARA: Dazed?

BOBBY: Stupefied.

CLARA: How did you two—

BOBBY: Meet? (*Gives her drinks.*) She didn't tell you?

CLARA: Sort of.

BOBBY: (*Sitting.*) November twelve. A year ago.

CLARA: Down to the day?

BOBBY: Steel trap. (*Drinks.*) I was sitting in my living room trying not to fall asleep over the front page of the Sunday *Times*—this was after another LA–New York no true food flight—and that song leaked through my door. My favorite song. My favorite album. Just a door away. I still had my LA openness on, so I put down my paper, knocked on the door, which, as if by magic, opened, and she was on the other side of it. Crying in the candlelight, drinking wine. She threw her arms around me and we danced and danced and thank god for phonographs because we heard that side of the album a couple of times, till our legs ached and my shoulder was soaked. Then she told me about Patrick, showed me his wedding announcement in the *Times*. The one he neglected to tell her about during their date earlier that week.

CLARA: I never liked him.

BOBBY: But, if it hadn't been for him, I wouldn't have met— (*The buzzer.*) That'll be Chinese. (*He goes to buzzer, talks.*) Spill it.

VOICE: (*Thick, snide, NY accent.*) Is this twenty-A?

BOBBY: It's twenty-B.

VOICE: (*Snidely.*) Oh. "Mr. Bennett." I thought you were—

BOBBY: I'm across the hall.

VOICE: You order Chinese?

BOBBY: Put it on the elevator.

VOICE: (*Snidely.*) Sure thing. "Mr. Bennett."

BOBBY: (*To Clara.*) Smart ass. I hate that night kid. So when's she going to be out?

CLARA: I don't know. After a year wouldn't you—

BOBBY: I've never been here when she wasn't here and I've never been here while she was in the shower. Do you prefer a plate or a fork? For your Chinese food? Out of the carton or—?

CLARA: Carton.

BOBBY: Get three forks. I'll be right back. (*He steps out of the door.*)

CLARA: Hey!

BOBBY: (*Pops back in.*) Hmmm?

CLARA: You don't look a thing like De Niro.

BOBBY: That's the dead give away.

(*The shower stops.*)

If you want a confab, I think she's drying.

(*He pops back out. Clara runs to the bathroom. As soon as she gets there, the blow-dryer starts. Clara yells at and yanks on the locked door.*)

CLARA: Jo? Joanna?! This guy says he's De Niro. Jo?!

JOANNA: (*Over blow-dryer.*) I'll be out in a few. I can't hear you!

CLARA: I said there's a guy out here and—

(*Bobby enters with bags of food and a picture, wrapped with paper and a bow.*)

BOBBY: She's getting the water out of her ears. With the blow-dryer. That I do know. Now, what I'd like to know is how she gets water in her ears in the first place. But—ours is not to wonder why…But you were wondering something, weren't you?

CLARA: No. No, I just—

BOBBY: You just what?

CLARA: Nothing.

BOBBY: Well, get ready to eat.

CLARA: I'm not hungry.

BOBBY: Are you sure?

CLARA: I've sort of lost my appetite.

BOBBY: (*Opening food.*) Excuse me while I—

CLARA: Go ahead.

BOBBY: It's been days since I've had Chinese. (*He digs in and eats.*) Lobster and shrimp with snow peas. You can order it in Chicago and demand it in L.A., but I'll tell you something. It never tastes like it does in the city so nice they named it twice.

(*Pause while he eats. She stares.*)

Say something so I don't have to talk with my mouth full.

CLARA: Ummmm...

BOBBY: Considering the amount of time you keep Joanna on the phone, the cat must've roasted your tongue over an open fire, huh?

CLARA: The amount of time I keep her on the phone? She's the one who—

BOBBY: Just checking. Slow down. Nobody accused you of cannibalism.

CLARA: I don't believe this.

BOBBY: You don't believe this. What don't you believe?

CLARA: ANY OF THIS! That you're who you two are saying you are. For god's sake! I watch you in movies! She doesn't meet people like you in her life.

BOBBY: I guess she did, though.

CLARA: (*Shakes head.*) Boy.

BOBBY: What? Trying to figure out how to tell Jack without sounding like you've lost your mind?

CLARA: No. Uh—Jack and I broke up this morning.

BOBBY: I'm so sorry to hear that. I know how much he meant to you.

CLARA: You do?

BOBBY: Of course. Joanna told me. (*Offers a tin.*) If you won't eat Chinese, at least you can have fudge.

CLARA: Oh, god, no. Thanks.

BOBBY: I made it for Joanna before I left, but she started accusing me of trying to fatten her up. Go ahead. Take one. They won't bite back! (*She takes one.*)

You have to take it *and* eat it, too. Not just take it. She looks great to me. I'll tell you something. (*Winks, looks over shoulder for eaves-droppers.*) A couple or few extra pounds feels good in your arms when you're dancing. And when you're—How's the fudge? Don't spread it around, but I sometimes like to venture into the kitchen. It's my father's recipe. You like?

CLARA: Do you love her? No, you can't love her. I mean, you date models and actresses and she's just—

BOBBY: "Just"? She's not "just."

CLARA: I mean—

BOBBY: I know what you mean. You want to know what I mean? When you're in love in first grade, you don't love like you do when you're twenty. Or twenty-nine. When you're a kid, what do you know. A pretty face could very well be a skinned knee. When I was a kid, I was in love with a little girl who always had bloody, scabby knees. Lola. Everybody in my class would laugh at my mole. Except Lola. Never even snickered. I asked her if she thought my mole looked funny. You know what she did? Lola looked right into my eyes and said, "What mole?" Threw a stick at me. I loved her. Little Lola.

CLARA: But—

BOBBY: But do I love Joanna?

CLARA: Yeah.

BOBBY: "Even though—"?

CLARA: Yeah.

BOBBY: You want to know what love is, Clara?

CLARA: Yeah.

BOBBY: Wish I knew. But I can tell you what it ain't. Love isn't a pretty face and a—excuse my Urdu—tight ass wrapped in Lycra. That's lust. Body attraction. The flesh and only the flesh. Regrets? Yeah. I've had a few. Bitten off more than I could et cetera et cetera. But I think love is flesh. And mind. And heart. All working together. All in synch. Dancing. You see? Love her? We dance good together. When you dance good together, everything else? Chocolate. Everything else is sweet. Go ahead. Have another piece. It's healthy fudge.

CLARA: Okay. Okay. Wait. Let's step back and look at this. Fact. You live across the hall. Fact. You met her the night she read in the *Times* that her boyfriend had gotten married. Fact. You dance with her. Fact. You're a movie star. Do I have that right? Is that more or less the way it is?

BOBBY: Yeah. Kinda restores your faith in the world and mankind, doesn't it.

CLARA: No. No. Not at all. You're not just any guy off the street. You're—

BOBBY: A guy with a heart. And any guy with a heart and a brain would be lucky to be in love with her.

CLARA: I can't believe you—

BOBBY: She's first in my heart. I love her every hour of every day. This is not an infatuation. This is the heart and the mind. This is the heart and the mind doing a tango. Or a dark basement in Motown sort of bump and grind thing. Moving together. In synch. Not two becoming one. Two becoming a million. A million beautiful things twinkling like diamonds. She walks into the room? It lights up. Everything becomes easier. Sweeter. Life is no longer a burden. It's a pleasure. She makes life's messiness bearable. Even though it's her messiness I hate. She's a slob. Forgive me. It's true.

CLARA: No. I know.

BOBBY: That and the red meat. Once a month *maybe*. As a self-indulgence. But more than that's potentially deadly. But, yeah. It's love.

CLARA: You don't know her! You've only danced a few times! That's all!

BOBBY: I don't know what she's told you, but it's been a hell of a lot more than a "few" times. A hell of a lot! And "only danced"? My parents met dancing. The parents of my parents met dancing. I remember being a little boy at my grandparents' house, sitting on the floor, watching them dance to something on the radio. I watched my parents dance me to sleep when I had a fever. Or a bad dream. And they would dance when they fought. The nights of their worst arguments. The ones that almost led to the violence of a fist against flesh. In a fight, you build up a wall. Put up a barrier. When you dance, you have to give a little. Lead some and follow if you must. Merge. Yield. You smell the neck. Press a spine. You hold and are held. Part of a team. You work together. Symbiosis. Capishe? Me and Joanna? We met dancing. We dance good together. When we dance, it's my parents. My grandparents. Strong. You can't hate your partner. Not for long. You breathe the same air. Occupy the same space. Move together through time. With never enough for the Holy Ghost between. Not when the song's right.

CLARA: When did you move across the hall?

BOBBY: About a year and change ago.

CLARA: Why here?

BOBBY: I like the music. (*He opens his fortune cookie.*) "If your desires are not extravagant, they will be granted." That's nice. Sounds like a prayer or something.

CLARA: Aren't *you* a little—

BOBBY: Extravagant? Me? No.

CLARA: But these things—

BOBBY: Okay. Guilty. But I think she needs spoiling. Look around.

CLARA: At what?

BOBBY: Not the things. The space between the things.

(*Pause. She is confused.*)
Tilt your head. From side to side.
(*She does. Slowly.*)
A little faster. Yeah. Do you see it?
CLARA: (*Still moving her head.*) What?
BOBBY: The way the room shines? Kind of sparkles?
CLARA: Yeah!
BOBBY: Know what it is?
CLARA: What?
BOBBY: That's what *I* wondered. We're twirling around, dancing. The room's shining. Dazzling. And I realize afterwards, "It's not shining because it's so clean. She's no June Cleaver. Un-unh. Silverfish."
CLARA: Silverfish?
BOBBY: Silverfish. What's left of them. They shine. Silverfish. Not roaches. Not waterbugs. Not fleas. Nothing run-of-the-mill. Nothing tolerable. Killable. She's gotta have an infestation of the nastiest, ugliest—ugh! (*A chill down his back.*) Excuse me. A woman who can live amid an infestation of the most disgusting little insects on God's green earth deserves extravagance. And I'll tell you something else. Emily Post does not tell you how to tell your hostess there's a silverfish in your tea.
CLARA: You talk a lot.
BOBBY: I do. I do. I started talking late. When I was three. I gotta admit it. I love the sound of my own voice. (*He laughs, rests, shrugs. Sings "When Joanna Loved Me" under his breath until he can bear the silence no longer.*) Guess me talking was better of two goods, huh? It feels good to talk. It's like eating. You move your mouth. Taste the words. Roll 'em around with your tongue. Work the jaw. You should try.
(*She spaces out and starts crying.*)
What? My breath?!
(*He laughs tentatively. She cries harder.*)
Is there anything…?
(*She waves him off.*)
Jack? Is it Jack?
(*She nods and cries harder.*)
CLARA: (*Through tears. Her voice and words are punctuated with sharp intakes of breath.*) I—I'm—I'm—I'm—sorry.

BOBBY: Oh, no no no. Sorry? What you're sorry? There's no sorry here. Your tears hurt me? No. Tears are good.

CLARA: He—He—He—

BOBBY: Take your time. Do you need a paper bag?

CLARA: He—He just said, "No more."

BOBBY: "No more"? What's "no more"? "No more" what?

CLARA: "No more love for me."

BOBBY: Awww, Clara.

CLARA: He said—

BOBBY: (*Gives her box of tissues.*) Shhh. It's okay.

CLARA: He said—

BOBBY: (*Gets fudge.*) Shhh.

CLARA: (*Eating fudge.*) How could he? Huh? How? I *loved* him!

BOBBY: I know.

CLARA: I really loved him.

BOBBY: It's gonna be all right. You were too good for him anyway.

CLARA: (*Stuffing her face.*) But we were so *right!* You know? So right!

BOBBY: I know.

CLARA: He said there was no— "romance." When we met, it was good. Real good. We sparked. You know?

BOBBY: I know. You want something to wash that down?

CLARA: Tequila.

BOBBY: (*Getting bottle.*) Aren't you afraid it'll—go down badly? In your stomach? I've got a cast-iron stomach and never not once have I been able to mix anything sweet with tequila.

CLARA: I need to puke. God, I wish I could puke.

BOBBY: No no no you don't want to do that, Clara!

CLARA: No romance? No romance? How could there be no romance? I'm the queen of romance! I get catalogs from Victoria's Secret! I've subscribed to Lingerie of the Month. I get something new and silky the seventh of every month! This month it was this! (*She holds up a strap through the collar opening in her shirt.*) And now he'll never see it! (*She cries harder.*) "No romance"?! I reek of it! I stink of moonlight and champagne! Look at me!
(*He does.*)
When you look at me, what do you think of?
(*He makes a grand thing out of looking at her. She has her mouth stuffed full of fudge, her makeup is running and smeared and she looks a mess. He pours her another shot. She shoots it.*)

I know I don't look great right now, but—

BOBBY: You look just fine.

CLARA: You were looking at me funny.

BOBBY: At you? No. I was wondering if you could stand hearing it.

CLARA: Hearing what?

BOBBY: The news.

(*He gives her another piece of fudge, puts down the tin, then decides to give her the entire tin, which she holds protectively on her lap.*)

CLARA: What is it? I can take it.

BOBBY: But can I? (*He sits by her.*) First somebody comes along and tells us the Earth isn't at the center of the universe. Then some other genius figures out the world isn't flat, and there are no monsters over the edge, waiting for boats to fall off. And another somebody gets the bright idea to put a man on the moon and prove it isn't just a ball of cheese. The most romantic thing in the world for eons, centuries and forever, then some wise guy's gotta walk all over it.

CLARA: Just sucking the romance out of everything.

BOBBY: There's even a special telescope now that can take the twinkle twinkle out of little stars. Can you imagine? So there's no romance left anywhere.

CLARA: But you don't understand, Bobby. For a while? It *was* there! It was really there!

BOBBY: It's always there. For a while. You know how you lose it?

(*She shakes her head.*)

Here.

(*Gives her his handkerchief, holds it up to her nose.*)

Blow.

(*She blows her nose and sounds like a trucker.*)

You look too hard at something, you examine it and examine it and you dissect it and you take it down to its lowest common denominator, and you know what happens then? You forget what made you think it looked good in the first place. You pick at it and pick at it and pouf! Gone. Gone like it wasn't ever really there and there's nothing left in that place to remind you the spaced used to be filled. You get what I'm saying to you?

(*She nods.*)

Blow.

(*She blows into hanky again, puts her head on his shoulder.*)

CLARA: I'm so tired.

BOBBY: It *is* getting late, isn't it?

CLARA: So you're De Niro.

BOBBY: I stand accused. I plead guilty on all counts.

CLARA: What's the worst thing about being you?

BOBBY: Besides giving interviews? Being doubted.

(*Now happy and comfy, she nuzzles into him, burying her face in his neck.*)

Uhhh, Clara—

CLARA: She was right. You really are great.

BOBBY: Thanks, but—

CLARA: No. You're really amazing. I can tell why Joanna is crazy about you…

(*She moves to kiss him. He quickly disengages and stands away from her.*)

What's wrong? Are you okay?

BOBBY: Are *you?* Look, you shouldn't—

CLARA: I just wanted someone to hold me. For you to hold me like you held her the night—

BOBBY: I can't hold you like that!? I don't do that. I don't believe in that. What are you thinking?

CLARA: I thought—

BOBBY: You're not thinking clearly, okay? Did you not hear me? Can you not hear me when I talk? Give me a sign. Close your mouth and nod your head.

(*She nods.*)

Okay.

(*The dryer stops. He gives bathroom door a hasty look.*)

I'll make it short. Are you her friend?

CLARA: Yes.

BOBBY: You're her friend?

CLARA: Yes.

BOBBY: You're telling me you're her friend.

CLARA: Yes?

BOBBY: You're not her friend. You know how the world is divided? There are your friends, acquaintances, and then there are the ones who are happiest after they've lodged a knife in your back. Your friends take it out, your acquaintances ignore it, and the person who put it in you in the first place? Tries to shove it in deeper. Do you know what we're taking about here?

(*She nods.*)

She doesn't know which one you are yet. But she will. These things have a way of—What is it? Disclosing themselves? Showing themselves. Making themselves known. Like silverfish.

(*Enter Joanna, putting on earrings. She is wearing a dress.*)

JOANNA: Hi! I thought I heard you!

(*He goes to kiss her.*)

BOBBY: Look at you! Are you losing weight?

JOANNA: Oh, stop it!

BOBBY: You look divine. A sight for sore eyes.

JOANNA: What brought you in here?

CLARA: I put the album on and he—waltzed right in. Just like you said.

JOANNA: You've been crying. What's wrong?

CLARA: What could possibly be wrong with me?

BOBBY: (*Gets picture wrapped in paper and bow.*) Hey! Look. I did this for you when I was out there. I wrote you a poem!

JOANNA: (*Unwrapping it.*) Oooh!

CLARA: A poem?

BOBBY: Yeah.

CLARA: Right.

JOANNA: Oh, read it!

BOBBY: Now? In front of—

JOANNA: Please?

BOBBY: (*Clears throat.*) "With thee conversing, I forget all time.
All seasons, and their change; all please alike.
Sweet is the breath of morn, his rising sweet,
With charm of earliest birds..."

CLARA: But Milton wrote that. It's from "Paradise Lost."

BOBBY: *I* wrote it. Look. (*He shows it to her.*) I do calligraphy in my spare time. Oh. You thought I—?! Oh, for crying out loud, Clara! Everybody knows Milton wrote that! What? You think I'm an idiot, something? Like I don't know what I know? Or if what I know is real? What I know is as real as what you know. Okay? Stop doubting me! I hate being doubted! (*To Joanna.*) Why not hang in here? It'll be enough out of the morning light but—You think?

JOANNA: I can't believe you! You thought he—

BOBBY: Hey! Hey! Shhh. Shhh. She didn't know. It's okay. It's okay. She didn't mean anything by it.

CLARA: He's not who he says he is, Joanna. You're fooling yourself. I hate to see him do this to you! He's making you look like a fool! I think—

JOANNA: I know what you think! You think I've lost my mind! You think nothing good ever happens to me! It only happens to you! He's not real? Fine. I've been dancing with the air. I've been dancing with nothing. Nothing's been giving me nothing, nothing loves me and nothing wants to share my bed. Happy? Does it make you happy to see me like this? This is me losing my mind, Clara. Go ahead. Call Patrick. Tell him I've never gotten over him. Call the men with those pretty little back-buckling jackets and tell them Joanna's lost it. Go on.

(*During this, Bobby has gone over to the stereo and turns on "Fly Me to the Moon."*)

Look! Oh my God! The stereo turned itself on!

(*Bobby has Joanna in his arms, making her dance.*)

Call 911! She's dancing with nothing and calling it love!

CLARA: He looks like him, talks like him, moves like him and everything, but—

JOANNA: But what? How could he love me? Is that it? Get out of here, Clara. Just get the hell out of here! Leave!

(*Clara exits.*)

BOBBY: Shhh.

JOANNA: I hate it! I just hate it! Why can't anybody let me be happy?

BOBBY: I know. I know. Shhh. Relax. We're dancing. Let me make you happy. (*Pause.*) You smell good.

JOANNA: Stop it.

BOBBY: You do.

JOANNA: I just got out of the shower. What is *with* her? She's usually not like that. She's usually so—

BOBBY: Who? I don't see anybody. I've got you in my arms, and that's all I care about. You in my arms, a song in my head, and look at that view.

(*They look out the fourth wall as they dance.*)

Say good-bye to New York nights for a while. I'm taking you away. I'll fly you to the moon.

JOANNA: On a plane?

BOBBY: First class.

JOANNA: Sleep in a hotel?

BOBBY: The best of the best.

JOANNA: Where are we going?

BOBBY: I told you. Didn't I tell you? I'll fly you to the moon.

JOANNA: What do they wear on the moon?

BOBBY: You mean what should you pack?

JOANNA: I've never had to pack light before.

BOBBY: Bring a toothbrush and a passport.

JOANNA: A passport?

BOBBY: Did I say a passport? I meant a passport. Bring your passport. And a toothbrush.

JOANNA: Where are we going?

BOBBY: Where do you want to go? I told you, Joanna. You want it? I want it for you. Plus a little bit more.

JOANNA: Bobby?

BOBBY: Yeah?

JOANNA: You're real, aren't you?

BOBBY: Me? Real as rain, baby. Realer than I need to be. Joanna?

JOANNA: Yeah?

BOBBY: You're real, too, aren't you?

JOANNA: Pinch me.

(*He does.*)

Owww! I don't think I'll be able to sleep.

BOBBY: Me, neither. Hey, Joanna?

JOANNA: Yeah?

BOBBY: Do you think my mole looks funny?

JOANNA: What mole?

BOBBY: So I'm real?

JOANNA: You're real.

BOBBY: Great. If this is what it feels like to be real, I think I'll keep it.

(*They kiss and dance in neat Fred Astaire–Ginger Rogers twirls as the lights dim to Black.*)

END OF PLAY

Sticks And Stones
by Drew McWeeny & Scott Swan

BIOGRAPHY

DREW McWEENY was born in New York but has lived all over the country in his first twentysomething years. His interest in film was initially sparked by *Star Wars,* and he spent most of his teen years watching any and every film he could get his hands on. He credits his imaginative skills to a mostly thrill free childhood.

SCOTT SWAN was born in Pittsburgh and raised in Washington, Pennsylvania. As an only child, he turned to his imagination early in life, writing stories and drawing their "storyboards" to entertain himself. At the age of ten, he utilized his talents writing, directing, and playing the lead role in his class play. An average student at best, Scott spent much of his time writing plays and studying on his own, educating himself in a way the school system could not. Inspired by the films of George Lucas and Steven Spielberg, Scott focused on screenwriting in his early teens.

Drew and Scott met while attending Armwood High School in Tampa, Florida, where they were the top Television Production students. Their work on a closed circuit morning show that was broadcast live to thousands of students each day (and garnered them several awards during the two years they worked on it) led them to collaborate on a screenplay together. Since moving to Los Angeles in 1990 they have written twenty feature length screenplays, two full-length plays, and four one-act plays. Their first produced work was *Sticks and Stones,* which snagged industry attention, leading them to a feature version of that play currently in development with Showtime and two original features currently in development with Avalon Films.

AUTHOR'S NOTE

As we sit down to write this, our first reaction is, "What more can we say that the piece itself didn't say?" We could tell you about the evolution of the piece from an original screenplay idea called *WOP.* Maybe we could tell you about our relationship with the original director of the piece, Jerry Levine. Maybe we could describe the miracle of casting that is Louis Mustillo, the original and (in our hearts) only Di Palma. We could discuss the wonders that *Sticks* has worked for our career, or the grueling development process we went through on the screenplay version.

Instead, though, we'd like to take a moment to consider the form itself. What is a one-act play? Some people seem to think that it's anything that is less than a full-length play. That's not accurate, though. A good one-act has to take a single moment in a character's life, a pivotal moment, and let the audience witness firsthand the change that occurs. It's that point where a character has been driven to react, and it's the reaction itself. It's also, in our opinion, got to take place on one set. We've seen one-acts with as many set changes as *Miss Saigon*, and that's just lunacy. The point is to let us in, to give us something real and charged and alive. You can't do that when the audience is sitting there thinking about how you made that wall move or how long it's taking to redress the set. You have to put them in a room with the people you're writing about and leave them there. The director, the stagehands, the writers...we're all invisible when a good one-act is on stage and working.

The first time we saw *Sticks* with an audience was better than any drugs. There was this immediacy, this electricity that came down off the stage and pulled us in. It was the single finest moment in our lives so far, and it's because we had a director and a cast that believed in the work, that trusted the words to be enough. There was nothing overstylized or hyper-theatrical about the presentation. Just the simple set and two men locked in combat over their words, over the weight of those words. It was theater at its best. It was as if we'd had nothing to do with actually writing it. While it was on stage, it simply lived.

We have a play running in this year's festival, *Broken Bones*, and I'm sure we'll continue to write for the stage in one form or another. Still, you don't get many perfect experiences in this business, and *Sticks* was one of them. We'll always be grateful to Jerry Levine, Risa Bramon Garcia, Michael Koopman, Jonathan Silverman, and Louis Mustillo, as well as Judy Pastore and anyone else we may be forgetting at this particular moment, for their efforts in helping us realize this particular dream. As you read it, you may be angered by Di Palma's words, or you may be moved by his predicament. The important thing, though, is that you feel something. We did. That's why we wrote it.

Enjoy.

ORIGINAL PRODUCTION

Sticks and Stones was originally directed by Jerry Levine with Jonathan Silverman as Klein and Louis Mustillo as DiPalma.

STICKS AND STONES

With the stage still dark, we hear:

KLEIN: Maureen, is my two o'clock here yet? Good…send him in.

Lights up.
A lawyer's office, well-decorated, comfortable. There are framed
headlines, signed photos on the wall. Alan Klein stands up from behind
his desk, walks around to his office door just as it swings open.
Salvatore Di Palma leans in, looks around. The men are obviously
from different worlds. Klein is confident, dressed well, in his mid-
thirties. Di Palma wears a rumpled, off-the-rack suit, fills it too full,
looks frazzled, sweaty. He's in his mid-forties.

KLEIN: Mr. Di Palma?
DI PALMA: Yeah…
KLEIN: I'm Alan Klein. Pleased to meet you. (*Klein offers Di Palma his*
    hand, which Di Palma shakes distractedly.)
DI PALMA: Wish I could say the same. (*Klein looks down at his hand as*
    he pulls it away.) Sorry about that. I've been sweating like a
    goddamn racehorse since I put this suit on.
KLEIN: Don't worry about it. Please…take a seat. Would you like a
    beverage? A soft drink, or maybe some water…?
DI PALMA: That's okay.
KLEIN: Really. Anything you want. I'll ask Maureen…

DI PALMA: I'm fine. I don't want anything.

KLEIN: You comfortable?

DI PALMA: Yes...I'm fine. Whattaya want here?

KLEIN: I'm asking because you're glowering.

DI PALMA: I'm what?

KLEIN: Glowering. You've got a look on your face like you want to strangle me. It's very disconcerting. (*The phone rings once.*) Excuse me...(*Answers it.*) Yes? Oh...right. I'll talk to him. Hold anything else, though, Maureen. Thanks. (*To Di Palma.*) This will just take a moment...(*Into phone.*)

Hello Marty. What do you want? Right. Sure. I'm going to tell you...no. No. Not a chance. I'll tell you what I think, Marty, and this is free advice, so listen well. You should cut your losses, get out now. Why? That's your call. I can't make that decision for you. Sometimes, you have to weigh what you will gain from somebody against what you could lose to them. (*Laughs.*) God, Marty... you're such a Jew. Fine. If that's what you want, fine. I'll talk to you later. I have someone here right now. I'm hanging up the phone, Marty. I'm hanging up. (*Hangs up.*) Schmuck's going to get his client the chair. (*To Di Palma.*) You're still glowering. This is a problem.

DI PALMA: I don't want to be here. I'm sorry I look like I'm not enjoying myself.

KLEIN: No one's asking you to enjoy yourself. Still, this doesn't have to be painful for you. After all, you are here for my help...

DI PALMA: Yeah...

KLEIN:...and I know exactly what you're going through.

DI PALMA: I doubt that.

KLEIN: You'd better *believe* that's true. You're depending on it. You're depending on my experience handling situations just like yours.

DI PALMA: Just like mine? There are no situations just like mine.

KLEIN: Okay, maybe the details are slightly different, but all the surrounding circumstances are the same, and those are what you need my help with. I have been exactly where you are right now.

DI PALMA: The fuck you have.

KLEIN: Excuse me?

DI PALMA: You heard me. You got no idea where I am right now. *I* don't even know where I am right now. How could you?

KLEIN: I've been through it before.

DI PALMA: You have? Or your clients have?

KLEIN: My clients have...

DI PALMA: Fuck that. Have you ever had charges filed against you? Have you ever been arrested?

KLEIN: No. I haven't.

DI PALMA: Then you ain't been here. (*Pause.*) Somebody...spit on me on the street this morning. Black bitch. In my fuckin' face. Called me a murdering bastard. Her husband got between us before I could react, told me I should be ashamed of myself. Goddammit, my son was with me...

KLEIN: I'm sorry.

DI PALMA: My life is so upside down and sideways from this thing...I'm tryin' to go one day without being on the front page of every newspaper in Los Angeles. My wife and kid see all this shit, all of it *wrong,* what are they supposed to think? God, they could end up hating me if I'm not careful.

KLEIN: Are you done?

DI PALMA: Done what?

KLEIN: Whining and crying.

DI PALMA: I'm not whining...

KLEIN: Sounds like it to me. What would you call it?

DI PALMA: I'm explaining...

KLEIN: And I'm telling you you don't need to. I've seen it more times than you know. You're living in a fishbowl, and I can help you handle it. You called me to set up this meeting. *You* called *me.* I assume you had a reason other than whining at me and arguing that I couldn't possibly understand how hard things are for you. Of course they're hard. You're in major trouble...nightly news size trouble, front-page photo and headline trouble...and you need someone in your corner. You need someone to save your life. And you called me.

DI PALMA: I need a good lawyer.

KLEIN: No, you don't. You need a *great* lawyer. You need Clarence Darrow and Daniel Webster tagteaming with Alan Dershowitz and Gregory Peck in *To Kill A Mockingbird.* You're not going to get them, though. I'm the best that's available.

DI PALMA: You think you can win this?

KLEIN: If anyone can, I can. It won't be easy, though...won't be easy at all. Getting you cleared in court might not be the end of it. The life you were living before all this happened...forget about it. It's over. Gone. You have a choice to make now about your new life, and how you're going to live it. You could end up in prison. You could even get convicted of murder in the first. This could go federal, get dragged through two or three separate trials...

DI PALMA: Jesus Christ...

KLEIN: ...or I could get you cleared, and you can retire, get out of the public eye. Maybe people will forget after some time has passed.

DI PALMA: Murder in the first?

KLEIN: It's possible.

DI PALMA: That's insane. This isn't about murder.

KLEIN: A boy is dead. You're responsible. If you did it on purpose, it's murder.

DI PALMA: The fuck it is. It was self-defense.

KLEIN: Not if the prosecutor can prove malice on your part.

DI PALMA: He drew a gun...

KLEIN: And you said something to him.

DI PALMA: That's what this is about.

KLEIN: That's right. Do you remember what you said to him?

DI PALMA: Yes.

KLEIN: Exactly what you said?

DI PALMA: Yes.

KLEIN: And did you, Mr. Di Palma, call that boy a nigger?

DI PALMA: Yes. So what? So I called some kid a nigger in the heat of the moment...now I'm this racist monster and that kid is a martyr? Bullshit on that. That kid was a fuckin' punk who'd have shot me if I gave him half a chance. I did my job.

KLEIN: If that's the truth, then you have no problem.

DI PALMA: Then I got no problem.

KLEIN: I have to admit, I was a bit surprised to get your call. I've been following your case in the papers...

DI PALMA: Yeah, well, all that stuff in the papers, it's all bullshit.

KLEIN: I thought the department had an attorney assigned to your case already.

DI PALMA: Fuck the department and their lawyer. The guy was a rat prick, getting at me from the minute I met him. Goddamn Hindu guy, Ram Dishnu or some shit like that. His whole attitude was that I was wrong and the easiest thing to do would just be roll over and apologize. They made me see the police shrink, too...

KLEIN: Standard procedure following a shooting...

DI PALMA: Fuck 'em. I was a cop for ten years in Chicago and eleven years here in L.A. They can't get behind me on this thing, fuck 'em.

KLEIN: So how did you come up with my name?

DI PALMA: I watch TV. I seen you on the news. You're startin' to get a rep for yourself.

KLEIN: I've been involved in some high profile cases...

DI PALMA: You're a camera hound. Admit it. That's fine. I know you play to win. That's what I want. Besides, I like your name. Klein. Good Jew name.

KLEIN: Okay...

DI PALMA: I'm sure you don't work for free, though. How much is this gonna set me back?

KLEIN: My billing averages three hundred dollars per hour...

DI PALMA: Three hundred per hour?!

KLEIN:...but for a case like yours, I might be willing to work something out.

DI PALMA: Gettin' fuckin' rich, aren't you?

KLEIN: I do well.

DI PALMA: You do better than well. That's fine, I respect that. It's not a crime to get rich.

KLEIN: What are you getting at, Mr. Di Palma?

DI PALMA: Nothin'...

KLEIN: Really? Because if you plan to sit here and make anti-Semitic comments...

DI PALMA: What'd I say?

KLEIN: "Klein. Good Jew name." Like that has anything to do with my ability as an attorney.

DI PALMA: Give me a fuckin' break. You should be glad I think that way. I came to you 'cos I want a Jew lawyer just like everyone in Beverly Hills wants a spic gardener. Different people do different things well. It's a fact.

KLEIN: So, that's it then. I'm a Jew, so I must be a good lawyer.

DI PALMA: Well, don't get lazy or nothin'. I mean, we're a long way from trial, and I still have to decide if I want you to represent me or not.

KLEIN: You sound pretty sure of yourself. How do you know I won't just turn your case down?

DI PALMA: Two things...money and prestige. You take on a case like this and you win, your price goes up, and your reputation grows a little more. You could write a book about it, sell the movie rights. I could *make* you. You want this case, and you want to win. This is a constitutional question with you on the side of right. How can you not get involved?

KLEIN: What makes you say this is a constitutional question?

DI PALMA: Freedom of fuckin' speech.

KLEIN: It's a little more complicated than that...

DI PALMA: Not really. I drew on a kid in self-defense, and I gave him every opportunity to freeze. I shot him because I had to...just like I was trained to.

KLEIN: That's what you say.

DI PALMA: That's the truth.

KLEIN: And so what if it is? You called him a *nigger.* Was that before or after you shot him?

DI PALMA: Both...I think.

KLEIN: Is that why you shot him? Because he was black?

DI PALMA: No.

KLEIN: Are you sure about that?

DI PALMA: You're startin' to sound like that rat prick from the department.

KLEIN: Just doing my job.

DI PALMA: It would make everything so easy if that's how it was. The big bad racist cop shot the poor little black boy. Boo fuckin' hoo. Too bad it's all bullshit.

KLEIN: That's what the witnesses are saying.

DI PALMA: Witnesses are gonna tell you what my goddamn motives were? They gonna tell you what's in my heart? They don't know what they saw...

KLEIN: They know what they heard. They remember you saying, "Nigger, freeze...or I'll blow your stupid nigger head off." You remember that?

DI PALMA: They black or white?

KLEIN: Who?

DI PALMA: The witnesses.

KLEIN: Doesn't matter.

DI PALMA: Of course it does. Niggers are gonna circle up, close ranks. They're gonna say I dropped the hammer on that kid in cold blood. White witnesses...they're gonna see the kid as the fuckin' animal that he was, and they're gonna thank me.

KLEIN: It's not as black and white as you think it is.

DI PALMA: So what color were they?

KLEIN: They were...African American.

DI PALMA: Fuckin' pussy answer. African American ain't a color. Fuckin' niggers don't appreciate what I did for them. That kid was a lump of shit...a nothin'.

KLEIN: How could you possibly know that?

DI PALMA: Be serious. He wasn't gonna cure cancer. He wasn't gonna be the next motherfuckin' President. Probably couldn't even bounce a basketball. He was *no fuckin' good,* and I did them a favor takin' him off the streets. He wasn't a brother to them...he was a burden, and I lightened the goddamn load. Where's the gratitude...huh?

KLEIN: Listen to you. You're amazing. The entire black community is calling for your head on a stick and you want them to throw you a parade. You've got some balls...

DI PALMA: 'Cos I'm on the side of right and justice will prevail.

KLEIN: I wonder if you have any idea what you're up against. A lot of pissed off people want to see you in jail or worse. A lot of people are saying an eye for an eye, a life for a life.

DI PALMA: Over what? Over something I fuckin' said?!

KLEIN: Yes!

DI PALMA: I was doing my job.

KLEIN: That's the excuse my grandfather told me the Nazis gave. "I was just doing my job."

DI PALMA: Fuck you. You callin' me a Nazi now?

KLEIN: I'm telling you how it sounds.

DI PALMA: I'm a cop. I do what I have to do to get the job done.

KLEIN: And what is your job?

DI PALMA: To protect and to serve.

KLEIN: Yeah? Who do you protect? Who do you serve?

DI PALMA: I protect and serve anyone who needs it.

KLEIN: Anyone? You protect black people?

DI PALMA: All the time?

KLEIN: Mexicans? Asians?

DI PALMA: I don't care what fuckin' color or religion they are.

KLEIN: But you use words like nigger and spic. I don't understand. Are you a racist, Mr. Di Palma?

Di Palma: Fuck you…

Klein: No, fuck you if that's how you plan on responding in court.

(*Simultaneously.*)

Klein: The judge isn't going to have much patience with your language.

Di Palma: Don't call me a racist…

Di Palma: Don't call me a racist! I'm so sick of that word being thrown around like a fucking football. I am what I was raised to be. It don't mean nothin'.

Klein: It's not just the words you use. It's how you use them. You're so full of hate.

Di Palma: Goddamn right I am. I hate criminals. I've got every right to hate them. If you could meet all the shitbag criminals I've ever had to deal with, you'd see where it comes from. I know what I've seen. I know what the real world is like. There are major differences between people. Does that make me a racist to point that out?

Klein: Tell you what Mr. Di Palma…maybe this'll put you at ease. I don't think you need to worry about the court case too much. I think you've got a valid angle. Hell, I think you're gonna win.

Di Palma: You do?

Klein: Yes. The boy had a weapon. Self-defense. End of story, right?

Di Palma: Right. That's what I've been sayin'…

Klein: Wrong. You have a filthy mouth. You can't use "fuck" in every other sentence in court.

Di Palma: Fine…

Klein: I don't think you can say "nigger," either.

Di Palma: What do you think I should say, then?

Klein: The preferred term is "African American."

Di Palma: Bullshit on that. They've been tryin' this same shit at work, with sensitivity training seminars and pamphlets on better race relations. "Watch what you say, watch how you say it, and watch who you say it to." It's all shit. They're just names, don't mean nothin'. At least I say what I'm sayin'…at least I say what I mean.

Klein: You don't understand how important this is.

Di Palma: I get it. I got trouble. I know why, too. It's because of who I am. I'm middle-class, white, Catholic…I'm the minority now. I'm the new nigger.

Klein: What are you talking about?

Di Palma: The whole world's been handed over to the blacks, the Mexicans, the chinks...everybody's got programs to protect 'em, groups to help 'em, everybody except me. Makes me fuckin' sick. If anybody else was bein' treated like this, they'd be raisin' hell, screaming for attention, cryin' "Where's mine? Huh? Where the fuck is *mine?*" You don't hear us cryin' though, do you? Hell, no. 'Cos I still got some pride in myself. I got a problem, so you know what I'm gonna do? I'm gonna fix it.

Klein: Mr. Di Palma, I can't help you.

Di Palma: Then fuck you. Who needs your help? Huh? I'm giving you a chance here, and all you can think to do is back down and lie. You might be able to live like that, but not me. I'm sick of bein' railroaded, pushed around by special interest groups.

Klein: At least make an effort. Use the words they want you to. An effort like that, it could sway the jury.

Di Palma: Why should I worry about swaying a jury? All I have to do is tell the truth.

Klein: You wish. This trial has already begun, months before you set foot in a courtroom. You are being tried by every single person who reads, watches, or hears anything about this case. You've heard some of the names people have for you. "Killer." "Hate Cop." You are being tried by the new American justice system. You know who the Supreme Court is today? Tom Brokaw, Peter Jennings, Dan Rather, and Connie Chung. The news is reality, whether it is or not.

Di Palma: What's that supposed to mean to me?

Klein: It means what it means. People accept what they see and read as fact. If it's in the newspaper or on TV, it *must* be true, and that's enough. If you want to win this case, you need to make people believe in you. You have to project the image you want them to see. If you sound like you're sorry...

Di Palma: No.

Klein:...then maybe people will listen to what you have to say.

Di Palma: They can listen if they want to. I'm here. I'm talking. Doesn't matter what words I use, they're gonna be wrong to someone. Besides, fuckin' niggers can't make up their mind what they want to be called. Today they're African-American, couple years ago, they were black...It's all the same goddamn thing. Whiny fuckin' loudmouths callin' themselves "leaders of the black community." Black community…what a joke. There *are* no leaders. They're just goin' around in circles, screamin' about how everyone else is the reason their lives are no fuckin' good…like it's *my* fault. (*Pause.*) They should take a lesson from you Jews. You guys been through some serious shit, and you're still here. Nazis couldn't kill you. The Egyptians didn't get you. You're fuckin' indestructible. You guys went out, you did what you had to do. I admire that. Niggers, though, they always point the finger at someone else, like it's an organized thing. They set themselves up for failure, and they say it's our fault. Bullshit, I say. Don't point your finger at me. Point it right back at your fuckin' self, 'cos that's where the problem is.

KLEIN: I can't believe what's coming out of your mouth.

DI PALMA: You've had these thoughts.

KLEIN: No…

DI PALMA: You may have dressed them up in your post-sixties liberal white guilt, but you've had them.

KLEIN: These people have every right to be heard. They just want what's fair.

DI PALMA: They've got it. All they have to do is take it. Get a fuckin' education, then get a fuckin' job. Be a productive member of society, I'll be glad to treat you like a neighbor. Then, it's fair.

KLEIN: Those things aren't available to everyone. You can't blame someone's environment on them. They didn't make their world…but they do have to live in it. You say I can't judge you? Fine. You can't judge them until you've lived like them.

DI PALMA: Shows what you fuckin' know. You don't have any idea what I've seen or what I've been through. I don't have to explain myself to anyone. You liberals love to hoot and holler about the First Amendment and how we have to protect it as long as it's convenient for you. The minute you hear something you disagree with, it's a different story. If I wanna call some kid a nigger, that's my fuckin' business, as long as it don't get in the way of the job. You can't say shit to me about the words I use. This is *America*…and I'm protected…just like they are, just like you are. It's all about freedom of speech. Anything goes. All except me. You don't like what I'm saying? So, fuck you. Fuck everyone. This is who I am, and I *will not* apologize to anyone for that.

KLEIN: Do you even care about winning?

DI PALMA: Of course. I plan on it.

KLEIN: I don't see how. The way you're talking to me, you don't stand a chance in court.

DI PALMA: You said you can do it.

KLEIN: What?

DI PALMA: Win.

KLEIN: You won't listen to me.

DI PALMA: I'll listen.

KLEIN: I know where you should start.

DI PALMA: Where?

KLEIN: Image.

DI PALMA: What about it?

KLEIN: Change it.

DI PALMA: You want me to do what? Pretend to be someone I'm not?

KLEIN: Yes. I do. I want you to be aware of how people react to you. Use the media instead of letting it hurt you. Get the papers on your side. Use TV to argue your case. You say you acted in self-defense. Convince me. Convince us all. You were heard using certain words, inflammatory words. The prosecution is going to use that against you. They're going to claim that the only reason that boy drew his gun was fear. He sees you chasing him, he hears you call out, "I'll kill you, nigger!" What's he supposed to think? He's going to run, whether he's guilty or not. This is Los Angeles, post Rodney King, post riots. This kid has grown up scared, worried every day that the color of his skin is going to get him killed. They're going to say that you made him draw that gun, and then you shot him because you wanted to. That's what you wanted all along. You hated him...because he was black.

DI PALMA: That's not true!

KLEIN: Prove it. All you've talked about since you came in here is "nigger this" and "nigger that." You've proved to me that you could have done this for the wrong reason. You seem like a racist to me.

DI PALMA: Do you know what that kid did?

KLEIN: You're a racist, so it doesn't matter.

DI PALMA: Of course it does. It all matters. Every detail. That kid was a sack of shit...

KLEIN: So you say. His mother says he was a saint. The media is on her side, so you shot a saint.

DI PALMA: Who cares?

KLEIN: *Everybody.* You're not listening to me. The media is public opinion. They shape it, they feed it, and then they reflect it. You should care, you stupid racist asshole.

DI PALMA: You call me a racist one more time, and I'm gonna hand you your fuckin' lungs.

KLEIN: Does that name bother you?

DI PALMA: What do you think?

KLEIN: It's just a name...*racist.*

DI PALMA: You fuckin'...

KLEIN: Look at you. One name and it gets personal.

DI PALMA: Shut the fuck up.

KLEIN: I could call you a wop. Or a dago.

DI PALMA: Shut your mouth.

KLEIN: I could talk about your mother, call her a whore.

(*Di Palma lunges for Klein.*)

DI PALMA: Little hymie fuck...I'll kill you.

(*Di Palma grabs Klein by his shirt front, pulls him close. They look each other in the eye, the moment thick with implied violence. Di Palma is on the verge of losing control.*)

KLEIN: (*Quiet.*) It's just words. Freedom of speech, right? Isn't that what you said?

(*Absolutely livid, Di Palma shoves Klein away, releasing him.*)

DI PALMA: You makin' a point here?

KLEIN: Sticks and stones may break your bones...but words do permanent damage.

DI PALMA: Am I supposed to see the light now? What do you think this is? PERRY fuckin' MASON? I'm not gonna have a change of heart and suddenly confess all my sins. I'm right, and that sets me free, man.

KLEIN: You'll get one hell of a fight.

DI PALMA: I can take it.

KLEIN: I don't doubt that. I have the feeling you might be looking forward to this in some perverse way. You want to argue this. You want your chance to talk.

DI PALMA: Goddamn right I do.

KLEIN: You can't win. Not your way.

DI PALMA: The fuck I can't.

KLEIN: You won't be allowed. You stepped over the line, and you're not sorry.

DI PALMA: I can't believe what a coward you are. You're so scared...most lawyers would see this as a challenge...somethin' to fuckin' fight for.

KLEIN: Most would. I have to sleep at night.

DI PALMA: You sound like you're afraid of trying.

KLEIN: I'm not afraid. I know my business, and I can see that you have a hard road ahead of you. It doesn't have to be this hard. I can make it easier on you, but I *won't* go your route with you.

DI PALMA: How? How can I make this easier?

KLEIN: You start by saying you're sorry.

DI PALMA: There's got to be another way...

KLEIN: I'm sorry. *I'm sorry.* Just like that.

DI PALMA: I'm...I can't. I can't say that. I'd feel like a liar if I said that. I'm glad I shot him. He deserved it. How am I supposed to hide the fact that it fuckin' delights me that he's dead?

KLEIN: You think about what's going to happen to you if this trial doesn't go your way. You think about the possibility of doing jail time. Hard time, in a federal pen, with some of the men you arrested...men who will come looking for you.

DI PALMA: You tryin' to scare me, Klein?

KLEIN: Yes.

DI PALMA: Good luck. You'd have to come up with somethin' truly disturbed to have any effect on me. I am...*saddened* by the shit I've seen. It makes me think we ain't got much of a future. The kid I shot...he was fourteen years old. He was just a baby. Man, when I was fourteen...

KLEIN: You grew up in a different world.

DI PALMA: Did I? Was it the world that changed? Or was it the kids? That kid was a regular full-time fuckin' gangster...no respect for nobody. That kid...all the other kids like him...*that's* the future. You wonder why I hate? Haven't I earned it? It's the only thing that keeps me goin' back out there and cleanin' up that fuckin' toilet every day. I hate what's going on, and I'll keep right on hating it till it changes.

KLEIN: *You*...you have to change.

DI PALMA: There's gotta be a way...

KLEIN: What? You give me an option, something that has even a prayer of working, and I'll do it. You have to give me something, though ...some reason to try.

DI PALMA: *I'm right.* You show them what that kid was really like. You said his momma's runnin' around talkin' about what a perfect little angel her baby was? You gotta show everyone how wrong she is. You think the papers or the TV really care who's right or wrong?

KLEIN: No. All they care about is drama.

DI PALMA: They gotta have a bad guy, and right now, that's me. You can give 'em a real bad guy. Tell everyone the truth about the kid. You tell them what he did…you tell them why I was chasing him.

KLEIN: You tell me.

DI PALMA: News been skipping that little detail, haven't they?

KLEIN: What did he do?

DI PALMA: Random act of violence, spur of the moment. He did it without thinking, the way he did everything…He robbed an old woman…Italian lady, about seventy-years-old. Rolled up on her while she was pullin' money out of an ATM. She probably never saw him comin'…He pushes her down from behind. She probably breaks something when she hits the pavement, so she's no threat. All this is goin' on right out in the open…but nobody cares. The kid takes the money from her. All he has to do is take off, the money's his. He can't do that, though. No…he has to hurt her. He has to *mark* her, just to prove that the whole thing was real. Otherwise, it could just be something he remembered from TV. So…he sticks a knife into her face and pulls it down, along the line of her nose, then over through one of her eyes. *Now* a few people are looking, startin' to pay attention, and this old woman is *screaming*, crying for help. He…steps on her until she stops making noise…then walks away, like nothing ever happened. That's how I saw him. He was strolling, like he had nowhere to go, not a worry in the world. He's got this old woman's blood all over his shoes, and he's leavin' these marks everywhere he steps…

KLEIN: Jesus Christ…

DI PALMA: He felt good. You could see it on him, like he'd just gotten laid. He hurt her because it made him feel alive. You tell that to the jury. She never even made it to the hospital…and I'm the animal? I'm the bad guy?

KLEIN: Tell me the truth…why did you shoot that boy?

DI PALMA: Because I had to.

KLEIN: But you said he was just *strolling* when you first saw him.

DI PALMA: That's right. I'm in my car, on break, and I see this kid walkin' towards me on the sidewalk. I'm lookin' at these marks he's leavin', thinking, "What's all over this kid's shoes?" when two things happen at the same time. One, my radio goes off, and it's the officer calling from the scene of the stabbing. She's got an ID already from some of the witnesses...and it's the kid, the one standing ten feet away from me. Okay, I go for my door. At the same time all this is goin' on, the kid makes me, sees me see him. Before I can even get my door open, he's gone. And this kid is like the fuckin' wind. One, two, I'm outa the car, I'm after him, and I've still got a visual on him. He's way out in front of me, like I said, and his feet aren't even touching the pavement he's moving so fast. I know there's no way I'm gonna catch him. This kid's movin' like Jesse Owens, I can't even catch my breath.

KLEIN: Did you tell him to stop?

DI PALMA: Are you fuckin' kidding me? All I'm doin' the whole time I'm chasin' him is screamin' at him to stop.

KLEIN: *What* did you scream at him? Exactly?

DI PALMA: "Police Officer! Freeze!"

KLEIN: That's it?

DI PALMA: I don't know! I called him a piece of shit, told him I'd shoot his dick off...I said a lot of things. What was I supposed to do?! He was *getting away* there was nothing I could do.

KLEIN: If he was that far ahead of you, how did you catch up to him?

DI PALMA: Stupid fucker made a mistake. He made a dodge down a blind alley, and before he could get out, I caught up to him and blocked his way.

KLEIN: Is that when you drew your gun?

DI PALMA: Goddamn straight it is. That kid turned around, there was a look in his eyes...I've seen it before. I was nothin' but a fuckin' obstacle in his way. He wasn't gonna waste his time talkin' to me.

KLEIN: What did you say?

DI PALMA: You don't know what it's like. Everything slows down. Every noise fades out. All you can hear is your own breathing. The kid turns around, and the look on his face, it's like somethin' outa some horror movie. Cold, man. Ice fuckin' cold. I don't even remember pulling my gun out...it's just in my hand, pointed at that kid's heart. "Freeze, you fuckin' nigger! I'll blow you away!" He...smiles. Like he ain't scared of me at all...like he don't even see the gun. He takes a step back...plants himself, like he's getting ready for a duel. My hands are slick with sweat…I can barely keep 'em still. "Don't fuck with me, kid. Don't do it." He's movin' his hands, reachin' behind him, and I'm screamin' "Put your hands on your head, nigger! I'll shoot you if you don't!" He keeps reachin', and reachin', and I think to myself, *fine…*this is what you want, then it's what I want too. *Give me a reason.* One little bit of the problem down, and all I have to do is pull the trigger. I squeeze off three shots, and the kid drops without a sound. He's layin' on the ground, and time comes crashin' back all around me. I hear the sound of sirens getting closer. I hear people yellin'. I can smell gunpowder burning my nose, feel it burning my eyes. I bend down to look at the kid's face…all that menace, all that cold pourin' offa him…there's nothin' there now. He's gone. (*Slowly, Sal comes back to the present, seems to snap out of it. He looks over at Klein, angry tears in his eyes.*) You tell me, Klein…if you were in that alley, just you and that kid, what would you have done? Would you let him shoot you? Everybody wants to judge me. Here's your chance. You tell me…him or you? What would you do? Don't just sit there starin' at me! TELL ME! WHAT THE FUCK WOULD YOU HAVE DONE?! WOULD YOU HAVE SHOT HIM?! YOU OR HIM?! YOU TELL ME!

(*Klein's phone rings. Once. Twice. For a moment, neither man seems sure how to react. Finally, it is Klein who gathers himself.*)

KLEIN: Excuse me…(*Answers it.*) Yes. Maureen…no. That won't be necessary. (*Klein hangs up, slowly turns back to Di Palma, who seems spent by his efforts.*) No offense, Mr. Di Palma…but I think you're garbage wrapped in skin. I listen to you…hear hate. The real thing. Not casual, inherited hate, but actual active loathing. That kid you shot…he's not the only one who's lost all respect for others. What are you supposed to stand for? Law and order?

DI PALMA: I did what I had to do. If you can't understand…

KLEIN: I understand perfectly. More than you do, probably. I pity you, Mr. Di Palma.

DI PALMA: Yeah? When did you have your big moral crisis?

KLEIN: It's an overall feeling.

DI PALMA: Fuckin' waste of time…

KLEIN: I'm sorry about that.

DI PALMA: Fuck you. I was straight with you.

KLEIN: And I'm trying to be the same with you.

DI PALMA: Shut the fuck up. I don't care what you think. I don't care what anyone thinks. I *know*...(*Quiet.*) I know who's right here. (*Di Palma turns his back on Klein, goes for the door.*) Fuckin' mistake to think a Jew'd understand, anyway...

KLEIN: I would have shot him. (*That stops Di Palma.*) That's right. I would have shot him. But I didn't...*you did.* (*Pause.*) My reasons, they'd have been different from yours. I would have tried to reach out to him first...help him, see if there was anything left to save. All you want is to get rid of them...all of them. That's what makes you different than me. That's what makes you wrong. You want me to represent you, Mr. Di Palma? (*Pause.*) Be here Monday morning at nine o'clock.

DI PALMA: What?

KLEIN: Like you said...it's a constitutional question with me on the side of right. How can I not get involved?

DI PALMA: But all that stuff you just said...

KLEIN: It won't be the first time I've defended filth...won't be the last, either.

DI PALMA: How can I thank you?

KLEIN: Don't bother. Pay me. That's enough.

DI PALMA: Monday mornin'...

KLEIN: Nine o'clock.

(*Di Palma nods, and with that, he is gone. Klein stands, goes to his window, looks out at Los Angeles for a long moment as he gathers himself. Finally, he walks back over to his desk, pushes a button on his phone.*)

KLEIN: Maureen? Cancel my afternoon...I think I need to take a walk.

(*Lights Down.*)

END OF PLAY

Jackie
by David Rasche

BIOGRAPHY

DAVID RASCHE. As a playwright: *A Meeting, Jackie, Scriptman, Moo, Friendly Greeting,* and *To Market, To Market.*

As a songwriter: "It Was Your Fault", "I Wish I Was Married to Your Wife", "Let's Play Doctor", "I'm a Mile High and I'm Not Even in Denver".

As a stage actor on Broadway: *Speed the Plow, Loose Ends,* and *The Shadow Box.*

As an actor off-Broadway: *Noone Will Be Immune* (Mamet), *Geniuses* (Reynolds), *A Sermon* (Mamet), and *Chicago: The Second City, Sexual Perversity in Chicago* (Mamet),

TV: *Sledge Hammer!, Barbarians at the Gate,* and *Nurses.*

Film: *An Innocent Man, Delirious, Manhattan, Bingo,* and *Best Defense.*

ORIGINAL PRODUCTION

Jackie was originally produced in New Your by the Ensemble Studio Theater, May 1993. It was directed by Peter Maloney with Cecelia DeWolf as Jackie and Ted Neustadt as Daniel.

It was subsequently produced in Los Angeles in the Act One Festival 1994 at the Met Theater. It was directed by David Rasche with Diana Bellamy as Jackie and Daniel Beer as Daniel.

JACKIE

Scene; A Los Angeles agent's office. In the center of the stage, facing the audience, sits Jackie at her desk. She is about 50 years old and, although not obese, seriously overweight. Hefty. A large woman. She wears a smart yellow suit with a collarless coat and an off-white blouse which also has no collar. Her jewelry is large enough to suit her size, but it is tasteful and dignified. Jackie is a chain-smoker and she is almost constantly either smoking a cigarette or holding a lit one. The room is decorated "Southwest" as L.A. understands it; that is, no sun-bleached skull or overtly sexual Georgia Okeefe prints, but Indian style throw rugs, a couch made of natural skinned pine logs, and everything in pinks and earth tones. At her feet, under the desk, are two piles of 8x10 glossy headshots. To the right of her desk is another chair, facing the audience, which is occupied by whomever is in to see her.

Jackie's thoughts turn on a dime, and often she is into the next idea before completing the one she is on, so she will leave it in an instant and not finish a sentence or phrase or idea. She has an engine which is at full throttle most of the time, which is not to say loud or inappropriately intense, but she has a great enthusiasm and zest for life, an energy big as Texas. Everything she says is important, often just because she says it. She is demonstrative, yet dignified. Jackie has no self-pity and at the end of the play, her struggle is one that makes her sad, even desperate, but it is a struggle she will not give up on and one she intends to win. She is basically telling the truth throughout this

piece, but she performs the truth. Her life and family are her clients.
She makes each actor she sees feel special and important.

Jackie's energy drives this piece and she never really hesitates,
because there is so much to say and everything is so terribly interesting.
There are almost no pauses throughout the piece. Daniel has almost no
opportunity to respond.

Daniel Rogers stands at an open door. He is a New York actor
unschooled in the ways of L.A., and he wears an inappropriate tweed
jacket, chinos, and a nice crew neck T-shirt or cotton crew neck seater.
He is a nice person, educated, and polite. He would be cast as the
young father or the lawyer or professor, but he can also play heavies. He
is good-looking, but not offensively so. He listens intently and enjoys
Jackie; he laughs at her jokes and is interested in her advice. He is
helpful and caring. He reacts throughout and tries to speak, but there is
seldom time to fit a word in.

As the lights go up Jackie is seated at her desk, working. Daniel stands
in the open door, waits a moment, hoping to get Jackie's attention, then
knocks gently.

DANIEL: Jackie? (*Jackie looks up, sees Daniel and, thrilled, rises.*)
JACKIE: Daniel Rogers, Daniel Rogers, Daniel Rogers, you, my friend,
you are…this man is…now I'm not going to say you're the greatest
actor in the world because that would be a lie. Greatest actor in the
world is Richard Burton, but you…darling, give me a hug and sit,
sit, sit.
(*She goes to him, gives him a hug, and takes him to his chair. He sits,*
she remains standing behind her desk.)
    How are…You were stunning. That is the truth. (*She calls off*
to her secretary in the anteroom.) Jeannie, didn't I say that? (*Back to*
Daniel.) We were both stunned, you are soooo gooood, *so* good
and you're cute and things, darlin', and you don't even know it, do
you? You don't even know how good you are, you don't know the
kind of future you have, God o God. Now, are you happy? Cause
you should be, if anybody has a reason it's you. Now are you
settled? I want your schedule.
(*She calls offstage to her secretary, Jeannie. She doesn't necessarily look*

to the door when she calls. It's automatic, and she keeps looking admiringly at Daniel as she calls.)

Jeannie, get his schedule, (*Back to Daniel.*) because I want to know where you are every single minute of every day, you darlin' sweetheart. Jackie is your guardian angel and by good God almighty I'm gonna guard you within an inch and ain' nobody else gettin' near you so just turn your thoughts to the straight and narrow, all right?

(*Daniel moves as if to speak to explain, but Jackie needs no answer and continues.*)

It's all right, jus long as you know, Jackie ain ever gon let you go. Jackie's gon' *be there,* Jackie's gon' *be* there and that's settled. (*She picks up a pack of cigarettes and takes one and prepares to light it.*) Now I have been talking about you and if your ears weren't ringing then there's something wrong because I have been singing your praises both high *and* low and (*she casually offers Daniel a cigarette.*) do you want a cigarette or have you...(*Before he can respond, Jackie knows the answer and calls.*) Jeannie, Daniel Rogers has quit smoking. You have, haven't you. (*Daniel nods affirmative.*) Well you are a darling, you have and I haven't, you're good and I'm bad. Well we already knew that. (*The most important thing in the world occurs to her.*) O God! I didn't even...Daniel, when your mind goes you just have to suffer with it. Daniel darling dear honey sweetie, have I got...I mean have I got for you, if this works, now I'm not saying it's going to work because I'm not a mind reader, but sweetheart, you've heard of James Brooks, you know, the biggest television producer in the history of humanity? (*Daniel nods, yes.*) Anyway that same James Brooks, and you are perfect for this, there is the...(*To Jeannie.*) Jeannie get me that thing for this wonderful actor Daniel Rogers. (*To Daniel.*) God is smilin', sweetheart, smilin' on you because you are *perfect,* just *perfect* for this, and I'm going to have Jeannie write all this down so you won't have to think of anything but this meeting and he is goin to *love* you, not like, if I'da meant like I'da said like but I didn't mean it so I didn't say it, I mean *love,* he is going to love you with all his heart soul and mind. Now your father is a minister, isn't that right, darlin? I remember, I remember, Jackie *will* remember if she needs to, and this is the part of a minister. It's got your name written all over it, it's going to fit you like a glove and go out and buy yourself a car because you are just about to make yourself a lot, and I mean a lot of money. Cold cash darlin, and I'm thrilled, I really am because you are...I mean you have...forget the past, forget the other suitors, you know what I mean, cuz darlin', Jackie hears. I hear and I see and I weep, but Jackie's been blest with...I'm a Taurus and we're determined. (*To Jeannie.*) Jeannie don't you want to marry him? Just marry him and take him, run him off? Well you can't because he's already married and besides I'm first in line. (*To Daniel.*) See it's not so bad here. I know, you you're a New Yorker, got to ride that subway, but it i'n bad, it i'n bad once you're here, and darlin, it i'n Texas either, I'd be the first to say, but you gotta go where the work is, right?

Now I won't be in next week because I am takin' a little trip with myself to a secret place I won't even tell *them* where it is because I don't want any phone calls and that secret place is Mexico. I'm treating myself, I deserve it and by God I'm going to take it while I can, but I am going to be thinkin' and prayin' for you, although really it's a prayer wasted because you're not going to need it, this match was made in heaven anyway. (*Coughs.*) Pardon me (*Coughs.*) pardon, pardon, thousand pardons (*Coughs.*) I'm coughin', can you tell? (*Coughs for a while and then recovers.*)

Now, you met John Schlessinger and I know, he is a nasty man, a nasty nasty man, but it's the way the world is darlin', we just have to move on and not let it get to us. Keep movin' and nothin' can bite you, it can nip at you but it can't get a good hold, if you know what I mean, can't do any real damage. Bonnie said she didn't think it was going to work out (*Daniel registers some disappointment.*) and I *know* you wanted that one, didn'tcha.

DANIEL: Well ...

JACKIE: I know, I could see your face on the phone you wanted it, but you know the truth, you know the god's honest truth? I was all the time hopin' you wouldn't get it 'cause I knew somethin better was goin' to come along and it did, din' it ...

DANIEL: We'll see ...

JACKIE: And if that would have happened we'da both been kicken' each other around two blocks fer bein s'damn stupid. Have you been to Mexico? This is goin to be new fer me. I mean when yer in Texas sometimes you may as well *be* in Mexico, s'many of them there, but I have never just stopped and said, now, I'm takin myself to

Mexico, and I don' care if the *Pope* says no, and I'm *not* goin ta drink the water, *just* gonna drink vodka, that's already been figured so I won't be bringing back any little parasite friends who might like this country so much they'll want to stay.

So darlin, now, you've got a car, well of course you got a car how you going to get around in LaLa land without a car, I'm jes bein' Jackie bein' concerned, thas all.

Now you know how I saw that show last night, I had another…see…another client was yer competition and so I was jes gonna have to do that channel switching thing all night and she told me not to miss the beginning, but, and if you tell her I will murder you in your bed on a cold and stormy night, I promise you, frankly it was pret'near the *dumbest* thing, and so I checked out you and I think I got there just after you killed the girl? and she was lying there? and the spooky music? Right? Isn't that what happened? See I wan't lyin', I watched it, and if it wouldna ended I'd *still* be watching the damn thing. I mean darlin' I got involved in a *big* way, and you were so evil, and oh I hated you, I *hated* you, I was thinkin' if you were in the room, then give me a knife, give me a blunt object, because hateful hateful. I don't know either for a nice man, I mean, I don't know who did what to you or who you met but Daniel Rogers you know things others of us don't and only find out because you tell us. I hope your chilren weren't watching that because, honey, you were so convincing, and that's a big compliment comin' from me because nothin scares me, honey. Jeannie do I ever …? (*Back to Daniel.*) I never scare. My daddy was huge and after that nothin can scare me could be the reason, but the hair on the back of my neck, but *literally,* and you were handsome, you have that handsome look and with that music and *you* believed it, didn't you, even *you* believed it, you could tell. And then, you little dickens, you had me feelin *sorry* fer ya. I'm sittin there sayin' "I hate this man," and I'm feelin *sorry* for him. He's done something very strange to me, and if you don't get a hundred thousand offers from that, then I've got some phone calls to make, because darlin' we handle everybody from Jack Nicholson on up to God himself and I go to these things and darlin' you—were – won-der-ful. How do you get so much of it when the rest of us didn't get any? And my mother, my *mother* called me up on the telephone, can you believe this? Can you believe that my mother is dialing her phone and calling me? Remember you met her at the awards? And so now I have to sit there and listen to her go on and on and I just said, "Mother, yer not tellin' me anything I don't already know."

All right now get out of here. It doesn't look like I'm going to shut up unless you just leave the room. Now don't hate us. I know we're those awful crude LA people but ya gotta love us cause we mean well and our hearts are in the right place. Now will you call? Will you call? You have to promise me you will call, now, not me 'cause I'm going to be drinking Margueritas, but call Jeannie and tell her *everything*, tell her the color of the *wallpaper*, and just do it, I'll call in…well you know how it will be, I'll get that guilt and it'll be about three days. I give myself about three days before I have a phone attack and I just give in, it happens every time so I've grown to expect it, and I just know it, I just say, "This is it, it's time," and I pick up the phone and it starts all over again, and I'm thinking why did I even bother with the airplane ticket and all, I never see anything, I just sit there by the pool and burn to a crisp and that *can't* be good, but you know how this business is, like an octopus and you jes feel strangled if you don't jes show em yer backside once in a while. 'Course if I had all that glorious talent like Mr. Daniel Rogers and made peoples' mothers call them up, and you didn't even want that, did you, you were all thinking, "O God, a bad guy," and I knew deep down and besides you can't know, you know, you can't know, you can *think* you know and there are things you *can know* but what will happen, it's always different for each individual thing and who knows, they may call you up five years from now or something and you have no idea, really the seeds you sow, and its what you make it anyway, i'n it, I think, and if I didn't think that I wouldn't be able to go on, darlin, not another day, not another step, 'cause that means yer workin fer them, du'n it, and yuh should be workin fer yerself, that's the only way to stay alive without jes existing. I mean come on, who is it for, who is it for in the end if it i'n for you, now thass jus common sense'll tell you that, but we start feelin' under and we get angry, we're always gettin angry, and then we're playin their game again, and they're changin' the rules all the time, so what's (*Coughs.*) what's the (*Coughs.*) what's the sense (*Coughs, coughs.*) and she's off (*Coughs.*) this'll take a minute (*She coughs for a while until it's over.*) There.

Well, you come from the theater, that's something money can't buy you and you look at God help'em those people who didn't work in the theater, and you can tell, you can just tell, there's something missin', darlin', no matter how fast they're out there a'dancin', it's as plain as the sun in the sky.

God I talk a lot, somebody stop me before I go all over myself. I'ss just my excitable nature and ain' nothin you or anybody else gon' do about it. I live with it just like my gone mind and my gone lungs if I keep this up, so sweetheart darlin' remember Jackie this weekend, I'll be takin' one major siesta by a pool filled with Mexican water probably jes full of little amoebas so I'm jes gon' keep my body out of that water and take no chances whatsoever as is my Jackie way. I'm jes a little girl, never fully grew up but what the hell can't have everything and who cares anyway, got this far, right? Damn right. Take it any way you can get it, even on the fly, darlin, even *on* the fly. Not you, yer married, you did the right thing, ya did it early, tha's yer good livin', tha's the way God intended it when he created it and tha's the way folks ought to leave it, God help'em they don't, but try to tell'em, now (*Cough.*) Pardon me, Pardon (*Coughs.*) o me o my, (*Coughs.*) this is a good one (*A rather worse cough.*) it'll pass (*a rather bad cough.*) That one came from my toes. (*She recovers.*)

Ok ok, I'm ok but do you remember the night I had to leave the theater because I was coughin' so much, I turned five shades of pale blue as I am sittin' in the front row, no, the front row, thank you very much is where they put me in their infinite wisdom and I, (*To Jeannie.*) Jeanne remember that? Were you with me? (*Back to Daniel.*) And here I was all set and not 5 minutes in I started to coughin' and carryin' on, like to have a fit and a half and I said to myself if I don't leave, no, and I mean right now, I'm goin' die right here in the front row of the Los Angeles Theater Center and they're going to have to carry me away in a damn box, because I was gone, darlin', totally and forever gone into the pit of darkness-coughin'-without ceasin' and, did you see me or hear me? I don' know how you could'a not, but I left then quietly as I could given the circumstances and then we got sa busy I never did get back which really killed me because I heard you were won-der-ful and Jeannie, does he have his appointment?

(*Back to Daniel.*) Have you ever met Jim Brooks? (*Daniel*

begins to respond in the negative.) No? Ok, so I'm cupid here, I'm cupid and I have the pleasure of shooting the dart, here I am I'm shooting the dart, (*She shoots a dart.*) Ping! (*To Jeannie.*)Jeanne the dart is shot, now I have to go Jim Brooks and shoot him a dart. (*Back to Daniel.*) You know iss good we're talkin' because how else do I know what you want to do, I can jabber on the phone to ya till *kingdom* come, but you can tell more from a person by looking square into their eyeballs and jes' try to convince my star client that they'll offer you gold, they'll offer you precious metals, but here's home for you! Do you want me to just (*Another coughing fit throughout next part.*) do you want me to say it (*Cough.*), excuse me, (*Cough, cough.*) I get to coughin' like this, (*Series of coughs.*) pardon me a thousand times, Kemosabe, but, (*Rather bad coughing and finish.*) Whew, did I get any on ya? My lungs are fightin' back darlin and there's no talkin to them they just won't listen after being mistreated for so many years, they're angry and they (*Cough.*)...excuse me, they don't (*Cough.*)...excuse me, they're not interested (*Cough.*)...oh this is a bad one, I had (*Cough.*)...hit my back would you, slap some sense into these lungs, those precious organs of life (*Cough.*)...(*He gets up and gently follows her instructions.*) just sit back and enjoy this because (*Cough.*) you don't have to (*Cough, and recovers. During the following she tries to pour a glass of water from the pitcher on her desk but it is empty.*) I'm fine darlin. I shoulda taken off earlier, but I have fierce loyalty, fierce, and I just couldn't (*Cough.*) get me some water over there, wouldya? (*He gets up, goes to the low table and pours a glass of water from a pitcher there and brings it to her.*) Thank you, thank you, you saved an agent's life. This is not going to look good on your record, you'll be drawn and quartered if this gets out, so we won't tell, will we, we'll jes' make it our little secret. Now we know something they don't, but doctors scare me, always have always will. (*Coughing fit is over.*) You are important to me, do you get that? God, I sound like Mr. Rogers here, but darlin' if reason will keep you I'll reason, if beggin will do it, I'll beg, cuz this California quicksand will swallow you up and I've quite frankly had some boats quite frankly ripped up their moorings here, so Jackie's just got to make sure all the sheep are in the flock. But you know I was so glad you came over for the awards, w'un that fun? Everybody had a ball and yer wife is such, such a sweetheart, I kin see why you snapped her up one two three and you look good together, you jest fit so well, and aren't my friends fun? Ya know, they're just people I've known since the beginning of creation and I can let my hair down and who cares what they think cause they known me fer sa long what's the difference, darlin, you know what I mean, let it all hang out and take a long, long look because I do not care, I really do not care at all, ask me and I'll tell ya so. And they loved you, yes, and they told me, they asked me about you and you jes fit in and those crazy awards, why do they even bother, it's so mad.

Not like the theater, darlin', is it...not like the theater. There it's yours, you're up there and you just say I'll take my good old sweet time 'cause who's gonn throw me off, right? 'Course there is nothing, no thing, not one thing as horrible, as tortured as sitting there and the lights go down and it starts and in about two seconds you *know*, you jes *know*, this is unbearable and it in' gon' end for two hours. No way you kin leave because one of your babies is up there in the mess, so just sit back and suffer, cause suffer yer gonna, dun' this happen? *God,* that's jes theater *hell.* Can't leave, cannot go, excruciating, endless, minutes turn into eternities, you look at yer damn watch and you think, "Only five minutes went by? Only five??? O God send immediate relief to the faithful, its awful, terrible, hideous, painful and laws should be passed by elected officials. I mean hang me, nail me to a tree, but don' make me watch a bad play, badly acted, badly badly badly everything, mercy mercy. Now you got yer time, you got the...Jeanne did you give him his li'l sheet? Got to have the li'l sheet so the actor dun' have to think about anything but his art and dun' get lost and end up in Needles, right? And you read that James Brooks thing and did she give you a copy? Jeannie he needs a copy, sweetheart, (*Back to Daniel.*) and now that you quit smoking you can be in it longer, (*To Jeannie.*) Jeannie make a note of that, lets make the contract a lifetime contract and we'll all get rich, he's gon' live to be a hundred and he's gon' do it in a James Brooks show, arn'cha. (*To Daniel.*) God it makes me feel good inside. This man makes me feel good. Ye'r healthy, married, three kids God blessem, soon to be a resident of California...you wait, you wait, I'll give you...it took me a year, no two years, really, truthfully, before I could actually get out of bed in the morning and say, "I live here." Know what I mean, and if you can do that the battle is won, and you'll meet people and school for the kids, everybody's here anyway, one by one, if the damn state doesn't sink lower in the water just from the weight of the sheer numbers of actors alone, not to mention every other damn person and his uncle and aunt and dog, and they say iss gon' get worse, oops, stupid Jackie from Texas, stupid, don't tell him iss gon' get worse, well it won't be worse where you live. Where do you think you'll want to live, cause darlin with the money you'll be makin you can live anywhere, believe me, now not up on the hill next to Spielberg, or Witt Thomas, not yet but soon, not yet but soon, lookin' down at us peons scratching in the dirt, you'll be gettin your award, and (*Another, worse coughing fit.*) this is a bad one, (*She has a fit of coughing which makes her hold onto the front of the desk and go down on one knee. Daniel goes to her to try to help. She motions to him.*) Close that door darlin'. (*He does and returns.*)

DANIEL: Jackie, are you …?

JACKIE: Jes hold my hand (*Daniel does. Jackie coughs.*) God help me, I lied to Disney and this is a judgment (*Terrible cough.*) This is all I need. Just get me to my chair. (*Daniel helps her to her chair behind the desk, and as he does, she says.*) You are a darlin'. (*She sits.*) Just my Jackie luck to get the son of a minister. You have a direct line, right, an 800 number to God? (*She coughs violently and spits into her tissue. She looks at it and does not like what she sees.*) Goddamit. Godamit.

DANIEL: Jackie, you gotta…

JACKIE: (*Quickly, and with great determination.*) Daniel, now listen to me. I am dealing with this. I've dealt with it and…I'm dealing with it. I should have dealt with it earlier, but I'm stupid, I'm stubborn as a damn mule and, frankly, I'm scared to hear what they have to tell me. I know, I'm dumbness. I put it off for too long, but I just was prayin' and ignorin', prayin' I was in the other fifty per cent. But…(*She smiles as she stifles tears.*) I'm upset can you tell? Now don't you ever, ever tell on me, promise me that, they'll bounce me faster than a bad check. And then my mother…(*She cries but stops herself.*) I been tryin' to put this off as long as I could, but it's catchin' up with me. Do me a favor, take these God awful things (*She stuffs a package of cigarettes into Daniel's hand.*) and tear 'em up. Go ahead, do it now. But leave me one just in case. (*She takes one cigarette and puts it on the desk. Daniel crushes the pack and throws them into the waste basket.*) Oh yer sweet, such a sweet man. If you'da met me a hundred years ago, would you have married me? Don't answer that. I'm going to assume. Aren't you glad you came just now? got to see this? I'm better. I am definitely better. Well, they say it's worse than heroin and I am the exception that proves the rule, it's filth, it stinks and here I am puffin' puffin', thinkin not me, everybody else but not me, you know how you do. Well, you smoked, you're one of us arncha, used to be. God I wish I could throw them all in the toilet and flush 'em once and for all, but you can hypnotize me, you can threaten me with a gun, I've got to have my cigarette and that's all. Now you better run along. Go on. I'll be all right. Did you get validated?

DANIEL: Oh, right…(*He searches his clothes for his ticket.*)

JACKIE: O darlin' don't forget that, they'll have you pay 16 dollars, *16 dollars,* to park yer car and you pay. Some of the biggest stars in Hollywood, and they didn't get validated and they paid, and he's Mexican down there and I guess they just told him, "That's it," so don't play with fire, do that on your way out (*Daniel goes to the door. Jackie stands.*) And Daniel…we have a relationship, darlin'. They'll offer you gold and precious metals of every hue, but yer lookin' at the one who sat here…who sat here and made the days turn into dollars for you. I can't force you and I can't marry you, but if you turn your back on me, if you forsake me for another…(*Daniel moves as if to protest.*) Don't have to respond…I don't know a thing…let me pretend…I'm jes gonna pretend it's like it always was. But just let me look at you one more time, I want to remember this, this is the before, this is the before picture, before he made a ton of money and got more famous than God. Run along. (*Daniel exits, as Jackie goes back to her work.*) Jeannie, would you come in here?

END OF PLAY

Iron Tommy
by James Ryan

*I would like to thank William Carden
who directed every production with inspiration and great skill,
and kept this wild bunch of men and woman
lovingly under control at all times.*

BIOGRAPHY

JAMES RYAN is a playwright and screenwriter. His plays include: *Dennis, Portrait of My Bikini, Arab Bride, Not Showing, South Pacific Snow, Door to Cuba, In Cahoots, Mink on a Gold Hook,* and *Iron Tommy,* among others. His work has been produced at Ensemble Studio Theatre, Los Angeles Theatre Center, The Playwright's Center in Minneapolis, Stage Three, Act One in Los Angeles, and the Berkeley Stage Company, among others. He is the recipient of Fellowships from the National Endowment for the Arts, New York Foundation for the Arts, McKnight Foundation and the Drama League Award. He has been commissioned by South Coast Repertory Company, Actors Theatre of Louisville, and the National Endowment for the Humanities.

He has adapted his play, *Arab Bride,* to the screen for Hollywood Pictures. His original screenplay, *Lucy,* has been purchased by Spring Creek Productions/Warner Bros. For television he has written for *The Days and Nights of Molly Dodd.*

As an actor he has appeared in over thirty productions Off and Off, Off, Broadway and in the films *Falling in Love, Five Corners,* and *Joe Vs. the Volcano.*

He has taught playwriting and screenwriting at Muhlenberg College, Playwrights Horizons Theatre Institute and The Playwright's Center in Minneapolis; he serves as a Teaching Artist at the Lincoln Center Theatre Institute; he has been Guest Artist at Columbia University, Graduate School of the Arts and Hunter College. He served as Executive Director and Artistic Director of Stage Three, a company dedicated to the production of New American Plays. He frequently moderates the Playwrights Unit at the HB Playwrights Foundation.

AUTHOR'S NOTE

An Author Shares his Secret...

This is how I came to write *Iron Tommy.*

My marriage ended and I cracked up. I seized the creative opportunity and went to therapy, studied Raja Yoga, played tennis four hours a day, travelled many Paths in Search. While on my Journey, I signed up for a "Men's Workshop" at the Open Center, a very nice alternative educational center in Soho, Manhattan.

I laughed, often, during the meetings. We had to meet six times; I made only three. When middle-aged men bang drums, read fairy tales and locate spots on their body where they hold an emotion, it just *is* very funny. It exemplifies how confused we all are about what it means to be a man or woman. One foot in the 50s, another in the 90s, shouldering centuries of claptrap about the supposed true nature of gender, our struggle to liberate and free ourselves becomes, many times, a wacky carnivalesque.

I really did write *Iron Tommy* in one night. I laughed until I had tears. Men crying is very funny for obvious and not so obvious reasons.

There is no sneer to my laughter, I hope. I love these men (and woman) for their courage and curiosity. They each have a very worthy ambition—a need to make oneself a better person.

We're all such fools, aren't we? It's wonderful, isn't it?

ORIGINAL PRODUCTION

Iron Tommy was developed with the help of many actors, producers and designers. The following is a list of its productions to date.

It received a staged reading in the Octoberfest, Ensemble Studio Theatre, Curt Dempster, Artistic Director, Kevin Confoy, Producer, in October, 1992. It was directed by William Carden.

Anthony	Jude Ciccolella
Barnett	John Gould Rubin
Edwin	Donald Berman
Rosco	Jay Patterson
Woody	Michael Mantel
Tommy	Paul Geier
Irene	Kayla Black

The first production of *Iron Tommy* was at the Westbank Cafe, New York, November 1992, Rand Forrester, Producer. It was directed by William Carden. The cast was as follows:

Anthony	Jude Ciccolella
Barnett	John Gould Rubin
Edwin	Donald Berman
Rosco	Jay Patterson
Woody	Michael Countryman
Tommy	Paul Geier
Irene	Kayla Black

The production returned to the Westbank in January of 1993. Everything was the same except for the role of Rosco. It was played by W.T. Martin.

The play was selected for the Marathon at Ensemble Studio Theatre and opened in May, 1993, directed by William Carden; Artistic Director, Curt Dempster, Producer, Kevin Confoy. The set was designed by Pete Foster, lights by Greg MacPherson, costumes by Julie Doyle, and sound by Jeffrey Taylor. The stage manager was Bethany Ford; assistant director was Lesile Windram. The cast was:

Anthony	Jude Ciccolella
Barnett	John Gould Rubin
Edwin	Donald Berman
Rosco	W.T. Martin
Woody	Michael Countryman
Tommy	Paul Geier
Irene	Ming Na Wen

It was staged in Los Angeles by Act One at the Met Theatre in May, 1994, and was directed by William Carden. Produced by Risa Bramon Garcia and Jerry Levine; the set was designed by Yael Pardess; lighting by Ken Booth; costume by Taylor Kincaid Cheek; sound by Peter Stenshoel; Charles Dayton and Thomas Connor; Kate Baggot and Michael E. Cerenzie were Associate Producers, and casting was by Mary Vernieu. The cast was as follows:

Anthony	Bruce McGill
Tommy	Vyto Ruginis
Barnett	Tim Choate
Irene	Charmaine Craig
Rosco	Jay Patterson
Woody	Richard Schiff
Edwin	Peter Van Norden

IRON TOMMY

A gathering of men sit on pillows in a softly lit room with art of various kinds on the wall: African, Zen, Islamic, etc.
Rosco, 30 to 40, a handsome actor, sits on a chair in the center and beats a large, standing drum. Softly. Fiercely. Softly. Alongside Rosco is Anthony, 30 to 40, a bear with fiery red hair and fists like fat tomatoes. He reads preciously from a book of Fairy Tales. The gathering listens intensely.

ANTHONY: The king looked at the cowlick. It had been prophesized that this boy would marry the King's daughter because of this cowlick. The King could not forget this. And even though he had tried to have the boy drowned at birth in the river, set aflame in the haystack, disemboweled with the sword shaped like a fishhook and, finally, have his hamstrings clipped, he stood before him.
(*He pauses. He looks at the gathering in worldly-wise way. Everyone shakes their head, mumbling in their own way: "yeah," "I hear you," "unbelievable" and so on.*)
His daughter, the Princess, gazed at the young man and burned with the fever of true love. The prophesy, it seems, had come true... (*He takes another dramatic pause and continues.*) "You must bring me three hairs from the head...
BARNETT: Excuse me... (*Barnett speaks up. He is a thin, pinched, and intense tree shrew, 30 to 40.*)

ANTHONY: Of the wild man…

BARNETT: Excuse me…

ANTHONY: (*Anthony has no patience for this guy. However, he tries.*) Yes?

BARNETT: I can't hear you.

ANTHONY: Pardon me?

BARNETT: I said I can't hear you.

ANTHONY: (*He looks to the group.*) Does anyone else among us have this problem?
(*Everyone shakes their head and mumbles "no".*)

ANTHONY: (*To Barnett.*) May I suggest you move closer.
(*Barnett moves closer. Next to the drum. Rosco beats it again. Barnett pinches his face in pain.*)

ANTHONY: You must bring me three hairs from the wild man…

BARNETT: Excuse me.

ANTHONY: who lives…

BARNETT: Excuse me.
(*Rosco stops. Anthony almost pops.*)

ANTHONY: What the fuc… (*Gets ahold.*)…yes?

BARNETT: (*Sensing his anger and correcting it.*) No, no. Excuse me.

ANTHONY: (*He accepts the correction.*) Yes.

BARNETT: It's the drum. I can't hear. The drum. It's a…(*His brow freezes, looking for the right thing to say.*)

ANTHONY: Okay. I hear you.

BARNETT: (*Still locked.*)…it's a…

ANTHONY: (*To Barnett.*) Okay, I hear you. (*To Rosco.*) Could you bring it down a bit?
(*Rosco obediently and loyally does so.*)
Better?

BARNETT: (*Feeling he has to say yes.*) Yeah. Alright.

ANTHONY: (*Returns to book.*) Three hairs from the wild man that lives in the cave…

BARNETT: (*Barnett stands, upset.*) Oh, this is ridiculous. I can't hear. I can't hear!

ROSCO: Ah, shit. (*Rosco loses it. The inspiration. The concentration. It causes him deep, deep pain.*)

BARNETT: I just simply can't hear.

ROSCO: Ah, shit.

ANTHONY: (*To Rosco.*) Alright. Take it easy.

BARNETT: I'm sure there are other people in this room…

ROSCO: Ah, shit. Shit!

ANTHONY: Take it easy.

BARNETT:…that might have the same problem. I'm sorry. The drum. It's not working.

(*Anthony' rubs Rosco's back. Rosco takes deep breaths.*)

ANTHONY: (*To Barnett.*) We got that. Okay? (*To Rosco.*) Take it easy.

ROSCO: Oh, man…shit!

ANTHONY: I hear you.

ROSCO: (*He stands. He stoops. He shakes his shoulders. He moves his jaw and growls.*) Ehhhhhhhhhh…Ehhhhhhhhhh…

WOODY: (*30 to 40, shaky voice, small frame and earnest.*) Excuse me. What is he doing?

ANTHONY: It's okay.

(*Rosco continues to growl.*)

WOODY: I need to know what he is doing. I am scared.

ANTHONY: Were you at the workshop on anger?

WOODY: No. I missed that one.

ANTHONY: The Lion's Roar. I'll explain it later.

(*Rosco gathers himself and can now breath normally.*)

BARNETT: I'm sorry…

ANTHONY: Alright, I hear you.

BARNETT: Maybe it's the room. That could be it. The room.

ANTHONY: I hear you. (*To Rosco, gently.*) You okay?

ROSCO: Yeah.

ANTHONY: Can we do it lower?

ROSCO: No. What's the point.

ANTHONY: You sure?

ROSCO: What's the point? Forget it. I'm not doing it now.

ANTHONY: Alright, I hear you.

ROSCO: I don't want to do it. That's it. I can't.

ANTHONY: Alright, I hear you.

(*Rosco sits with his arms crossed and pouts and sneers at Barnett. Barnett is a bit guilty.*)

BARNETT: I'm sorry. I had to be honest. That's all.

ANTHONY: I hear you. (*To Rosco.*) May I ask if you are okay?

Rosco. I thank you. I am okay.

ANTHONY: May I ask you what you feel?

ROSCO: Forget it, that's all. Just forget. Like WOW!!! FORGET IT! FORGET ITTTTT!!!!

ANTHONY: (*Pause.*) Alright, I hear you.

(*Rosco stands, hunched, shakes his shoulders and growls.*)

ROSCO: (*Shaking out the fear.*) Ehhhhhhhhhhhh... (*Rosco sits. Calm.*)

ANTHONY: Alright, I hear you.

BARNETT: No. Now, wait a minute. No, no. Let's wait one minute.

ANTHONY: Alright.

BARNETT: The drumming was loud. It really was. And it was bad. It was annoying. I wasn't being honest.

ANTHONY: (*To Barnett.*) Alright, I hear you. (*To the Gathering.*) Everyone keep breathing.

(*Everyone lets out some breath.*)

BARNETT: When I cannot hear, I need to hear. Is that so wrong?

ANTHONY: No. I hear you.

BARNETT: And if someone is not going to protect me. If my father did not protect me. If he did not stand up for me I will stand up for myself!! I CANNOT HEAR!! LET IT BE KNOWN TO THE WORLD! OKAY?!! I CANNOT HEAR! You hear me?!! I cannot hear! I need those limits respected!

ANTHONY: (*Beat.*) Alright, I hear you.

(*Everyone cools down. Anthony proceeds.*)

WOODY: Ahhhh...oh boy. I'm anxious. I'm scared.

ANTHONY: Okay. I hear you.

WOODY: I'm uncomfortable. I really am.

ANTHONY: Okay.

WOODY: Can we take a vow?

ANTHONY: If you so desire.

WOODY: Can we take a vow not to be violent?

ANTHONY: Okay. I hear you. Do you desire a consensus?

WOODY: Yes. I would like that.

ANTHONY: Okay. Let's have a show of hands. All those who can vow not to be violent raise your hand.

(*No one raises their hand. Everyone looks down in shame.*)

(*To Woody.*) It cannot be done. (*He continues to read.*) The boy went on his way and entered the land of the ice caves. At the mouth of the cave was an old witch.

WOODY: Excuse me.

ANTHONY: Yes.

WOODY: Could I try the drum?

ANTHONY: Pardon me?

WOODY: Could I try the drum? I have this impulse.

ANTHONY: (*Pause. He thinks about this.*) I do not have a response to that.

WOODY: I mean, no one's doing it right now. Maybe I can do it differently. You know. Just a suggestion.

ANTHONY: Okay. I hear you.

WOODY: We don't have to abandon it entirely, do we? It does a lot for me. Really. You know. Like ritual wise.

ANTHONY: Okay. I hear you. (*To Rosco.*) Rosco, how do you feel about that?

(*Rosco stares at the floor and pouts.*)

Rosco?

(*He jumps out of his seat and sits at a distant spot on the circle.*)

ROSCO: It's not my drum. I don't own it. Fuck it. I don't give a shit.

ANTHONY: The message is mixed for me, Rosco. Are you indifferent to this suggestion?

ROSCO: If it is your desire to shame me, I will not be part of it.

WOODY: No, no, that's not what I meant.

ANTHONY: Okay, I hear you.

WOODY: I didn't mean that.

ANTHONY: Okay, I hear you.

ROSCO: Then what the fuck did you mean? Get honest. I mean reallllly.

WOODY: I didn't mean that. No, no, you're taking it all wrong.

ANTHONY: (*To Woody.*) Okay, I hear you! Do you hear me Woody...I hear you!

(*Pause. Everyone chills.*)

WOODY: (*Timidly.*) Sorry.

ANTHONY: Rosco. Are you or are you not indifferent to this?

ROSCO: No. I am not indifferent. But I yield.

ANTHONY: Okay. I hear that. (*Anthony looks at Woody.*) Well?

(*Woody takes a chance and darts to Rosco's seat and feels the drum. Anthony looks at him. Woody begins a light tap. Barnett gets pissed.*)

BARNETT: Oh, Christ.

(*He moves out of the circle. Woody taps with a new-found glee.*)

ANTHONY: (*Back to business.*) The witch was the mother of the wild man. She looked at the boy and said, "You are not one of us." He said, "That is true, but I need your help just the same." She looked at his cowlick. She said "I will help you. Follow me." He did so and entered the cave. (*He holds forth.*) Alright I'm gonna stop here.

(*Woody is into his drumming. Anthony glares at him.*)
Woody.

WOODY: (*Gets ahold of himself.*) Oh. (*Woody stops.*)

ANTHONY: (*Portentously.*) How many people here would trust the witch? Raise your hands.

(*No one raises their hands.*)

How many of you would not trust her?

(*Everyone instantly raises their hands. He grins.*)

Okay. Alright. I hear that.

TOMMY: (*Tommy is impeccably dressed in Armani casual wear. He is 30 to 40. A wide mouth with a John Gotti accent.*) Wait a minute. C'mon, now. This whole thing. It is getting…I don't know…

ANTHONY: Okay…

TOMMY: You. For instance. "You hear us?" People were raising or not raising their hands and you said you heard us. No one said a word. Why are you always saying you hear us?

ANTHONY: (*He exhales anger. Pause.*) I meant I felt what they had to say.

TOMMY: Felt? You felt? So you feel something and then tell someone you hear it? Excuse me if I'm being picky. But if I was the leader of a group about communication I would learn how to communicate.

ANTHONY: I am not a leader. I am a facilitator.

TOMMY: Okay. Alright. You say two-mott-oh, I say two-may-toe.

EDWIN: (*30 to 40, very big, soft, he is high-strung and speaks with a lisp.*) Oh, please. Please. Don't start this.

TOMMY: Don't start what?

EDWIN: Don't start being so male.

TOMMY: What? This is a men's meeting. Where the fuck am I gonna be male if I can't be male here?

EDWIN: (*Bitchy.*) At your mother's house.

ANTHONY: Alright now…

TOMMY: Hey. What did you say?

EDWIN: Never mind.

TOMMY: No, what did you say?

EDWIN: (*Flips out.*) I said male. Like hierarchical. One up, one down. Protect your ground. Take orders, give orders. Guard your independence! Display your knowledge! Never admit to failure! The whole boring trip!

TOMMY: Really? Okay. Great. I read the same fucking book.

EDWIN: It doesn't show.

TOMMY: What does show with you is that your mind has been conquered like Morocco or something. You haven't said an original thing yet.

EDWIN: Really? Take a look at your outfit. Talk about painting by numbers.

TOMMY: I can read. Okay? Woopy-fucking-doo. So you read a book. Do you therefore lose your mind because of it? (*To Anthony.*) I mean who the fuck has said an original thing here yet? It's like you're talking in tongues. Channeling Houdini or something.

ANTHONY: Okay. I hear you. The question I have is: Why must one always be original?

TOMMY: What? What the fuck does that mean?

ANTHONY: Maybe we're just the light, not the light bulb.

TOMMY: Hey. Tell it to the Japs, okay?

ANTHONY: Alright. I hear that.

TOMMY: What I'm saying is: I don't understand. This story for instance. Are you saying we're to trust this wicked bitch whose son is the guy he's suppose to pluck hairs from? That's bullshit.

ANTHONY: Did I give you that impression?

TOMMY: Yes.

ANTHONY: Could perhaps that impression be inside yourself?

TOMMY: Oh fuck you.

ANTHONY: Okay. I did not say you had to trust her. I honor you. Whatever you feel.

TOMMY: What if I say I don't feel jack shit?

EDWIN: Wouldn't surprise me...

ANTHONY: Okay. I honor that.

TOMMY: (*Dismissive.*) Oh. Okay, great. What a surprise.

ANTHONY: May I ask you a question?

TOMMY: That's another thing. "May I ask you a question." "I hear you." "May I do this, may I do that." What is this shit? Who talks like that? People don't talk to you like that. Unless they're a Stepford Wife.

ANTHONY: May I ask you a question?

TOMMY: Okay. Good. Very good. Sure go ahead.

ANTHONY: Are you trying to start a fight because you are scared?

TOMMY: Scared? I'm horrified.

ANTHONY: Does this scare you?

TOMMY: Fuck you. You ain't asking me a question. You're telling me what I think. And no one tells me what I think. Fuck you!

ANTHONY: Okay. I hear that.

TOMMY: I mean look at this room. Where are the blacks? I don't see any blacks. Do you see any blacks? No. I mean if we had some blacks at least we'd have a decent drumbeat.

ROSCO: (*Goes into primal release of his feelings, shaking and growling.*) Ehhhhhh...Ehhhhh...

TOMMY: This gathering doesn't appear to be very ecumenical. You know what I mean?

ANTHONY: Alright, I hear that.

ROSCO: Ehhhhhh...ehhhhhh...

TOMMY: (*To Rosco.*) Yeah. Go ahead. Growl. You don't need a men's group. You need a exorcist.

ANTHONY: Alright, I hear that.

ROSCO: Ehhhhhh...ehhhhhhh...

ANTHONY: May I ask you a question?

TOMMY: Oh, shit...are we gonna continue to talk like this?

ANTHONY: May I ask you a question?

TOMMY: Alright! Yeah! Fine! Sure! You may ask me a question!

ANTHONY: May I ask you what your name is?

TOMMY: Tommy.

(*Edwin breaks out into giggles.*)

What's your problem, numb nuts?

EDWIN: It's a funny name.

TOMMY: Fuck you.

EDWIN: (*Seeking approval.*) A joyful, funny name.

TOMMY: Fuck you again.

ANTHONY: Welcome Tommy.

TOMMY: Yeah. Thanks.

(*Edwin reaches out and squeezes his hand.*)

EDWIN: Welcome.

TOMMY: (*Tommy bats it away.*) Get your fucking hand off me.

ANTHONY: Tommy, may I ask you why you came to this meeting?

TOMMY: Okay. Sure. My girlfriend bought the ticket. Drove me to the front door and watched me walk in. It felt like the first day of school with my mother for christsakes.

ANTHONY: May I ask you who took you to school on the first day?

TOMMY: Well, it wasn't the nanny.

ANTHONY: Was it the mother?

TOMMY: "The mother?" Yeah, it was "the mother." My mother. Der Mutter. What is the game around here? You gotta become a Jungian to become a man? Is that it?

ANTHONY: Did your mother make you do things you did not want to do?

TOMMY: Fuck you! You ain't a psychiatrist!

EDWIN: Why is it always the mother? I wanna know. Mommy, mommy, mommy. Why not daddy once in awhile? Huh? Daddy! (*He bursts into tears.*) That bastard!

ANTHONY: Okay. I hear that.

TOMMY: Holy shit...

ANTHONY: Tommy, do you desire to ask more questions?

TOMMY: Questions? Yeah, I got questions. Lots of them. But you could make it a lot easier for me if...when you talked...you used a CONTRACTION once in a while!

Anthony. Okay. I hear that.

TOMMY: I mean what is going on here? I made a million and a half last year playing tick, tack, fuck on Wall Street. The bubble bursts and I get this notice from the girlfriend. I'm on probation till I can get touchy feely. What is this shit? What does she know? She was a model for christsakes. Ahhhh, this country. It's going right down the drain. Look at this shit. Grown men. I can't fucking believe what's happened to me.

ANTHONY: Tommy, look...you are a beautiful man.

TOMMY: Really? You think I'm beautiful? It's been a long winter, huh?

ANTHONY: You have beautiful, dark eyebrows. I find them attractive. Beautiful lips. Full and ruby.

TOMMY: So what does that mean? If we were in prison together you would be my best buddy?

ANTHONY: Is that how you feel?

TOMMY: Fuck you!

ANTHONY: Do you feel sexual?

TOMMY: Stop telling me how I feel!

ANTHONY: Okay, I hear that. What you feel is what you feel. I honor that. That is all I know about this movement we have. To honor each other's feelings. Man to man. We are out of practice.
(*Everyone mumbles.*)

We are way out of practice. Centuries out of practice. Dynasties out of practice.

WOODY: It's been a long, long time.

(*Everyone mumbles.*)

ANTHONY: So here we practice.

EDWIN: That's what we do.

ANTHONY: Here we are safe. And with enough practice who knows. Maybe the next time your girlfriend asks you how you feel, Tommy, you will be able to tell her.

TOMMY: In my entire life I have never met a woman who has ever asked me how I felt. As a matter of fact, I showed one my feelings one time and she ran out of the room.

EDWIN: That doesn't surprise me either...

ANTHONY: Alright, Tommy...

TOMMY: I mean let's get real here. This whole thing looks to me like an updated version of the He-Man Women Haters Club.

ANTHONY: Tommy...

TOMMY: A room full of white men...

ANTHONY: Tommy...

TOMMY: Who read this book by a guy who looks like Grandpa Walton and get their rocks off by playing strip poker in a sweatlodge together...

ANTHONY: Alright, Tommy, I gonna have to stop you right there!

TOMMY: Fuck you! I'm not stopping!

ANTHONY: Fuck you, you are stopping!

TOMMY: Fuck you I am not!

ANTHONY: Fuck you, you are! You are a fucking boy, Tommy! There is a tiny thread that's holding the two halves of your brain together, and you don't know it yet, but you are in the immediate danger of having it snap at any moment! I will not have soft fascists here! I had an Italian family that told me what to do all my life! I will protect everyone from that! I will joust you down, man! Joust you down!!!!

(*Anthony growls at him. Tommy stops. Anthony breathes. He bursts into tears. He cries for awhile.*)

Tommy...Tommy...I'm sorry...Tommy I'm sorry...may I hug you?

TOMMY: What?

ANTHONY: May I hug you?

TOMMY: That's what I thought you said. Ah, shit. I'm getting out of here.

ANTHONY: Please, Tommy. I need to hug you! I respect your opposition. I see the beauty of your strength. May I hug you? (*He stands before Tommy.*)

TOMMY: Alright, fine. Hug me. Jesus.
(*He does so.*)

ANTHONY: You are beautiful, Tommy. You are a beautiful man. (*He kisses him.*)

TOMMY: Hey. Take it easy.

ANTHONY: You are not my enemy.

TOMMY: Alright. Thanks. I agree. I'm beautiful. Now let go of me.
(*Anthony hugs him tighter and cries hard.*)
Oh, shit.
(*Edwin begins to cry.*)
Oh, shit.

EDWIN: I just need to say that I own my balls. I am proud of these balls! I can feel the hair on them standing up right now! They're mine and no one is gonna take them away from me!
(*Woody begins to cry. Then Rosco joins him. Anthony lets go of Tommy and walks to Rosco and ministers to him.*)

ANTHONY: May I know your grief?

ROSCO: Yes. You may.

ANTHONY: Why do you grieve?

ROSCO: I wanted to play the drum.
(*Rosco cries harder. Anthony embraces him. Woody and Edwin cry harder and embrace.*)

TOMMY: Oh, shit…(*He gathers his coat. There are several knocks on the door. Tommy looks around the room of crying men.*) Yeah? Come in.
(*A beautiful woman, 28, natural and fresh, opens the door and enters. Her name is Irene.*)

IRENE: Excuse me…

TOMMY: (*He is dumbstruck with the possibilities of this.*) Yeah?

IRENE: I'm sorry. Am I interrupting something?

TOMMY: No, no. Come in.
(*Woody is the first to notice her and stops immediately. He raps Edwin who looks at her and stops dead. Both wipe their eyes and pull themselves together.*)

WOODY: (*Alerting Anthony.*) Anthony…Anthony.

(Anthony spots her and recoils from his embrace with Rosco. Both men clam up.)

IRENE: Sorry…are you sure I'm not interrupting something?
     (There is a long silence.)
ANTHONY: May I help you?
IRENE: I'm lost. I think. Is this the tea house?
ANTHONY: No. It is not.
IRENE: Oh, no…I'm looking for the tea house.
ANTHONY: That's the Institute's Annex. Four blocks down on tenth.
IRENE: Oh. Okay. Thanks. *(She tentatively heads for the door.)*
TOMMY: Hey. You okay?
IRENE: Yeah. Thanks. This neighborhood. It's a bit…isolated.
WOODY: Yeah.
IRENE: *(To Anthony.)* Come to think of it. Do you think someone could do me a favor and walk me over.
ANTHONY: Pardon me?
IRENE: You know. An escort. Just to feel safe. Would you mind?
     (There is a tense silence in the room. Anthony becomes very solemn.)
ANTHONY: No. I am sorry. That cannot be done.
IRENE: Oh. Okay. I just thought…you know. It'll only take a minute.
ANTHONY: No. I am sorry. It cannot be done. I would suggest you search for the warrior within yourself.
IRENE: Pardon me? The warrior? I don't understand.
ANTHONY: I am further saddened to hear that. I cannot explain. "No" will have to be a complete enough answer.
IRENE: Okay.
TOMMY: Hey. Don't worry hon, I'll take you over.
IRENE: Thanks…but it's okay. It's not really necessary. Come to think of it.
TOMMY: Look. I'm heading out. I'll take you over there. No problem.
WOODY: *(Jumps up eagerly.)* Have you been to that building before, Tommy?
TOMMY: What?
WOODY: The building. Nine eighty. On tenth. Have you been there before?
TOMMY: Yeah.
WOODY: What's it look like?
TOMMY: What is this, my SAT's? What do you mean what does it look like. It's a building.

WOODY: (*To Irene with a big grin on his face.*) This guy's such a card. (*Holding the grin.*) What's it look like, Tommy?

TOMMY: I said a building.

WOODY: (*To Irene.*) This guy's such a card. (*To Tommy.*) Tommy, you shouldn't make things up on something like this. It's not nice. This is a situation for trust.

TOMMY: Hey, look. Weasel. (*He gets ahold of himself.*)

WOODY: (*To Tommy.*) Yeah?

(*Tommy clams up.*)

(*To Irene.*) Look. I'll take you over. I know where it is. It's the building with the Buddha on top.

IRENE: Oh. Okay. Alright. Thanks. That would be great.

TOMMY: (*Very pleasant.*) Woody, I'm dressed. I'll take her.

IRENE: No, it's okay. Thanks alot. But I'd rather, well...go with him. You know. He's been there before.

TOMMY: Okay. (*He sits.*) Okay.

(*Woody puts on his coat and exits with Irene.*)

WOODY: (*Exiting, to Anthony.*) I'll give you a call about the stuff I missed.

ANTHONY: Okay.

IRENE: What's your name?

WOODY: Woody.

(*Everyone is seated. Dumbstruck. Woody got a woman. Or so it appears. They stare abstractly into space. Suddenly, oddly, Tommy begins to weep. All the men look his way and then burst into tears as well. Lights fade on these weeping men.*)

END OF PLAY

Wish Fulfillment
by David Simpatico

To my father, with deep love.

BIOGRAPHY

DAVID SIMPATICO'S most recent play, *The Secret of Life,* enjoyed a Spring run at the Westbank Cafe Theatre. He was a Guest Artist at Syracuse University and Dartmouth College, and he received fellowship residencies at both the Yaddo and Macdowell colonies. His full-length play, *Macs,* was the featured play for the First Look Series Benefit for Ensemble Studio Theatre.

David has performed *Cavalcade of Scars,* his one-man show about the psychoneurotic multiple-personality plight of a New Jersey lounge lizard, at the New York Theatre Workshop's *O Solo Mio* Festival and most recently as the recipient of the Emerging Artist Award at the Franklin Furnace in Exile Emerging Artists Series at the New School. During 1992–93, David was named an NEA Playwriting Finalist; Guest Artist at both the New York Public Library and Dartmouth College; and a recipient of the Franklin Furnace Emerging Artist Grant. Recent resident fellowships include the Edna St. Vincent Millay Arts Colony and the Edward Albee Colony at Montauk.

His work has been featured in the Baca Downtown Festival, the Key West Theatre Festival, the West Coast Playwrights' Conference, and the New York Theatre Workshop.

Other projects include *Glen or Glenda!,* a musical concerning a cross-dressing schizophrenic homicidal maniac; *Contact,* a full-length play in which six characters free-fall through the polarities of contemporary society and land in Dr. Kitty's Interpersonal Training Workshop; *Nanna,* a three person play dealing with incest survivors, children of alcoholic parents, necrophilia, and the Mother Goddess; and *Prom Queen,* a play about two high school girls whose pursuit of beauty takes them from eating disorder to vampirism.

A Resident Playwright for the New York based Barrow Group, he is also a member of The Dramatists Guild, The Drama Club, The New York Theatre Workshop Usual Suspects, and the Playwrights'/ Directors' Unit at the Actors' Studio. He has studied acting with Sanford Meisner and Greg Zittel, and playwriting with John Wulp in the Advanced Playwrights' Workshop at Playwrights Horizons. David graduated Northeastern University ('83) with a BS in Theater. He was seen recently performing in *The Rocky Horror Show* National Tour, appearing nightly as Eddie/Dr. Scott.

Author's Note

Wish Fulfillment examines the few split seconds of fantasy that explode across your brain just before those three little words, "Dad, I'm gay" tumble out of your mouth and change your life forever.

Speed is a key ingredient. I wrote the piece in a torrential five hours; that same rush of compact, focussed energy pertains to the performance as well. The variations build one upon the other, gaining a steady momentum that ultimately erupts in violence. Ideally, the comic and tragic elements co-exist in the same breath, in such a way that the humor serves as a conduit into the darker issues raised.

Special thanks to Judy Boals, my agent steadfast and true; to Act One and Showtime, for selecting my play from a multitude of riches; to Edward Albee and the William Flanagan Memorial Creative Persons Center in Montauk, New York, where I wrote the play; to Cal Skaggs and the Stillwaters Theatre Company, for taking an early interest; to Kirk Baltz and Jack Wallace, two powerful actors who put their hearts in the line of fire; to Jenny Sullivan, whose compassionate and insightful direction taught me much about grace under fire; and most especially to Robert C. Strickstein, my lover and best friend who gave me the strength, encouragement, and support I needed to sit down and, once and for all, talk with my father.

836

Truth is as old as God–
His Twin identity
And will endure as long as He
A Co-Eternity–

And perish on the Day
Himself is borne away
From Mansion of the Universe
A lifeless Deity.

— *Emily Dickinson*

ORIGINAL PRODUCTION

Wish Fulfillment was originally directed by Jenny Sullivan with Kirk Baltz as The Son and Jack Wallace as The Father.

WISH FULFILLMENT

ONE

Two chairs face each other. An end-table between them. The Son rocks nervously in his chair. The Father walks in, holding a double scotch. He sits opposite the Son.

FATHER: Your mother said you wanted to talk to me.
SON: Dad.
FATHER: Yeah.
SON: I got something I need to tell you.
FATHER: What is it.
SON: Mom already knows.
FATHER: What is it.
SON: This is not easy for me.
FATHER: What is it.
SON: Uhm…
FATHER: Yes—
SON: Uhm I…
FATHER: WHAT IS IT?
SON: DAD I'M GAY.
    (*They don't move. They stare at each other in tense silence. Slowly, the Father cracks into a mask of tears, sobbing pitifully.*)
SON: Daddy—

(A Siren wails. The Father rises, walks around the chair and starts the scene again.)

Two

The Son rocks nervously. The Father walks in, holding his drink. He sits opposite his Son. [Note: Each time the scene starts over, we should see the same ritual of The Son waiting and The Father entering, with occasional variations.]

FATHER: Your mother said you had something you wanted to tell me.
SON: Dad.
FATHER: Yeah.
SON: I got something I need to tell you.
FATHER: What is it.
SON: Mom already knows.
FATHER: What is it.
SON: It's hard, Dad.
FATHER: What is it.
SON: This is not easy for me.
FATHER: Yes—
SON: Uhm I…
FATHER: WHAT IS IT?
SON: DAD I'M GAY.
FATHER: Oh my God.
SON: Dad—
FATHER: So am I!
      (Jumps on his son, devouring him in a deep, taboo kiss. Siren wails.)

THREE

The Son rocks. The Father enters holding his drink.

FATHER: Your mother said you wanted to talk to me.
SON: Dad.
FATHER: Yeah.
SON: I got something I need to tell you.

FATHER: What is it.

SON: Mom already knows.

FATHER: What is it.

SON: It's hard, Dad.

FATHER: What is it.

SON: This is not easy for me.

FATHER: Yes—

SON: Uhm I...

FATHER: WHAT IS IT?

SON: DAD I'M GAY.

FATHER: Is that all?

SON: Dad—

FATHER: I always thought you might be, ever since you were little. I'm glad you finally feel comfortable enough about your sexuality that you can admit it to yourself. Your mother and I just want you to be happy.

SON: Wow.

FATHER: And healthy. Do you practice safe sex?

SON: Absolutely.

FATHER: Well then. As long as you're happy, that's all that matters.

SON: I don't know what to say.

FATHER: You've already said it.

SON: But you're being so cool.

FATHER: Hey now, don't sell your father short. Just because I personally don't ascribe to your sexual orientation, I would never have the pomposity to morally condemn something simply because it is out of the realm of my own personal experience.

SON: Wow. When I grow up, I want to be just like you.

FATHER: I just want you to be happy. Your father loves you.

SON: Dad—

(*They are about to embrace, but the Siren wails. They start the scene again.*)

FOUR

The Son rocks. The Father enters, holding his drink.

FATHER: Your mother said you wanted to talk to me.

SON: Dad.
FATHER: Yeah.
SON: I got something I need to tell you.
FATHER: What is it.
SON: Mom already knows.
FATHER: What is it.
SON: Uhm…
FATHER: Yes.
SON: I mean—
FATHER: Yes.
SON: Uhm I…
FATHER: What is it son? (*Takes a drink.*)
SON: Dad, I'm gay.
  (*The Father spits out his drink in a violent spume of disbelief, sopping his son with his double scotch.*)
  (*The Siren wails. They start the scene again.*)

FIVE

The Son rocks. The Father enters with a new drink.

FATHER: Your mother said you wanted to talk to me.
SON: Dad.
FATHER: Yeah.
SON: I got something I need to tell you.
FATHER: What is it.
SON: Mom already knows.
FATHER: What is it.
SON: It's hard, Dad.
FATHER: What is it.
SON: This is not easy for me.
FATHER: Yes—
SON: I mean I—
FATHER: WHAT IS IT?
SON: Dad, I'm gay.
  (*The Father's drink dribbles out of his mouth.*)
  Dad—
  (*The Father clutches his heart, suffers a massive coronary, collapses to*

the floor shaking in agony. The Son races to his father's side, alternately pounding on his chest and giving him mouth-to-mouth.)

No—Daddy please don't die, it's all my fault, I didn't mean it, I'll change, I was kidding—don't die Daddy please don't die—Daddy please—

(*With a final horrific shudder, the Father dies.*)

SON: I'VE KILLED MY FATHER!

(*He throws himself weeping across his father's corpse. The Siren wails. They start the scene again.*)

SIX

The Son rocks in his chair. The Father enters, holding his drink.

FATHER: Your mother said you wanted to talk to me.
SON: Dad.
FATHER: Yeah.
SON: I got something I need to tell you.
FATHER: What is it.
SON: Mom already knows.
FATHER: What is it.
SON: It's hard, Dad.
FATHER: What is it.
SON: This is not easy for me.
FATHER: Yes—
SON: Uhm I…
FATHER: WHAT IS IT?
SON: DAD, I'M GAY.

(*A tense beat of stillness. Suddenly, the Father takes out a gun. Shoots his son in the head. The Son does a backward tumble out of the chair and shakes in postmortem frenzy. The Father methodically empties the gun into his son's body. The Siren wails. The Father sneaks one last bullet into the corpse before they start the scene again.*)

SEVEN

The Son rocks. The Father enters, holding his drink.

FATHER: Your mother said you wanted to talk to me.
SON: Dad.
FATHER: Yeah.
SON: I got something I need to tell you.
FATHER: What is it.
SON: Mom already knows.
FATHER: What is it.
SON: It's hard, Dad.
FATHER: What is it.
SON: What I have to tell you.
FATHER: WHAT IS IT—
SON: Can you please stop yelling at me—
FATHER: I AM NOT YELLING—
SON: YES YOU ARE TOO YOU'RE ALWAYS YELLING I CAN'T STAND IT ANYMORE JUST STOP YELLING FOR CHRIST'S SAKE—
FATHER: What the hell did you want to tell me already—
SON: NONE OF YOUR STUPID MOTHERFUCKING BUSINESS OK, GET THE FUCK OFF MY BACK AND LEAVE ME ALONE ALL YOU EVER DO IS YELL AT ME MY WHOLE LIFE WHY CAN'T WE JUST TALK SO FUCK YOU AND YOUR BIG FUCKING MOUTH OK—
FATHER: DON'T YOU EVER TALK TO YOUR FATHER LIKE THAT, I DON'T CARE HOW BIG YOU ARE I AM STILL YOUR FATHER DO YOU UNDERSTAND ME (*Slaps him.*) DO YOU UNDERSTAND ME (*Slaps him.*) DO YOU UNDERSTAND ME (*Slaps him.*)
(*The Son shakes his head "Yes."*)
(*Gently.*) Now what did you want to tell me?
(*The Siren wails. They start the scene again.*)

EIGHT

The Son rocks. The Father enters, holding his drink.

FATHER: Your mother said you wanted to talk to me.
SON: Dad.
FATHER: Yes.
SON: I got something I need to tell you.
FATHER: What is it?
SON: I love you Dad.
FATHER: What is it?
SON: I love you.
FATHER: What did you want to talk about?
SON: Do you love me?
FATHER: Is this what you wanted to talk about?
SON: Do you love me, Dad?
FATHER: I'm your father.
SON: Do you love me?
FATHER: Yes, I love you.
SON: No matter what.
FATHER: I love you I love you.
SON: No matter what.
FATHER: What is it?
SON: Well, Dad, I'm gay.
　　(*Silence.*)
FATHER: I don't want to hear this.
　　(*The Siren wails. They start the scene again.*)

NINE

The Son rocks. The Father enters, holding his drink.

FATHER: Your mother said you wanted to talk to me.
SON: Dad, I'm gay.
FATHER: I don't want to hear this.
SON: Well I am.
FATHER: I don't want to hear this.
SON: I'm gay.

FATHER: You just told me the worst thing in the world.
SON: Thanks Dad. You still love me?
FATHER: Don't ask me that like I'm on trial here.
SON: It's a simple question.
FATHER: You just threw a brick in my face.
SON: Do you still love me?
FATHER: You will always be a part of this family, but in my honest opinion, you belong on the other side of the street in the gutter with the freaks.
SON: So I'm a freak.
FATHER: You're being honest, I'm being honest.
SON: You just called your son a freak.
FATHER: You don't like the truth.
SON: You just threw a brick in my face.
FATHER: Truth hurts don't it.
SON: Do you still love me?
FATHER: You're my son.
SON: I thought I was a freak.
  (*The Siren wails. They start the scene again.*)

TEN

  The Son rocks. The Father enters, holding his drink.

FATHER: Your mother said you wanted to talk to me.
SON: I'm gay Dad.
FATHER: Your mother said you wanted—
SON: Dad I'm gay.
FATHER: Your mother said you—
SON: I'm gay Dad.
FATHER: Your mother said—
SON: I'm gay Dad.
FATHER: Your mother said you wanted—
SON: I'm gay Dad.
FATHER: Your mother said you—
SON: I'm gay, Dad.
FATHER: Your mother said you—
SON: I'm gay, Dad.

FATHER: Your mother said you wanted to talk to me.

SON: Forget it.

    (*Pause.*)

FATHER: You can get help you know.

    (*The Siren wails. They start the scene again.*)

ELEVEN

    The Son rocks. The Father enters, holding a two-by-four.

FATHER: Your mother said you wanted to talk to me.

SON: Dad.

FATHER: Yeah.

SON: I got something I need to tell you.

FATHER: What is it.

SON: Mom already knows.

FATHER: What is it.

SON: It's hard, Dad.

FATHER: What is it.

SON: This is not easy for me.

FATHER: You can tell me I'm your father.

SON: It's really really hard for me.

FATHER: I'm your father, I love you.

SON: Well Dad I'm gay.

    (*Instantly, the Father brings the two-by-four down on the table between them, destroying it.*)

FATHER: I'm sorry, what?

SON: I said I'm gay.

FATHER: As in Homosexual.

SON: As in Homosexual.

    (*The Father slams the wood down again, finishing off whatever is left of the table. They jump up, face off.*)

FATHER: My son, prepare to die.

    (*He swings, barely misses his son, who fends him off throughout.*)

SON: I thought you loved me.

FATHER: I thought I knew you.

SON: You do know me. Now you know me better.

FATHER: No I don't.

SON: Why because I'm gay?

FATHER: No, because you're a goddamn freak that's gonna wind up dead in the gutter at the end of a two-by-four because someday soon you're gonna pinch the wrong behind and he's gonna turn around and rip the eye right outta your friggen head and I hope to God I'm there to see it, goddamn AIDS carrier—(*Swings, wings his son.*)—to think you played with your own godson right here in this house, if that kid gets sick I am coming for you—

SON: I am not an AIDS carrier—

FATHER: You're a goddamn faggot is what you are and all faggots are AIDS carriers—(*Slams, just missing his son's skull.*)

SON: I knew you'd be upset.

FATHER: How the hell are you gonna be happy—

SON: How is anyone happy how are you happy—

FATHER: Oh but I am not happy. (*Swing and a miss.*) I used to think I was happy but see I used to think I kinda knew my son, (*Swing and a miss.*) I used to think I had something in common with the boy I raised. (*Swing and a miss.*) I used to think I could teach him something and maybe someday see a little part of me growing up inside of him.

SON: There's a lot of you in me.

FATHER: Don't tell me that!—(*Swings, knocking his son to the floor.*) I never even suspected—

SON: (*Slowly rising.*) So what were you seeing I mean I'm lost here, Dad, if me telling you that I'm gay changes everything then what was there before that's going to change. You're letting one part of who I am completely change who I was so tell me, really, who was I, who were you seeing all that time that you don't see now—

FATHER: I gotta be honest I got no idea and that's what scares me it's like I'm looking at a big blank like the past twenty years means nothing like all the sweat and blood and worry I put into raising you means nothing like you're spitting in my face and telling me it's all my fault and I should smile and accept and I am sorry kiddo but just because you got my blood in your veins don't mean I got to stand back with my thumb up my ass watchin while you piss on everything I built my life around—I am telling you I will not accept!

SON: (*Approaching him.*) Daddy—

FATHER: I WILL NOT ACCEPT—(*He sends his son for a homer.*) I am

so humiliated my whole life means nothing without a son I can't be a father so who the hell am I and who are you I want my goddamn son back and it's all my fault—(*Slam his son across the spine.*) it's all my fault—(*Slam.*) it's all my fault—(*Slams.*)
(*He drops the wood and sucks in breath, standing over the corpse of his son. The Siren wails. They jump up to start the scene again.*)

TWELVE

The Son picks himself up. As the Father enters, the Son also picks up the two-by-four.

FATHER: Your mother said you wanted to talk to—
   (*The Son takes a powerful savage swipe at his Father, knocking him in the ribs. The Father crumbles to the ground, crawls away from his attacking son.*)
FATHER: Why do you always have to attack your father—
SON: I'm not attacking, I'm fighting back.
FATHER: But I'm your father.
SON: Fuck you. (*Kicks him in the ribs.*) You're nothing but a bad dream that rolled over in his sleep years ago and slipped it in my mother and I'm the result, (*Grabs his father's hair.*) do you understand me—answer me—
FATHER: But I love you—
SON: Bullshit. (*Slams his father's head into the floor; the father rolls away in pain, trying to evade his son's assault.*) You stopped loving me when I was three fucking years old and you came home from work and I ran up and hugged your legs because I was so happy to see Daddy because Daddy was so big and so strong and so tall and Daddy always brought home a candy bar hiding in his pocket and so I grabbed it but instead I grabbed your cock didn't I Daddy and you knocked me down and beat me black-and-blue didn't you Daddy because I was three years old and I had to learn never to touch another man's cock because it was sick and bad and from that second on you wouldn't even let me hug you because you wanted me to be normal and well-adjusted so you kept pushing me away and pushing me away because you were too scared to let me hug you again—stop running away from me. I want to hug you. Daddy, I want to knock your teeth down your fucking throat—

FATHER: I was just trying to be a good father—

SON: You think this is easy for me—(*Swing and a miss.*)

FATHER: How are you gonna be happy—

SON: How is anyone happy how are you happy—(*Swing and a miss.*)

FATHER: Oh but I am not happy.

SON: Well neither am I. (*Connects, sends the father across stage.*) I'm looking back on my life and all I see is a big blank, I don't know who you are Dad what did we ever talk about I can't remember and I want my father back because I feel like I wasn't there, like I was always pretending, sitting around smiling and being the good boy and all the time about to explode with a deep dark perverted secret that no one could understand and made me a freak in the eyes of God and so I became a freak and lived like a freak and treated myself like a freak so I could live up to your expectations drowning in the sewer but I can't live by your rules anymore because I am exploding now and I can't stop and I want my life back and I want to be happy because I am not a freak, Daddy, do you understand me, I am not a freak—

FATHER: It's all my fault—

SON: (*Slams him across the head.*) It's nobody's fault Dad It's not good and it's not bad, it just is—and it is about me, it is not about you—stop being so self-centered and think about what I'm telling you and what I'm going through because I am the one who is going through it, not you, and I need love right now you motherfucking piece of shit, understand, I need love—

FATHER: I wanted to teach you how to fight.

SON: Well you did a good job because that's all I know how to do –

FATHER: (*Feebly on his knees.*) Your father loves you—

SON: NO—(*Big smash, sends the father to the floor; pounds away.*) I don't know who you are—I have no father. I have only myself. I am finally in control. (*Smash.*) My father is dead and I am free. I am free of his anger. (*Smash.*) I am free of his hate. (*Smash.*) I am free of his love. (*Smash.*) I am free of him. (*Smash.*)

(*He drops the wood. Sucks in air. Realizes he is standing over his father's body. He suddenly and sadly sees how much his father's son he truly is. A Siren wails. They rise and start the scene again.*)

THIRTEEN

The Son rocks in his chair. The Father enters, holding his drink.

FATHER: Your mother said you wanted to talk to me.
   (*Silence. They say nothing.*)
   (*Black out.*)

END OF PLAY

A Death In Bethany
by Garry Williams

BIOGRAPHY

GARRY WILLIAMS is the co-author of *Rebels* (with Steven H Ridenour), 1988 winner of the Festival of Emerging American Theatre; *Rain*, 1991 winner of the Alliance One-Act Festival and recipient of the Drama-Logue Critic's Award for Playwriting. *Rain* was chosen to appear in New York's Ensemble Studio Theatre's 1995 Marathon. He also wrote *A Blooming of Ivy* and has two screenplays currently under studio option.

AUTHOR'S NOTE

When I sat down, all I knew was I wanted to write a ten-page play. I had been hearing about the form and was curious to try it. I wondered if I could find the kind of economy to tell a full story with beginning, middle, and end in that short an amount of time.

I made two initial, very mundane decisions: to establish a recognizable situation quickly, and to spring at least one surprise. The image of a man locked out of his house and demanding to see his kids struck me as an opening that contained a lot of information. We would instinctively know much about that situation in a very few lines. That got me pondering why the man needed to see his kids. And why tonight, why right now? The death of the man's father gave me that reason and, if revealed at the right time, would possibly satisfy the element of surprise that I wanted. I started writing on those decisions alone.

Then I got lucky. I found out while writing that there was another surprise to come. I also found out that the death of Henry's dad gives him more than a reason for wanting the comfort of seeing his kids. It ultimately causes him to realize why he had walked out on his marriage, his children, everything that is dear to him.

It would be easy to view Henry's emotional state as a breakdown of sorts, a cry of, "Please let me come home, I'm hurting". As a matter of fact, that's what I initially thought I was writing. But then his last monologue unfolded and I knew I had something more. The realizations that Henry eventually comes to about his father lifts the play to a level of redemption, of enlightenment for him. With Henry having a break*through* rather than a breakdown, the ending is not about Roz being too nice a person to kick him out when he's this distraught. It's about Roz seeing growth in her husband and deciding to find out where that growth might take them as a couple, as a family.

A reviewer wondered if this play wasn't just the climactic scene of a longer piece. I don't know if that should trouble me or not. If this ten minutes reverberated in his mind as part of a larger canvas, maybe it did its job. What I do know is that while I undertook the play as an exercise in brevity and economy, I feel I came to know and care as deeply about these characters and their problems as any I have written to date.

ORIGINAL PRODUCTION

A Death in Bethany was originally produced at the Showtime's Act-One 1994 Festival. It was directed by Heidi Helen David, assistant to the director was Brigitte Mahaney, original music was by Robert Buckingham with the following cast:

Roz . . . . Kellie Overbey
Henry . . . . David Packer
Monty . . . . Clem Jeffreys

A DEATH IN
BETHANY

*It is night. In the dim light of street lamps we can see a small living
room (or the theatrical hint of one), cheaply furnished. It is tidy, but
very little money went into the place.*
*There is a knocking at the offstage front door. It comes again, louder.
Then again, louder.*

HENRY: (*Offstage.*) Roz? Roz, open the door.
    (*A woman of twenty-five or so comes out from the wings—or an
    onstage door— wrapping a robe tightly around her body. She moves
    silently toward the front door and stands in the darkness.*)
HENRY: (*Offstage.*) Roz, I know you're in there, open the door! (*After a
    beat, roaring.*) You want me through the picture window?
ROZ: Go away, Henry.
HENRY: (*Offstage; quieter now.*) I want to see the kids.
ROZ: Well, they don't want to see you.
HENRY: (*Offstage.*) Bullshit. I want to see my kids, Roz. I'm not goin'
    away till I see my kids. I won't even wake 'em up.
ROZ: You'da woke 'em already if they were here. They're not here.
HENRY: (*Offstage.*) Bullshit.
ROZ: They're not, Henry. They're at my mom's. Go to a phone booth
    and call her, she'll tell you.

HENRY: Yeah, I know what she'd tell me.

(*There is a sadness in Henry's voice; a resignation of sorts that belies the bravado of his words. Consciously or unconsciously, Roz reacts to it.*)

ROZ: Go home. Sleep it off, you can see 'em tomorrow.

HENRY: I wanta see 'em *now!*

ROZ: No, Henry. You're drunk, just go home.

HENRY: I *am* home. And I'm not drunk. Now, you let me in or I'm comin' through a window. I mean it, Roz. You know I'll do it.

ROZ: I'll call the cops.

HENRY: Weasel and Billy are doin' nights this month. And they'll just tell you to let me in.

(*There must be truth to this, because she goes to the door and unlocks it. Henry is a young man, mid-twenties, dressed in factory overalls and steel-toed black shoes. He looks around at the darkened living room.*)

HENRY: You sleepin'?

ROZ: It's night, isn't it? Yeah I was sleepin'. How come you're not at work?

HENRY: I was. You sure the kids aren't here?

ROZ: If they were here I'd let you see 'em, okay?

HENRY: Why they at your mom's?

ROZ: Hank's been havin' his nightmares again. He thinks he won't have 'em if he's over there.

HENRY: How often's he havin' 'em?

ROZ: They come and go, like before.

(*Henry sighs.*)

HENRY: Damn. Damn. Hey, can we turn on some lights here, or what?

ROZ: Henry, I can't be staying up talking, okay, I have to work in the morning.

(*Henry turns on a lamp anyway and slumps on the couch.*)

HENRY: You got any coffee?

ROZ: I'm not your maid, either.

HENRY: Oh, come on, Roz, gimme a break, willya?

ROZ: You want coffee, you know who can make it for you.

(*Henry sags. He puts his face in his hands, then runs them aimlessly through his hair. Then he slumps sideways onto the couch, curling into a loose fetal position.*)

HENRY: You still got that blanket in the closet there? The one with the ducks on it?

ROZ: No.

HENRY: Oh, come on, you know you do.

ROZ: You're not gonna sleep here.

HENRY: I wanta be here when the kids come.

ROZ: In your work clothes on the couch. They'll think you were drunk.

HENRY: No they won't.

ROZ: What else would they think?

HENRY: (*Sitting up, with emphasis.*) That I missed them. That I needed to see them. That maybe I'm not such a terrible guy.

ROZ: (*A beat.*) They'll think you were drunk.

HENRY: (*Laying back down.*) Thanks, Roz. I really needed that.

ROZ: Henry, I'm not kidding, now, get up.

HENRY: You won't even know I'm here. Just go back to bed. I won't come in or nothin', I swear.

ROZ: What'd she do, kick you out?

HENRY: I'm so tired, Roz. I feel like I'm melting somewhere, way down inside.

ROZ: Henry . . .

HENRY: My dad died, Roz.

ROZ: (*A whisper.*) What?

HENRY: Heart attack, they think. Just died, right there at the punch press.

ROZ: Oh, God, Henry.

HENRY: They called me on the loud speaker. Told me to get to section four real quick. I knew it as I ran.

ROZ: I'm so sorry.

HENRY: I never saw a dead person before. I mean, just dead, right there in the real world, you know? I mean, I've seen those wax-lookin' bodies in caskets, but I've never seen anyone dead in the real world. And it was my dad.

(*Roz kneels tentatively beside him. She reaches a hand out and strokes his hair.*)

I think somethin' melted inside me, Roz. Somethin' scary and important. I thought it was gonna run all over the floor, like blood or pee or somethin'. That it was gonna mess my dad up. He was all clean and dead, you know, and somethin' was gonna come out of me and mess him all up.

(*Roz keeps stroking his hair, gently and softly as she would a child.*)

I'll never ask you for nothin' else, Roz, if you'll just let me sleep here and wait for the kids.

ROZ: Henry…

HENRY: Please, Roz.

(*She stays at his side for a long moment. Then she rises slowly and walks to the bedroom. She opens the door and Monty, a young man her age steps out. Quietly, but with no attempt at concealing his presence, he walks toward the front door. Henry rises slowly to a sitting position, never taking his eyes from Monty.*)

MONTY: I'm, uh, sorry, Henry. I'm sorry about your dad.

(*Henry stands slowly and walks around the couch, standing between Monty and the front door. Monty remains completely still.*)

ROZ: (*Quietly.*) Henry. Henry, don't.

MONTY: I'm not gonna fight you, Henry. We go back too far for that.

(*With an explosion of rage, Henry dives on Monty. Grappling, Monty ends up on his back with Henry on top. Roz is right in the thick of it, trying to get Henry off, and we hear her clearly above the guttural cursing of the men.*)

ROZ: Six months ago. You left me six…months…ago!

(*The primal urgency of her voice seems to freeze the men in place. Struck by the truth of her words Henry breaks away, stands and paces off some of the adrenaline. Then he sits on a coffee table, his back to the audience. Roz walks around and posts herself right in front of him. She lifts his face roughly and locks eyes with him.*)

I'm a real person, Henry. *I* am a *real person.*

(*Monty rises slowly. He turns toward Henry and Roz, but their eyes are locked on each other. Knowing this isn't about him anymore, he wanders almost absently out the front door. Closes it behind him. Roz holds Henry's gaze a moment longer, then steps back. Speaks quietly.*)

I'm, um…I'm gonna go take a shower. You be okay for a minute?

(*She starts to go but Henry's voice stops her.*)

ROZ: (*Quietly.*) I'm gonna go take a shower. You be okay for a minute?

HENRY: Hank's nightmares…?

ROZ: Yeah?

HENRY: I'd take 'em away if I could. I'd take 'em on myself.

ROZ: I know.

(*He reaches out and holds a corner of her robe.*)

HENRY: I came over here to ask if I could come back.

ROZ: I know.

HENRY: Were you gonna let me?

ROZ: No.

HENRY: Because of Monty?

ROZ: No.

HENRY: Because of Alicia?

ROZ: No.

HENRY: Then why?

ROZ: I don't know. I wanted to hate you and I hadn't started hating you yet. I figured I deserved awhile of that.

(*He nods. She tries to go but he holds tightly to her robe.*)

HENRY: My mom gave herself twenty years of it. You figure it'll take you that long.

ROZ: I don't know. I'm not your mom.

HENRY: And I'm not my dad. Hell of a way to realize you're not somebody else, look at 'em dead on a floor. I just kept lookin' at him layin' there, sayin', "Can't we do somethin'? Can't we do somethin'?" And Al Johnson said, "He don't need nothin' now, Henry." And I thought, he never *did* need nothin'. You know it, Roz? He never needed nothin'. Not me or Johnny or Mitzi or mom or nothin'. Him dead on the floor was no different than him alive standin' at that punch press, 'cause he didn't need nothin' either way. (*He's starting to cry.*) The son of a bitch has been dead for twenty years. I shoulda known it back then. I shoulda known it when he left home. I spent my whole life tryin' to be a dead man. A dead man who lived across town. (*And now the tears can't be stopped.*) Goddammit. Goddammit, I didn't want to do this.

ROZ: It's okay.

HENRY: No, it isn't. I didn't want to do this. (*He stands, wiping madly at the tears, but they keep coming.*) I just wanted to see the kids. I just wanted to look at 'em while they were sleepin'. (*He's pacing now, looking for something.*) I'll get out of here in a minute, I just gotta find my jacket.

ROZ: Stay, Henry.

HENRY: Look, I'm gonna get my jacket and get outta here. I'll see the kids tomorrow.

ROZ: Stay, Henry.

HENRY: Just help me find my jacket.

ROZ: You didn't have one, honey.

HENRY: (*Crying harder.*) Oh, God, look at me. This shit's melting inside me and it's gonna get all over the place. It's gonna come out and mess everything up.

Roz: It's all right.

Henry: No, it's not. It's comin' out all over the place. Jesus God, let it stay inside me…

(*She goes to him and holds him.*)

Roz: We'll get in the shower, okay? We'll get in the shower and it can all come out. It can all come out and won't mess up a thing.

Henry: I'm scared.

Roz: I know.

Henry: I never needed nothin' before.

Roz: I know.

Henry: I don't know how to do it.

Roz: Sure you do, Henry. Sure you do. The kids'll be home tomorrow. The sun'll come up and the kid's'll be home.

Henry: I need a shower, Roz. I think I need a shower.

(*Lights out.*)

END OF PLAY